Medical and Psychological Aspects
of Disability

Publication Number 868

AMERICAN LECTURE SERIES®

A Publication in

The BANNERSTONE DIVISION *of*
AMERICAN LECTURES IN SOCIAL
AND REHABILITATION PSYCHOLOGY

Consulting Editors

JOHN G. CULL, Ph.D.

Director, Regional Counselor Training Program
Department of Rehabilitation Counseling
Virginia Commonwealth University
Fishersville, Virginia

and

RICHARD E. HARDY, Ed.D.

Chairman, Department of Rehabilitation Counseling
Virginia Commonwealth University
Richmond, Virginia

The American Lecture Series in Social and Rehabilitation Psychology offers books which are concerned with man's role in his milieu. Emphasis is placed on how this role can be made more effective in a time of social conflict and a deteriorating physical environment. The books are oriented toward descriptions of what future roles should be and are not concerned exclusively with the delineation and definition of contemporary behavior. Contributors are concerned to a considerable extent with prediction through the use of a functional view of man as opposed to a descriptive, anatomical point of view.

Books in this series are written mainly for the professional practitioner; however, the academician will find them of considerable value in both undergraduate and graduate courses in the helping services.

Medical and Psychological Aspects of Disability

By

A. BEATRIX COBB, Ph.D.

Horn Professor of Psychology
Director, Research and Training Center in Mental Retardation
Texas Tech University
Lubbock, Texas

CHARLES C THOMAS • PUBLISHER
Springfield • Illinois • U.S.A.

Published and Distributed Throughout the World by
CHARLES C THOMAS • PUBLISHER
BANNERSTONE HOUSE
301-327 East Lawrence Avenue, Springfield, Illinois, U.S.A.

© *1973, by* CHARLES C THOMAS • PUBLISHER
ISBN 0-398-02653-X
Library of Congress Catalog Card Number: 72-86997

With THOMAS BOOKS *careful attention is given to all details of*
manufacturing and design. It is the Publisher's desire to present books
that are satisfactory as to their physical qualities and artistic possibilities
and appropriate for their particular use. THOMAS BOOKS *will be true*
to those laws of quality that assure a good name and good will.

Printed in the United States of America
JJ-23

CONTRIBUTORS

Joan L. Bardach, Ph.D., Director Psychological Services, Institute Rehabilitation Medicine, Associate Professor in Clinical Rehabilitation Medicine (Psychology), New York University Medical Center, New York, New York.

Lewis Barnes, M.D., Psychiatrist, Lubbock, Texas (deceased).

Beverly W. Bell, A.B., Social Science Analyst, Office of Research and Demonstrations, Social and Rehabilitation Service, Washington, D. C.

D. Bruce Bell, Ph.D., Research Analyst, Office of Research and Statistics, Social Security Administration, Washington, D. C.

A. Beatrix Cobb, Ph.D., Horn Professor of Psychology, Acting Director, Research and Training Center in Mental Retardation, Texas Tech University, Lubbock, Texas.

Patrice M. Costello, Ed.D., Texas Tech University, Lubbock, Texas; Consultant, Area of the Deaf, Dixon State School, Dixon, Illinois.

John G. Cull, Ph.D., Director, Regional Counselor Training Program and Professor, Department of Rehabilitation, School of Community Services, Virginia Commonwealth University, Fishersville, Virginia.

Eric Denhoff, M.D., Co-Director, Governor Medical Center, Medical Director, Meeting Street Children's Rehabilitation Center, Providence, Rhode Island.

John R. Healy, A.B., Project Coordinator, Curative Workshop of Milwaukee, Milwaukee, Wisconsin.

A. Lee Hewitt, M.D., Urologist, Lubbock, Texas.

Stanley Holgate, Ph.D., Lubbock, Texas.

O. Brandon Hull, M.D., F.A.C.P., Diplomate American Board of Internal Medicine, Internal Medicine and Cardiology, Lubbock, Texas.

v

John W. Knapstein, Ph.D., Counseling Psychologist, John Cochran V. A. Hospital, St. Louis, Missouri; Assistant Professor, Southern Illinois University, Edwardsville, Illinois.

Alan Krasnoff, Ph.D., Psychologist, Chairman, Department of Psychology, The University of Missouri at St. Louis, St. Louis, Missouri.

G. Frank Lawlis, Ph.D., Director Rehabilitation Counseling Program, Texas Tech University, Lubbock, Texas.

Franklin D. Lewis, Ph.D., Senior Psychologist, Ouachita Regional Counseling and Mental Health Center, Hot Springs, Arkansas.

Royce C. Lewis, Jr., M.D., F.A.C.S., Diplomate American Board Orthopedic Surgery, Associate Clinical Professor of Orthopedics, Director Hand Surgery Department, Texas Tech University School of Medicine, Lubbock, Texas.

James R. Matthews, M.D., Lubbock, Texas.

Alfred A. Nisbet, M.D., Ophthalmologist, San Antonio, Texas.

Robert P. Overs, Ph.D., Research Coordinator of the Curative Workshop of Milwaukee, Milwaukee, Wisconsin.

Isabel P. Robinault, Ph.D., Supervisor, Research Utilization Laboratory, ICD Rehabilitation and Research Center, New York, N. Y.

John H. Selby, M.D., Diplomate American Board of Surgery, Diplomate American Board of Thoracic Surgery, Thoracic Surgeon, Lubbock, Texas.

Lloyd A. Storrs, M.D., Lubbock, Texas, Guest Lecturer in Otology, University of Pittsburgh, Pittsburgh, Pennsylvania.

To my mother,

whose loving life taught me the meaning of caring

and

my brother,

whose brave endurance of unceasing pain for nine weary years turned my professional career to the field of rehabilitation.

EDITOR'S FOREWORD

In the many fields of rehabilitation, thorough understanding of disability is essential. The various aspects of disability are complex and a challenge to understand. When the psychological aspects of a particular disability are superimposed upon that disability, many professional practitioners are overwhelmed. Yet to serve an individual adequately through the rehabilitation process, it is required that the professional practitioner have a thorough understanding of the social, psychological, and vocational implications of a disability as well as the medical aspects of that disability.

In this book, Dr. Cobb has been able to organize a large, complex body of knowledge in such a fashion as to make it very manageable to the reader. The student will find this text of great value, while the practitioner in the field will gain a useful reference guide. Most other texts written in this area tend to lump together all the various concomitants of a disability. Dr. Cobb has taken a somewhat innovative approach, in that her structure is to discuss the medical aspects of a disability in one chapter (these include anatomical concerns, disease processes, trauma, diagnostic symptoms, treatment, and surgery) followed by a chapter which treats the social, psychological, and vocational aspects of the disability. These psychologically oriented chapters also include statements and guides relating to the rehabilitation of persons with these disabilities.

We feel this book will become a landmark publication, as will the companion volume to this text. This book covers the disabling conditions of heart disease, stroke, cerebral palsy, amputations, respiratory diseases, kidney disorders, disorders of the gastrointestinal system, convulsive disorders, hearing disorders, and visual impairments. The companion text is concerned with the social and psychological disorders and their rehabilitation implications. The areas covered in the second text include attitudes toward disability, motivational factors, alcoholism, drug abuse, the public offender, cultural deprivation, the emotional disability, mental retardation and aging, chronic illness, and neurological disabilities.

We are quite pleased to have this addition to the American Lecture Series in Social and Rehabilitation Psychology. These two texts will find widespread use in the university courses which train professional practitioners in understanding the medical and psychological aspects of disability as well as having wide usage as reference material for professionals in a wide range of rehabilitation and rehabilitation-oriented settings.

Stuarts Draft, Virginia   JOHN G. CULL, Ph.D.
                                               RICHARD E. HARDY, Ed.D.
                                               Consulting Editors

PREFACE

In this volume, an effort has been made to face the challenge of multidisciplinary communication in a specific setting—rehabilitation. We seek to transmit some of the most pertinent medical and psychosocial concepts surrounding common disabilities with which the rehabilitation counselor must work. One of the primary goals is to make it possible for the rehabilitation counselor to develop a medical and psychosocial vocabulary in order to expedite his ability to communicate with the physicians, psychologists, and other professionals on the team. A secondary hope is these people will also read the material and in this way improve their in-depth understanding of the total rehabilitation process.

In the pursuit of this undertaking, I wish to acknowledge the significant contributions of those who have made the book possible. First, I wish to express deep appreciation to the Lubbock-Crosby-Garza County Medical Society. Through the past fourteen years, this society has contributed the teaching staff of physicians for the graduate course in Medical Aspects of Disability (Psychology 5326). Most of the medical chapters were written by these teacher-physicians after working through the years with rehabilitation counselors-in-training. Without this basic contribution, the volume could never have been.

Second, the contribution of the psychologists and educators who brought together the educational, psychological, and rehabilitation factors related to each disease or dysfunction is deeply appreciated. These individuals, despite crowded schedules, responded graciously from New York, St. Louis, and Milwaukee as well as within Texas because they realized the urgent need for bridges across the communication gap to expedite the delivery of rehabilitation services.

Third, the eagerness of the students to learn to communicate meaningfully with other professionals on the rehabilitation staff, as they have worked through the class assignments each of the fourteen years, has made a tremendous contribution by inspiring renewed effort on the part of the editor and the authors. Reports back from the field, as these students became working counselors, to the effect that the course and the material had assisted them in more effective team communication and client service has served to reinforce the effort.

Finally, I wish to acknowledge the dedicated contribution made by Mrs. Mary Dillon, who typed the final manuscript. Her contribution goes far beyond technical production. Her interest, careful proofreading, and revision suggestions were invaluable.

A. BEATRIX COBB

CONTENTS

Medical and Psychological Aspects
of Disability

The following books have appeared in the American Lecture Series in Social and Rehabilitation Psychology:

Vocational Rehabilitation: Profession and Process
  John G. Cull, Ph.D., and Richard E. Hardy, Ed.D.
Contemporary Field Work Practices in Rehabilitation
  John G. Cull, Ph.D., and Craig R. Colvin, M.Ed.
Social and Rehabilitation Services for the Blind
  Richard E. Hardy, Ed.D., and John G. Cull, Ph.D.
Fundamentals of Criminal Behavior and Correctional Systems
  John G. Cull, Ph.D., and Richard E. Hardy, Ed.D.
Introduction to Correctional Rehabilitation
  Richard E. Hardy, Ed.D., and John G. Cull, Ph.D.
Drug Dependence and Rehabilitation Approaches
  Richard E. Hardy, Ed.D., and John G. Cull, Ph.D.
Vocational Evaluation for Rehabilitation Services
  Richard E. Hardy, Ed.D., and John G. Cull, Ph.D.
Adjustment to Work
  John G. Cull, Ph.D., and Richard E. Hardy, Ed.D.
Applied Volunteerism in Community Development
  Richard E. Hardy, Ed.D., and John G. Cull, Ph.D.
*The Big Welfare Mess: Public Assistance and Rehabilitation
  Approaches*
  John G. Cull, Ph.D., and Richard E. Hardy, Ed.D.

Chapter I

AN APPROACH TO INTERDISCIPLINARY COMMUNICATION IN REHABILITATION

A. BEATRIX COBB

Interdisciplinary communication is recognized as probably the most urgent problem in the delivery of services to individuals where multiprofessional teamwork is essential. In the field of rehabilitation, this problem is acute. The rehabilitation team may include an internist, a surgeon, a psychiatrist, a social worker, a psychologist, a work evaluator, a training leader, and the rehabilitation counselor. Each member of this team tends to be carrying a heavy case load; consequently, little time can be spent in joint consultation where each member could learn firsthand the contributions and methods of the other.

The usual physician is frank enough to confess only vague conceptions of the total rehabilitation process. Nor does he claim to be cognizant of the theoretical framework and practical procedures of the evaluators, educators, psychologists, and counselors on the case. On the other hand, the usual psychologist, evaluator, educator, and counselor knows even less of the medical terminology and procedures employed. Although each profession as a whole, and each team member as an individual, gives lip service to the need for communication among and between the professions, little has been done to expedite this flow of meaning.

To bridge this interdisciplinary communication gap is not an easy task. Although rehabilitation is not a new concept (the National Office celebrated its fiftieth anniversary in 1970) and despite the fact that at the local level numerous rehabilitation teams have learned to work together effectively, the techniques of communication used have not been formalized. The usual procedure seems to be that two or three professional people, while working to alleviate or solve the problems of a mutual client, grow to understand the work of the other. This is indeed a slow and often frustrating process.

It would seem that long before fifty years of teamwork had elapsed, some communication aids would have evolved. In fact, a number of books have been written over the years with this thought in mind (Bellak, 1952; Garrett and Levine, 1962; Healey, 1970; McDaniel, 1969; and others). The "catch" seems to be that all of the professions do not read these books. Healey (1970, pp. 182-183) points out that you cannot get physicians to read books or articles written by members of other disciplines. This is not just an indictment of members of the medical team. Each profession spawns such a plethora of material each year that the individual is hard-pressed to read the mandatory research in his own field. This, however, should not preclude work on the interface of one profession with the other if meaningful material has been developed and presented.

In an approach to this communication problem, three national interdisciplinary conferences on "Rehabilitation of the Patient with Cancer" were held in 1967, 1968, and 1969 (Healey, 1970). These conferences brought together representatives from the wide band of medical services, psychologists, social workers, nurses, and educators. It is fascinating to note that even in-depth discussions covering four days at each conference and considering only *one* disease entity (cancer), there seemed to be little interdisciplinary consensus of thought.

The major area of agreement was on the *need* for rehabilitation. There were sharply divergent opinions as to *who* does rehabilitation. Some participants viewed rehabilitation as a "special aspect" of all good medical practice, with the physician as captain of the team. Others saw it as a specialized effort extending medical practice to the world of work and requiring a more complex organizational arrangement. Some of the physicians did not understand the need for, or role of, the rehabilitation counselor. Several disclaimed need for the services of the psychiatrist and psychologist on the team.

Again, all agreed that the goal was more effective care of the total patient and that at times this required the services of trained multidisciplinary teams. Healey (1970, p. vi) brought into focus the crucial problem when he pointed out the following:

> During the discussions some cancerologists confessed their ignorance of rehabilitation measures; rehabilitation experts voiced their ignorance of the relevant surgical problems; and the educators deplored the lack of training of physicians in cancer as well as the lack of communication among the various disciplines.

These three conferences brought into focus the basic rehabilitation principle ". . . that it is not enough to be content with saving lives. . . . There should be more concern with bringing those lives to optimal functioning again . . . physical, mental and social" (Healey, 1970, p. v). *But,* the conferences closed with the major topic of multidisciplinary communication merely opened. The problem is far too basic and widespread to be solved in conferences. Fundamental vocabularies and principles cutting across the disciplines must be shared and experienced at a personal level and then published for others to share in order to bridge this widening chasm of communication among the disciplines.

As the newest member of the team and serving as coordinator of all services delivered to the rehabilitation client, the rehabilitation counselor feels a pressing need for these interdisciplinary communication skills. Rehabilitation educators throughout the nation, training individuals to assume leadership roles in the field, also expressed this need from the standpoint of securing and organizing pertinent information in order to prepare students for their working role.

The purpose of this book is to assemble and integrate pertinent medical and psychosocial information on nine* of the major chronic disabilities that result in a need for rehabilitation services. It is designed to meet a twofold objective. First, it is arranged to serve as a textbook for a course in medical-psychosocial aspects of rehabilitation for rehabilitation counselors-in-training (or other related professionals), to give them practical and basic inter-

---

*The more specialized problem areas for which rehabilitation is responsible (i.e., drug addiction, alcoholism, the public offender, cultural deprivation, mental retardation, emotional disabilities, etc.) will be treated in a separate volume, *Special Problems in Rehabilitation: Medical and Psychological Considerations.*

disciplinary knowledge before they enter the field. Second, it is planned to contribute to the effectiveness of the working re-habilitation counselor (or other related professionals) as a resource or reference volume in the field.

The aim throughout is multidisciplinary communication. The rehabilitation worker must have a basic medical vocabulary pertinent to the disability of his client before he can communicate effectively with the physician and understand the living and working implications of the disability on his client's future. Equally as urgent is the knowledge and integration of the psychosocial impact, progress, and residual of the disease on the client by both the counselor and the physician.

In order to expedite this realistic and practical purpose, the book has been written by individuals intimately acquainted with rehabilitation problems in the field. The chapters dealing with medical information were written by physicians who have lectured to classes of rehabilitation counselor trainees over a period of 10 to 15 years and who have worked as consultants with the local rehabilitation agencies. The psychologists, educators, and counselors who wrote the sections dealing with psychosocial concepts are, or have been, actually involved in work in the field. The book, therefore, has been written *for* practitioners in the field *by* practitioners in the field.

The material is organized in such a fashion as to be readily adaptable to classroom assignments of one semester's length. Medical and psychosocial factors of each disease entity have been integrated or placed adjacent to each other, so that the student may get a holistic view of the total impact of the disability on the client. This arrangement also makes for convenient utilization of the book by a counselor in the field who may need to acquaint himself with, or review, major problem areas related to a specific disease prior to work with a new referral.

Again, the purpose of this volume is to face the challenge of interdisciplinary communication in rehabilitation and assume some responsibility toward the solution of the problem. The major goal is to make available to rehabilitation counselors in training and in the field pertinent medical and psychosocial information, which it is hoped will enhance the quality of communication among members of the rehabilitation team and result in more effective delivery of service to the client.

REFERENCES

Bellak, L.: *Psychology of Physical Illness.* New York, Grune and Stratton, 1952.

Garrett, J. F. and Levine, S. E.: *Psychological Practice with the Physically Disabled.* New York, Columbia University Press, 1962.

Healey, J. E., Jr.: *Ecology of the Cancer Patient.* Washington, D.C., The Interdisciplinary Communication Associates, Inc., 1970.

McDaniel, J. W.: *Physical Disability and Human Behavior.* New York, Pergamon Press, 1969.

Chapter II

MEDICAL ASPECTS OF HEART DISEASE

O. Brandon Hull

GENERAL INFORMATION

Heart disease is an interesting and fascinating subject. The fact that some form of cardiovascular disease causes between 50 and 55 percent of the deaths in this country each year makes people conscious of its importance. President Eisenhower's heart attack focused national attention on coronary heart disease. Since then, volumes have been written by columnists, and everyone has assumed that it is his right to discuss the subject. All news media have felt free to treat it at great length. Yet it is surprising at times that in spite of the exposure, the public seems to have little knowledge of heart disease.

The human heart is a wonderful and amazing organ. It is designed to work 24 hours a day, 365 days a year, and in isolated instances has done so for 100 years or more. In a 70-year life span, the ordinary heart will beat about 2½ billion times, pumping anywhere from 60 to 300 gallons of blood each hour, depending upon the activity habits of an individual. This amounts to several hundred million gallons during a lifetime. It performs this staggering feat without once stopping for a rest.

ANATOMY OF THE HEART

Before we get into the study of particular diseases, we should review some of the anatomy and physiology of the heart.

The heart is a hollow muscular organ somewhat conical in shape and roughly about the size of one's fist. It is situated in the middle of the chest area, with the apex (left ventricle) extending well into the left side of the chest cavity. The heart consists of four chambers: two *atria* (auricles) and two *ventricles*. All chambers are divided by walls and/or heart valves. For simplicity, the heart may be thought of as divided into two symmetrical halves

8

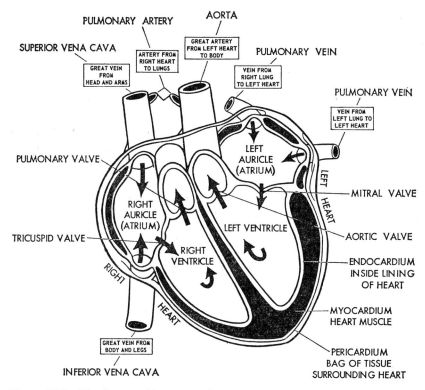

PULMONARY ARTERY AORTA

SUPERIOR VENA CAVA

GREAT ARTERY
FROM LEFT HEART
TO BODY

ARTERY FROM
RIGHT HEART
TO LUNGS

GREAT VEIN
FROM
HEAD AND ARMS

PULMONARY VEIN

VEIN FROM
RIGHT LUNG
TO LEFT HEART

PULMONARY VEIN

VEIN FROM
LEFT LUNG TO
LEFT HEART

PULMONARY VALVE

LEFT
AURICLE
(ATRIUM)

LEFT HEART

MITRAL VALVE

RIGHT
AURICLE
(ATRIUM)

LEFT VENTRICLE

HEART

TRICUSPID VALVE

AORTIC VALVE

RIGHT
VENTRICLE

RIGHT HEART

ENDOCARDIUM
INSIDE LINING
OF HEART

MYOCARDIUM
HEART MUSCLE

GREAT VEIN FROM
BODY AND LEGS

INFERIOR VENA CAVA

PERICARDIUM
BAG OF TISSUE
SURROUNDING HEART

Figure II.1. The heart. (Courtesy of U. S. Department of Health, Education, and Welfare. *Descriptions of Common Impairments.* Washington, D.C., U. S. Govt. Printing Office, 1959.)

because each half has a slightly different function. The upper portions of each half of the heart are the atria. These receive the blood. From the atria (auricles), the blood flows through valves into the lower portion of each half of the heart, the ventricles. The ventricles are the heavy muscular portions of the heart; they do most of the pumping. The right half of the heart receives venous blood—blood which has lost its nutrients (e.g. oxygen, etc.) and has picked up cell excretions (e.g. carbon dioxide, etc.) and pumps the blood into the lungs where carbon dioxide is given off and oxygen is received. The left half of the heart receives blood from the lungs and pumps it into the aorta (the large artery supplying the entire body with fresh blood). The coronary arteries which supply the heart muscle itself with fresh blood are branches of the aorta.

DISEASES OF THE CARDIOVASCULAR SYSTEM

There are many different types of heart disease. Perhaps it is easier to study them if they are presented in chronological order according to the types of heart disease we might see from birth through old age. Congenital heart disease, naturally, is the most common type of infancy. Rheumatic heart disease as the result of rheumatic fever is most common around the age of nine or ten, and we generally see this through the early twenties. After the early twenties, hypertension, or hypertensive cardiovascular disease, is the most common type. Occurring a little bit later, but almost concurrently, in the mid-forties and on into later life is atherosclerotic heart disease. There are many other kinds of heart disease due to infections and nutritional and metabolic disturbances, but they make up only a very small percentage of cases. Depending on age, time, and whose figures one might be quoting, approximately 90 percent of all heart disease is made up of three types: rheumatic, hypertensive, and atherosclerotic. Each type will be briefly described.

Congenital Heart Disease

The etiology of congenital heart disease is unknown except in about 35 percent of cases. When a pregnant woman has a viral infection, especially German measles or so-called "three-day measles," during the first trimester, there is a high incidence of congenital heart disease and congenital anomalies in general. Any type of viral infection which causes a high fever, certain nutritional deficiencies, vitamin deficiencies, etc., may play a part. Other than this, there is no known direct cause of congenital heart disease.

Congenital heart disease commanded very little attention among doctors until 1939. At this time, Dr. Gross in Boston tied off a patent *ductus arteriosus*, and since then, congenital heart disease has become very important to recognize and diagnose. One must realize that certain congenital anomalies may produce symptoms during the first few hours or the first few weeks after birth. Great strides in diagnosis and treatment have been made and are being made every day, so that the picture changes constantly. There are some congenital defects that allow a person to lead practically a full and normal life. In between, there are all gradations of defects, some of which can be corrected surgically, and the patient can be operated on as soon as they are diagnosed. There are others that need only to be studied and observed so that proper advice can be given at the time, depending on the technique that has been improved upon and developed through the preceding months or years. In other words, the picture changes constantly with medical advances.

Recent discoveries in medicine, particularly the advent of the sulfa drugs in 1938 and 1939 and penicillin in 1940, have allowed surgeons to operate within the chest cavity, where before, infections had prevented any definitive treatment. New developments in anesthesiology, a new understanding of cardiopulmonary physiology, and the ability of surgeons, anesthetists, and medical men to work together as a team have allowed procedures to be done now that would have been undreamed of as recently as 20 years ago. These advances have brought forth a whole new field of medicine and in fact have created a subspecialist in surgery— the chest and cardiovascular surgeon.

In fetal life, there is small communication between the pulmonary artery and the aorta. The fact that before birth the fetus is not breathing any air into the lungs makes it unnecessary for the blood to be pumped through the lungs, and so this *ductus arteriosus* acts as a shunt. The blood is pumped from the pulmonary artery into the aorta by way of this shunt and hence is distributed through the body and back to the heart again but bypassing the lungs. Normally this closes at birth or within a few hours afterwards—certainly within the first three to four days. Occasionally, however, in some infants it remains open. This was the type of surgery that was first performed by Dr. Gross in 1939. Some people with this defect are able to lead perfectly normal lives, but the natural history in the great majority of such cases is for them to go into congestive heart failure sometimes in their middle twenties or early thirties and die because of this defect with its resulting pathophysiology. Since this now can be corrected surgically, and it is one of the lesions that requires surgery when first diagnosed, after surgery the individual can be expected to lead a perfectly normal life.

Pulmonary stenosis is a narrowing of the outflow tract of the right ventricle somewhere between the pulmonary valve and the branches of the pulmonary artery. When this tract is narrowed, or stenosed, it causes an increased work load on the right side of the heart, and youngsters or young adults with this affliction can get into difficulty with heart failure sometime later in life, again depending on the degree of the stenosis, or narrowing.

Coarctation of the aorta is a narrowing of the aortic arch that occurs most commonly just past the takeoff of the left subclavian artery; however, it may be proximal to this and may vary in size from a small stricture or contraction to an inch or two in length or even longer. This causes high blood pressure above and low blood pressure plus absent pulsations in the arteries below the point of narrowing.

The two disabilities mentioned so far are really outside the heart and not inside the heart itself. Actually, the most common defect statistically is failure of closure between the walls of the two upper chambers of the heart, the atria. This is called an *atrial septal defect.* The next most common, and varying with statistics, is an opening between the two lower chambers of the heart, the ventricles. This is called a ventricular septal defect. Both of these lesions are compatible with life, depending on the size of the opening, but because of improvements in technique, the heart may now be opened and the openings can be closed successfully. Such operations are being done every day. Again, the changing circumstances in the day-to-day, month-to-month, and year-to-year improvement in this type of surgery must be noted.

Another common type of congenital defect is *tetralogy of Fallot.* This was originally described by Dr. Fallot and is a combination of congenital defects, namely: (a) pulmonic stenosis, (b) ventricular septal defect, (c) dextraposition of the aorta, so that it receives blood from the right as well as from the left ventricle, and (d) hypertrophy of the right ventricle. There are different types of procedure and operations to correct this defect with improving results through the years with added experience.

It must be added that there are many other combinations and possibilities of congenital heart disease. Those discussed above are the more common ones, the ones which at the present time are being treated most successfully. With newer advances, techniques, and experience, others will be added to this list.

Rheumatic Heart Disease

After congenital heart disease found in children to the age of nine, we may find rheumatic heart disease, which is the result of rheumatic fever. The cause of rheumatic fever is not known. It is believed to result from an infection with the beta hemolytic streptococcus and possibly other infectious conditions. The disease causes disability in any one or more of several ways. When inflammation develops in the heart, it may take the form of inflammation of the inner lining of the heart or *endocardium (endocarditis)* of the heart valves *(valvulitis)* of the heart muscle or *myocardium (myocarditis)* or of the sac enveloping the heart or *pericardium (pericarditis)*. Endocarditis is used to indicate not only the inflammation of the lining of the heart but of the valve and the valve structure.

When the damage is to the valve, the healing of the inflammation may be accompanied by scar formation, with the result that the valve may become thickened and distorted. These changes may prevent proper closure, thus permitting some of the blood to slip back through the valve. The defect is called *valvular insufficiency* or *regurgitation,* and usually produces a characteristic heart murmur (sound that the blood makes as it leaks back through the valve). The valves most frequently affected are those on the left side of the heart—the mitral valve and the aortic valve. The mitral valve separates the left auricle or upper portion of the left side of the heart from the left ventricle, which is essentially the pumping portion of the left side of the heart. The blood that is purified leaves the lungs through the pulmonary veins which take the blood to the left auricle. Then the pure blood passes from the auricle through the mitral valve to the ventricle, where it is pumped to the rest of the body through the aorta and its branches. When the mitral valve is inflamed, thickened, and scarred, and is prevented from closing efficiently, the doctor calls this *mitral insufficiency.* If the aortic valve is affected, the condition is called *aortic insufficiency.* In mitral insufficiency (*regurgitation*), the improper closing of this valve permits some of the blood to regurgitate back through the valve and into the auricle, thereby increasing the pressure in the blood vessels of the lung. Also, the left ventricle has to work more, since some of the blood it pumps is going the wrong way. When the heart is unable to keep up with this additional workload effectively, congestive heart failure results, with "backing up of blood." In extreme cases, the air sacs of the lungs may become filled with fluid from the blood, which may seriously interfere with breathing capacity. This condition is known as *pulmonary edema.*

Sometimes the inflammation causes not only a scarring but a partial fusion of the edges of the valves. This, in effect, reduces the size of the valve opening, limiting the amount of blood that can be forced through. This condition is known as *stenosis,* hence *mitral stenosis.* Narrowing of the mitral valve causes back pressure in the left auricle and pulmonary vein. This pressure prevents proper lung functioning and causes shortness of breath and edema in the lungs and other body tissues as in the case of mitral insufficiency. Valvular defects may produce a greater than normal burden on the heart muscle. When a valve leaks, the same blood has to be repumped, and when there is stenosis, the heart has to pump with greater force in order to supply sufficient blood to the body. The mechanism of compensation for this and other defects, whereby the heart muscle makes up for the damage, will be discussed later.

If mitral stenosis or mitral insufficiency persists for a period of time with repeated pulmonary congestion ("left-sided" heart failure), the increase in back pressure in the pulmonary vessels is transmitted back into the pulmonary artery, and this may in turn strain the right side of the heart, resulting in "right-sided" heart failure.

Occasionally heart valves which have been damaged by rheumatic fever become the seat of a bacterial infection, the bacteria usually having gained entrance to the bloodstream through an infected tooth or some other infection and then lodged in the diseased heart valve. This condition is known as *bacterial endocarditis.* This is, in essence, a severe infectious illness, with fever, weight loss, weakness, and the usual signs of a systemic infection. Pieces of the infected valvular material may break off, enter the circulation, and occlude the vessels to vital organs causing serious and permanent damage (e.g. in the kidneys or brain).

A typical history of rheumatic fever might be of a youngster around the age of nine who develops the symptoms of a cold or sore throat. This may clear up in a matter of seven to eight days, or it may last a little bit longer than usual. In any event, it need not be severe or seemingly worse than a common upper respiratory infection. Sometime within the next two to six weeks he may not have returned to normal, may tire a little more easily, may run a low-grade temperature, and may start having some vague complaints around the joints, especially in the knees, ankles, elbows, wrists, with what may have been called "growing pains" in the past, or at least confused with such. It is this continued lack of normal activity and vague complaints which call the parents' attention to the fact that something may be going on other than just a common sore throat. It must be stated that having an infection with rheumatic fever does not per se necessitate rheumatic heart disease. Fortunately only a small percentage of people with rheumatic fever will develop valvular damage, but again, all too many develop difficulty.

During this time, the youngster may develop a heart murmur and a doctor may find some slight heart enlargement. Certain blood tests, such as a routine blood count, may show that the child is slightly anemic, and the white blood count may be elevated. The sedimentation rate is increased, and a test called the antistreptolysin titer may be higher than it should be, indicating a previous streptococcic infection. All these things suggest rheumatic fever and, depending on the type of murmur that is heard, would indicate particular valve damage.

There is a saying that "rheumatic fever licks the joints and bites the heart." The valves of the heart are almost tissue-paper thin and open and close with each heart beat. They should be free to open and close in the bloodstream just like the billowing of sails on a ship. In one who has had a rheumatic infection, there is scarring of the valves so that they do not open and close freely. The valve does not open as wide as it should normally, and we say that this valve is narrowed, or stenosed. Because of this valve damage, the leaflets cannot approximate each other and make a tight valve. So they begin to leak. When this happens, it is called an insufficient valve. Some valves may show only a stenosis, others only insufficiency, and some may show both stenosis and insufficiency. The valves most commonly affected with rheumatic fever are the mitral and aortic valves, or a combination of the two.

The youngster with rheumatic infection who develops rheumatic heart disease may get completely well after a period of two or three weeks, or the disease can be drawn out in a chronic illness and last several months, even up to a year or two. If there is permanent valvular damage, this is a "from-now-on situation," and depending on the degree, the individual may be able to lead a perfectly normal life or may be handicapped with certain limitations according to the pathophysiology of the valves involved.

The specific treatment consists of rest, adequate diet, vitamins, antibiotics, usually penicillin (the drug of choice) in the acute infections, and after the recovery the patient may or may not be restricted as to activity. The continued use of prophylactic penicillin to prevent recurrences of infection again depends on each individual case, and the doctor must decide on the best treatment.

Through the years, the scarring of the valves slowly increases. When the mitral valve is stenosed, surgical correction may or may not be needed to free the leaflets of this valve. This is another type of surgery which has been most successful and was first performed in 1949.

Surgery on the aortic valve is much less successful. At the present time, several artificial valves are being used, but these to date are not without fault and must be reserved for the patient who is in serious trouble.

Hypertension

When one speaks of hypertension, referring to high blood pressure, he is speaking of an elevation in either the systolic or the diastolic blood pressure. When the blood pressure is taken, the cuff is put around the arm and the rubber band inflated until no blood gets past the cuff. The physician listens with a stethoscope immediately below this point, releases the pressure, and then reads it on a column of mercury, or if the instrument happens to be an aneroid type, then just reads the dial. In listening, one notices when the blood first starts coming through, and this is read as the upper figure when the heart is beating, or contracting. This is called the *systolic* pressure. The air pressure is allowed to decrease, and when the sound changes or disappears, this is read as the *diastolic* or the lower figure. Taking thousands of blood pressure readings for a norm, physicians arbitrarily state that anything above 140 mm Hg systolic is high blood pressure or that anything over 90 for the lower diastolic reading is high blood pressure.

More concern is associated with the lower figure than the upper figure, because this is the one that does the damage through the years. The upper figure, or systolic pressure, fluctuates widely, and if the blood pressure of a person is taken twenty times a day it might be noticed that there is as much as 20 to 40 mm difference, depending on the circumstances or emotion, fatigue, and so forth. There is also a difference in the reading according to body position. A reading taken in the sitting position, in which most blood pressures are taken (and one that is usually quoted as an average), can change immediately when the patient stands up. On standing, a lot of blood drops into the lower extremities and abdomen; there is an immediate fall in pressure, as much as 20 points; and it takes a few seconds for the arteries to contract and the pulse to speed up a little in order to maintain a normal pressure. On squatting, the pressure increases as much as 20 to 30 points, and so when one changes from a squatting to a standing position, there may be a difference of from 30 to 60 mm Hg in the systolic pressure.

Blood pressures also vary somewhat according to age, sex, and states of physical and mental activity. With advancing age and consequent blood vessel changes, there is a tendency for the blood pressure to rise. Since one is generally dealing with an older population in a disability program, he might consider that the maximum normal blood pressure is approximately 150/90 for the older age group. Women tend to have slightly lower blood pressures. The 150 designates the systolic pressure which accompanies the contraction of the heart. The 90 designates the diastolic pressure or the pressure remaining in the arterial system during relaxation of the heart.

When the blood pressure rises above the normal level persistently during physical and mental rest, *hypertension* exists. There are numerous causes of elevated blood pressure, or hypertension, during rest. Diseases of the glandular system or endocrine system, diseases of the kidney, diseases of vessels themselves, or emotional diseases may produce elevations in blood pressure. Hypertension in these diseases is generally termed "secondary hypertension" and may usually be cured by treating the underlying disease.

There is another form of hypertension where the cause is not known or cannot be removed. This form is by far the most common. It should be noted that as knowledge of this disease has progressed, a number of conditions that were once not remediable have turned out to be secondary hypertension and can be cured. (It is important to realize that the diastolic pressure correlates better with unfavorable prognosis of course. This is not to imply that the systolic blood pressure is without significance.)

Hypertension may exist for many years before it begins to produce organic changes of a more permanent nature. This period may vary from 1 to 40 years, but is usually less than 10. Hypertension becomes disabling, usually due to changes in vessels.

Organs most commonly involved are the brain, heart, and kidney. Disturbances of the organs result in malfunction. Also, the hypertension produces an increased workload on the heart. When this work exceeds the ability of the heart to perform its function, the heart begins to fail and congestive heart failure develops. (Congestive failure will be discussed separately.) We might spend just a few moments discussing the effects of the changes in the arteries upon the functioning of the different organs.

In the brain, occlusion of a blood vessel, insufficient supply, or bleeding may occur. This results in abnormal function or death of certain nerve cells with observable neurological changes. When occlusion or hemorrhage occurs, it is referred to as a *cerebrovascular accident* (CVA) or "stroke."

By looking at the blood vessels of the retina (the light-sensitive area of the eye), one may see spasms of these vessels or other abnormalities which signify end organ eye changes. In more advanced cases, hemorrhages may be seen, and in the most advanced cases, one may see edema of the optic disk (bulging due to retention of fluid). This edema of the structure in the optic disk is called *papilledema*. When one has marked elevations in blood pressure with papilledema, it is usually a sign of a poor prognosis.

The normal kidney maintains a proper chemical balance in the body. In hypertensive disease with significant damage to this organ, the chemical balance or regulatory function is disturbed. As a result, waste products accumulate which interfere with normal functions of the body. When extreme, the condition first reduces ability to function and may lead to death from uremia.

The *etiology of hypertension* is extremely varied. In only approximately 15 percent of cases, the actual cause can be determined. This may be due to endocrine disturbances; to brain tumors; to coarctation of the aorta, as mentioned in extremely young individuals; and to certain specific kidney lesions. In the last few years, it has become increasingly important to consider hardening of the renal arteries which reduces the blood supply to one or both kidneys, and this in turn can produce high blood pressure. However, we lump the great majority of cases under the term *essential hypertension* because people have high blood pressure and we cannot find the cause.

There is no doubt that emotions play a considerable part in producing high blood pressure, especially in younger individuals from their twenties to their forties. This can be seen when a young man goes in for his physical before going into the service. He may be a little bit tense, his palms a little bit sweaty, his pulse increased, and his blood pressure elevated. The same phenomenon occurs in people coming for insurance examinations. If they are allowed to rest, their pressure may drop down to a normal level within 15 to 20 minutes. However, a small percentage of people may be what we call hyperreactors in the sense that they continue to run a higher blood pressure at these times, and it is difficult to ever get a normal reading when around the doctor or at times of tension and anxiety. If we were able to take their blood pressure at home, it might be within normal limits. However, these people overact to stress and through the years are more prone to develop high blood pressure than those who are not of this nervous temperament. Although they may be more likely to develop high blood pressure, they are also generally perfectionists and take good care of themselves, and their chances of living a normal life or even longer are better than most people's because they seek medical advice early.

Treatment

As has been suggested, the course of hypertensive cardiovascular disease (that is, hypertension which has resulted in damage to the heart and blood vessels, brain, or kidneys) may run a highly variable course, and usually the hypertension exists for a considerable period of time before cardiovascular damage is seen. A rapidly progressing disease ending in death within six to eight months is called *malignant hypertension*. It should be pointed out that this develops in a minority of cases of hypertension and is generally found in younger people between the ages of 20 and 40.

There are numerous drugs today which are used to treat hypertensive vascular disease. It is the consensus that these drugs change the course of the disease. Secondary hypertension is treated by caring for the underlying disease. Surgical procedures are also available for certain cases of hypertension.

People with high blood pressure over a period of years generally get into trouble with (a) congestive heart failure, (b) heart attacks (myocardial infarction), (c) nephrosclerosis producing uremia, (d) cerebral vascular accident or stroke, or (e) any combination of the previous four. Consequently it is important for anyone who has high blood pressure to be under medical attention through the years in order to keep his pressure within normal limits and delay or forestall any of the above complications.

Atherosclerotic Heart Disease

Although it is possible to have atherosclerosis without high blood pressure, people with high blood pressure always have atherosclerosis. The elevation of blood pressure seems to speed up the process of atherosclerosis and arteriosclerosis (hardening of the arteries). The fact that these two generally go together means that we can discuss many of the possible etiological factors together.

In arteriosclerotic heart disease, there is disease of the coronary arteries (blood vessels supplying the heart). There is abnormal deposition of fatty material including calcium and cholesterol in the walls of the blood vessels. These structural changes are referred to as "degenerative" changes and result in reduction of the calibre (lumen) of the blood vessel. With reduction of the blood vessel lumen, there is a diminution of blood supply to the heart muscle, especially during activity. The extent of the disease process will determine the extent of reduction in blood supply and of muscle ability to remain healthy and work. The heart requires oxygen and other nutrients carried by the blood to maintain normal structure and function. With the diminishing of the blood supply, as occurs in this disease process, the heart muscle suffers for want of nutrients. At first only the strength or function of the heart muscle may be affected, but as the disease progresses, there may be definite structural and chemical changes in the organ itself.

There are five important factors in the etiology of atherosclerosis. These include heredity, high blood pressure, obesity or overweight, diet, and stress.

HEREDITY. If there is a strong history of heart disease in the family, especially occurring in members around forty or so, this is a significant point. Heart disease that has developed in the late fifties or early sixties is also important, but so many people get atherosclerosis after the age of sixty that it used to be thought that this was just a normal process of aging. With more and more investigation going on, it is uncertain whether this is true.

HIGH BLOOD PRESSURE. As mentioned above, high blood pressure speeds up the process of atherosclerosis, and so it is important that blood pressure be controlled.

OBESITY OR OVERWEIGHT. It seems that some people can carry extra weight without any trouble, and yet of a thousand overweight people, statistics show that more of them are likely to get heart trouble than a thousand skinny people. At the same time there are fat people who never have heart trouble and thin people who may, but physicians are unable at the present time to single out the fat ones that will get in trouble; consequently, they may make the general statement that it is better for people to maintain an average weight or a little below because there are certain other diseases that are apparently brought on by obesity.

DIET. Here one encounters the conflicting evidence about cholesterol, fats, etc. One could fill a large room with journals, both pro and con, and after having read all of them, one would probably still be undecided as to what part cholesterol and fat metabolism may play in the etiology of atherosclerosis. After reading the literature of the last few years, one might think that this information is new; however, it has been known for over a hundred years that cholesterol may be deposited in the lining of the arteries. The problem is whether it plays a part and why it is deposited in the lining of the vessels in the first place.

People are confused because of what they read. Many people come into a doctor's office just wanting to have a cholesterol test done, or after he has examined them, the patients say, "Aren't you going to test my cholesterol?" And it is difficult to explain to them that although many doctors believe that cholesterol may be important, just as many believe that it is not. This obviously provides reason for the patient to wonder.

It is important to point out that cholesterol level, as measured in the blood, may be anywhere from 200 to 250 as a normal limit, with 250 probably being a rough average. Because it is an extremely difficult test to do accurately, one test may be off as much as 15 to 20 percent. The cholesterol level fluctuates markedly from day to day. It apparently goes up at times of stress or tension. It has been shown that people playing bridge, if they are really intense bridge players, may have a higher cholesterol. Students taking examinations have elevated cholesterols, and certified public accountants will run higher blood cholesterols when they are busy working on income tax forms from January 1 to April 15 than they do the other months of the year. Consequently, to have a blood cholesterol checked on one occasion and to find that it is high or low may be inaccurate according to what that individual may average if several levels are taken over a period of time. This is probably the only accurate way to do it in order to get a baseline for a particular individual.

When we try to summarize the importance of diet, fats, and cholesterol, about all that we can say is that one should not be overweight and should not be a heavy fat eater, especially of animal fats or fats that are solid at room temperature. This is why the polyunsaturated fats such as found in vegetable oils have been so highly advertised.

STRESS. We must include smoking as stress. In considering smoking and stress one wonders whether an individual smokes because he is under stress or is under tension because he smokes or what. In any event, the tense, anxious, heavy-smoking, high-pressure individual seems to get into trouble more than the calm, composed, relaxed person. Again, this may be difficult to substantiate statistically, but it is the high-pressure type of individual who is competitive in nature and has to strive constantly to be at the top, regardless of his vocation, who gets into trouble.

There are also other names for atherosclerotic heart disease. The term generally refers to the blood vessels that supply the heart or the coronary arteries, and so doctors speak of coronary artery disease, coronary heart disease, and atherosclerotic heart disease.

The person with atherosclerotic heart disease generally has symptoms starting out with what is called *angina pectoris*. This is described as a heavy, pressure-like sensation in the middle of the chest, which may go up into the throat or into the arms. But generally, simple angina is located in the chest and throat. This usually comes on at times of exertion when a person tries to do things in a hurry such as climbing stairs, walking, running fast, or any ordinary type of exercise. It is more likely to occur when one is under emotional tension or walks into the wind on a cold day or has eaten too much or has had something cold to drink. It only lasts for a matter of three to four minutes; if he stops to rest, the pains disappear, or a nitroglycerin tablet under the tongue brings almost immediate relief. Some people may have as many as one hundred attacks a day requiring as many as one hundred nitroglycerin tablets in extreme cases. Again, it is most important that people learn to live with this in order to stay out of trouble.

The next symptom is the same type of pain but more severe, and instead of lasting only three to five minutes, it may last for a period of thirty minutes to three or four hours. The patient may have excruciating pain, break out in a cold, clammy sweat, be pale, and have a drop in blood pressure. In this case, it is very difficult to say whether the patient has or has not had a *myocardial infarction* (heart attack); consequently, he has to be put into the hospital and treated as if he has until proved otherwise.

The third and more severe pain is as described above, but actual evidence of heart muscle damage shows on the electrocardiogram. Also the patient runs a temperature and has an increased blood count, sedimentation rate, and a transaminase of serum glutamic pyruvic transaminase (SGPT) test. These patients are the ones who actually have had a heart attack with heart muscle damage. When doctors speak of a heart attack, this is all they are referring to, for a fast heart rate or simple angina or coronary artery insufficiency is not a heart attack as such.

After one has had one of the coronary arteries plugged off and has an area of heart muscle damage, this area of damage is called a *myocardial infarction.* (A myocardial infarction may be defined as an area of dead tissue in which the blood supply has been cut off through the plugging off of an artery.) Consequently, the cause of this plugging off may be a myocardial infarction, a coronary occlusion (if the vessel has just become occluded), or a thrombus, in which case the term *coronary thrombosis* is used. All of these are the same type of thing and deal only with the immediate pathology, but the end result is the same.

A person who has had a heart attack is just like someone who has broken a leg. People realize that breaking a leg means it will take a period of from eight to ten weeks time for the fracture to heal and that it is going to have to be in a cast. The same thing is true with the heart; it takes three to six weeks for it to heal with a hard, firm scar in the area of heart muscle damage, but we cannot take the heart out and put it in a cast; we cannot turn it off to heal. Consequently, the only way we can give the heart an opportunity to heal is to keep an individual in bed and to keep him quiet for a period of two to four weeks with gradual increase in activity.

The most dangerous time is from onset to the fourteenth day, and for this reason we generally keep patients in the hospital for two weeks or so, then send them home for about the same amount of activity for another two weeks, then try having them go to the table to eat, go to the bathroom, and be up and around a little each morning and afternoon by the end of the sixth week after they first had their attack. The next six weeks are spent in gradually increased activity so that in the majority of cases the patients are back at their old jobs three months later.

The majority of people, about eight out of ten, can return to their old activities, provided that they have no more angina, heart enlargement, or heart failure. Again, the single most important thing is for them to learn to live with their situation and try to lead as normal a life as they did previously but take a little better care of themselves without letting themselves get tired; trying to do things too hard, too fast, or too long; having emotional upsets, etc.

Congestive Heart Failure

It has been suggested in the foregoing discussion that most heart diseases, including arteriosclerotic heart disease, hypertensive heart disease, rheumatic heart disease, etc., may progress to congestive heart failure. In the above diseases, it was noted that the heart or heart musculature (myocardium) is placed under increased stress. The heart reacts to this added stress as follows. The heart muscle enlarges in size *(hypertrophy)* just as the arm muscles of a weight lifter enlarge. With the increase in muscle mass, there is also an increased demand by this musculature for blood, which is supplied by an increase in the coronary blood flow. The heart chamber size increases by a greater relaxation of muscle (cardiac dilation), and this allows, up to a certain point, a stronger contraction and ejection of a larger amount of blood per contraction. The heart thus maintains a continued fairly normal circulation of blood; this is called *cardiac compensation.*

As the stress persists for a period of time, the heart can no longer continue to hypertrophy; and its musculature gradually loses its ability to perform its appointed task and begins to fail. This is termed *cardiac decompensation* and results in the clinical picture of *congestive heart failure.*

The next step is to understand what is meant by the word "congestive," as used in the term "congestive heart failure." Let us take an example and we shall see why this word has been used. In a person with long-standing valve or heart disease, the heart has become hypertrophied and dilated. The coronary blood flow is insufficient to meet the requirements of the changed heart. As a result, the heart begins to fail—*it cannot fulfill its task.* Failure is frequently limited first to the left ventricle, although both ventricles may fail simultaneously. As the left ventricle fails, it (the ventricle) is not well emptied with each ventricular contraction. The consequence of this incomplete emptying is that the blood in the left atrium which empties into the left ventricle is placed under increased pressure. The increased pressure in the left atrium is in turn transmitted via the pulmonary vein to the small blood vessels (capillaries) of the lung. These small blood vessels may be quite distended, as their walls are very thin. The increased pressure in the left atrium and pulmonary vein (a back pressure from the left ventricle) leads to the accumulation of blood in the small blood vessels of the lungs. These blood vessels become distended and engorged with blood. These changes (due to pressure and other subtle phenomena) produce leakage of blood into the tissue spaces of the lung, causing congestion. This fluid in the lung tissue is called *pulmonary edema.*

As the left ventricle begins to fail more and more, the back pressure is transmitted all the way to the right ventricle (from the left ventricle to the left atrium, from the left atrium via the pulmonary vein to the lungs, from the lungs via the pulmonary artery to the right ventricle). This back pressure places a stress upon the right ventricle which may become sufficient to make the right ventricle fail. The failure in turn produces increased pressure in the great veins leading from the head and arms and from the body and legs (superior vena cava and inferior vena cava). Increased pressure in the superior vena cava may be transmitted to the liver where the smaller blood vessels (capillaries) become engorged. Again, edema may result, as was the case in the lungs. Liver engorgement and edema result in liver enlargement.

Increased pressure also may be transmitted to the capillaries of the lower extremities where edema may be formed, producing swelling of the lower extremities. Thus, it should become clear that with heart failure there is a tendency for blood pressure to "back up," as it were, producing congestion of organs and formation of edema fluid. There are factors other than pressure changes which play a part in decompensation and edema formation.

The above discussion would become too lengthy and complex if all mechanisms of failure were properly discussed. We have considered one pressure and traced it backwards against the bloodstream. In the medical literature, this type of failure is termed "backward failure," as opposed to another type called "forward failure." The mechanism is less important in evaluating work capacity than in appreciating the slow and relentless progression of decompensation over a period of years ending in irreversible anatomical changes and an irremediable manifestation. An example of this would be dyspnea with mild exercise and later even at rest, terminating finally in death.

In some diseases, the stress may be almost exclusively upon the right ventricle, but this is comparatively rare. This contributes to the total picture of congestive failure. In such diseases, the right ventricle may fail without the left ventricle failing. Such a situation—right failure without left failure—would usually be transient.

One of the most common symptoms of congestive failure is shortness of breath. Shortness of breath experienced as a feeling is called *dyspnea*. Generally, dyspnea will become more severe as the pulmonary congestion and edema formation becomes more marked. Of course, dyspnea is a subjective personal feeling and therefore need not especially parallel the severity of the lung congestion. When shortness of breath or dyspnea is experienced while lying down, it is called *orthopnea*. When the shortness of breath occurs intermittently at night it is called *paroxysmal nocturnal dyspnea*.

Congestive heart failure does not mean the end of activity. Digitalis is a drug which is used because it increases the strength of the muscular contraction of the heart. Restriction of dietary sodium intake (table salt, etc.) and the use of diuretics help the elimination of fluid by way of the kidneys. There are many diuretics. Mercurials and ammonium chloride are old standbys, but new, excellent diuretics are continuing to appear. With the judicious use of drugs, diet, and restriction of physical activity, a state of compensation may again be attained. Eventually, however, even with these measures the heart may no longer be able to maintain a stable state of compensation; here we have a condition which is referred to in our guides as *established congestive heart failure*.

A type of right heart failure is produced by lung disease. Resistance to flow of blood through the lungs may produce enlargement of the pulmonary artery and right side of the heart. Eventually failure of the right side of the heart occurs as discussed above. This condition is called *"cor pulmonale"* or *"pulmonary heart disease"* and is discussed briefly in the section on lung disease. Similar to other forms of right heart failure, it does not yield so readily to treatment as the more common types of heart failure.

Cardiovascular Syphilis

The syphilis organism (spirochete) may cause damage in the wall of the aorta or in the valve between the heart and the aorta. This valve is called the aortic valve. The aorta is the main artery leading from the left ventricle and carrying fresh blood to all parts of the body. The following are the principal ways in which the cardiovascular syphilis results in disability.

When the spirochete localizes in the wall of the aorta, it damages and weakens the wall. When the blood from the heart pumps into the aorta, the pressure causes the aorta to dilate. This dilatation, or enlargement, is called an *aneurysm*. The aneurysm may be painful and interfere with normal functions. It may cause various disturbances by exerting pressure on neighboring structures. It may rupture causing death by hemorrhage.

The syphilitic process may also involve the aorta at the side of origin of the coronary arteries, interfering with the opening and function of the coronary arteries. This may deprive the heart of its necessary blood supply, resulting in angina pectoris, heart failure, or myocardial infarction, comparable in a way to arteriosclerotic coronary artery disease.

Another way in which cardiovascular syphilis may cause disability is by the damage the spirochete causes to the aortic valve. The valve may be damaged to the extent that it becomes unable to close completely. The blood pumped from the heart into the aorta then leaks back into the heart. In this way, the heart has to do more pumping to maintain an adequate blood supply for the body. Because of this continuous strain, the heart may begin to fail, and congestive heart failure results.

Other Cardiovascular Diseases

Buerger's disease or *thromboangiitis obliterans* is of unknown etiology. It was originally described by Dr. Leo Buerger, who had many Jewish patients, and it was thought that this disease occurred only in Jews, especially in those originating in the area of the Black Sea. It is now thought that smoking definitely plays a very great part in this illness and that it is an inflammatory reaction involving the arterioles of the extremities, which can cause gangrene of the fingers and toes and even loss of limb. People with this disease are sensitive to tobacco and never do well unless they quit smoking.

Raynaud's disease has to do with the nerve supply to the arterioles, where people get vasoconstriction with narrowing of the vessels. This disease usually is seen in women, especially around the age of menopause. The afflicted are more sensitive to cold; for example, reaching into the refrigerator for a bottle of milk may trigger off an episode of blanching of the hand, which turns white due to the painful constriction of the arterioles. An emotional factor is also involved, and, again, we do not know the etiology of this.

Endocarditis is an inflammation of the lining or valves of the heart. This is usually superimposed on a congenital lesion or on an old valvular lesion of rheumatic heart disease. Whenever a person goes through the simple process of chewing food, he gets a shower of bacteria into the blood; if he happens to have a rough surface upon which bacteria may lodge, such as a damaged heart valve, then such an individual is more prone to infection. Before the days of antibiotics, these cases were practically always fatal, but now, depending on the type of bacteria, as many as 90 percent of them can be saved; however, if it happens to be a viral and staphylococcus infection, this figure may be lowered to 5 percent. So much depends on the virulence and type of bacteria.

DIAGNOSTIC SYMPTOMS IN HEART DISEASE

There are certain symptoms which are similar in all types of heart disease: shortness of breath on exertion, tiring more easily with activity, waking up in the middle of the night short of breath, having to sit up to breathe (this may last only a few minutes at a time), increased gaseousness or sense of fullness in the stomach, and swelling of the ankles. These are all symptoms of heart failure. Heart failure means that the myocardium (the heart muscles) reaches a point where it has difficulty in maintaining adequate circulation. The blood is not pumped fast enough in adequate quantities to supply the tissues of the body, and this begins to tell with increased venous pressure, with the filtering out of fluid into the tissues, and with the symptoms mentioned above.

The relation of congenital heart disease to cyanosis, which indicates inadequate oxygenation and which leads one to suspect the possibility of certain types of congenital heart disease, is of special interest. In other cases, one may suspect congestive failure, if an inadequate oxygen supply is being carried to the tissues.

Certain physical findings help us determine the type of congenital or rheumatic lesion. Whenever the heart contracts and the blood is forced through the heart in a pumping action, there are certain sounds, normally described as "lub-dub," produced by the contraction of the muscle and the closing of the valves. If the blood happens to be going through a larger or a smaller opening such as those produced by stenosis or insufficiency; or if there is a congenital opening such as a patent ductus or septal defect, as discussed under congenital and rheumatic heart disease, then there are differences in the heart sounds. These are called murmurs. It is like having a garden hose without a nozzle on it, for the water comes out and does not make much noise. However, if one places the thumb over the end of the hose, then there is a swishing sound. A murmur is a swishing sound produced by the blood going over or through an abnormal opening or a roughened area. Instead of having the sound of "lub-dub," it may "swish-dub" or "lub-swish," depending on whether it is in systole or diastole; or it may be in both. The location, the type of sound, its intensity, whether it is harsh or soft, blowing or rough, all help determine the etiology and what valve or defect might be present.

Heart enlargement is the most important single thing in physical findings as far as heart disease is concerned. Heart enlargement always means trouble. This does not mean that one cannot live for years with a grossly enlarged heart, but it does signify that pathology is present—enough to make the heart enlarge. This is determined by physical examination, although it is only a rough measure and is more accurately done with fluoroscopy and x-ray of the chest. In this way, the particular chamber of the heart involved can be noticed and help establish the diagnosis and etiology.

The electrocardiogram has helped greatly in diagnosing particular types of disturbance of heart rhythm termed *arrhythmias*. This may be only an occasional ectopic beat; that is, when one beat comes in a little bit too soon. Or this may occur when the upper part of the heart beats independently of the lower part of the heart, in which case we call it an atrial flutter or atrial fibrillation, depending on the type; in other words, these are two different types of arrhythmias.

A complete heart block may occur, depending on the area of damage in the conduction system of the heart. When this occurs with the slowing of the pulse to 20 to 30 and with symptoms of fainting, artificial pacemakers are used.

In heart catheterization, a catheter is passed generally through the veins directly into the heart or sometimes into the femoral artery and into the aorta or into the left side of the heart, depending on what lesion the doctor is trying to diagnose. This is not done without some hazard, but again the risk is minimized when one realizes that these people are headed for trouble and that definitive surgery could cure them. In good hands, complications are minimal. Cineradiography or aortography, in which dye is injected and x-rays are taken as it goes through a particular vessel or the heart, also helps us understand the physiology better and helps make accurate diagnoses.

Atherosclerosis of the peripheral vessels generally in the feet and legs may cause a narrowing and an inadequate blood supply to the muscles of the legs and feet. When one has inadequate blood supply to the leg muscles, he experiences pain similar to angina. In other words, a person walking will develop leg cramps, but when he stops to rest, the pain disappears. This is similar to angina pectoris and is described under coronary heart disease. At times it may progress to actual gangrene of the toes and is generally worse in people who have diabetes since it is one of the complications that accompanies this illness.

In evaluating any type of heart disease, a careful history and physical examination are necessary. A chest x-ray, electrocardiogram (EKG), and other laboratory studies are frequently helpful.

A full diagnosis of heart disease usually includes a statement of cause or etiology, description of the anatomical lesion (structural change), physiologic changes, and therapeutic implications including functional restrictions.

CLASSIFICATION OF HEART CONDITION

There are frequent references to the functional and therapeutic classification of the American Heart Association. The *functional* portion of this classification refers to the degree of activity which patients may endure without symptoms. This classification also describes the level of activity when the symptom begins. The following functional classification is quoted directly from the American Heart Association's publication, "Returning Cardiacs to Work," published in 1952. More recently, six classifications have been described; however, these generally are not used.

Class I. Patients with cardiac disease but without resulting limitation of physical activity. Ordinary physical activity does not cause undue fatigue, palpitation, dyspnea, or anginal pain.

Class II. Patients with cardiac disease resulting in slight limitation of physical activity. They are comfortable at rest.

Ordinary physical activity results in fatigue, palpitation, dyspnea, or anginal pain.

Class III. Patients with cardiac disease resulting in marked limitation of physical activity. They are comfortable at rest. Less than ordinary activity causes fatigue, palpitation, dyspnea, or anginal pain.

Class IV. Patients with cardiac disease resulting in inability to carry on any physical activity without discomfort. Symptoms of cardiac insufficiency or of anginal syndrome are present even at rest. If any physical activity is undertaken, discomfort is increased (p. 32).

The *therapeutic* classification refers to the type of activity prescribed for the patient as being of optimal benefit to such a patient. The following therapeutic classification is also quoted from "Returning Cardiacs to Work."

Class A. Patients with cardiac disease whose physical activity need not be restricted.

Class B. Patients with cardiac disease whose ordinary physical activity need not be restricted, but who should be advised against severe or competitive physical efforts.

Class C. Patients with cardiac disease whose ordinary physical activity should be moderately restricted and whose more strenuous efforts should be discontinued.

Class D. Patients with cardiac disease whose ordinary physical activity should be markedly restricted.

Class E. Patients with cardiac disease who should be at complete rest, confined to bed or chair (p. 45).

A complete diagnosis, therefore, might be stated as follows: etiologic, rheumatic heart disease; anatomic, mitral stenosis; physiologic, compensated; functional, Class I; therapeutic, Class A.

Such a complete diagnosis and functional classification may be a transient one insofar as physiologic, functional, and therapeutic implications are concerned. For purposes of disability benefits, it must be established from the evidence in the individual case whether the condition is transient subject to change, or whether a stable or slowly progressive condition has been reached. The functional portion of the classification is also subject to individual variation both from the standpoint of the classifier and from the standpoint of the applicant or patient presenting his problem. Some people have little pain and complain much; others have much pain and complain little. Some people have little dyspnea and complain much, while others have severe dyspnea and complain little.

It is commonly believed that a person suffering from heart disease is destined to a life of inactivity. This is far from true. A majority of these people can live entirely useful, and very often active, lives.

REHABILITATION

When it comes to actual rehabilitation of heart patients, roughly 72 to 80 percent can get back to some kind of work. This same group can return to their old jobs. You will have all the facts, figures, and advice from the physician on what these people will be able to do as far as their work capacity is concerned, and you will be one part of the team in making the decision about their return to work and their capabilities.

In general, it is best if they can get back to their old jobs as soon as possible, depending on their symptoms and physical findings and varying with their type of illness.

The contents of this chapter is intended to promote an interest in cardiovascular diseases in general. It was originally presented informally to small classes, usually 12 to 15 graduate students, in two two-hour discussions. Designed to call attention to the types of condition they might see most commonly in rehabilitation, it was delivered extemporaneously to promote questions.

It is not considered to be a scientific treatise on heart disease and no bibliography is provided. However, four reference books are listed which will give far more information than anyone working in rehabilitation can ever use. The references are excellent resource material, supplying information, descriptions of procedures, and a philosophy toward heart disease and rehabilitation.

REFERENCES

Hurst, X. and Logg, X.: *The Heart,* 2nd ed. New York, McGraw-Hill, 1970.

Netter, X.: *Heart.* The Ciba Collection of Medical Illustrations. Summit, New Jersey, Ciba, 1969, Vol. V.

Returning cardiacs to work. *American Heart Association,* 1952.

Wood, P.: *Diseases of the Heart,* 3rd ed. London, Eyre and Spottiswoode, 1968.

Chapter III

PSYCHOLOGICAL ASPECTS OF HEART DISEASE—IMPLICATIONS FOR REHABILITATION WORKERS

D. Bruce Bell, Beverly W. Bell and Franklin D. Lewis

A "*heart*warming" sight or she "died of a broken *heart*" are common expressions and illustrate quite clearly the symbolic importance the heart has for each of us. As the popular song says, "you gotta have *heart!*" This symbolic relationship underlies a complex interplay between organic and psychological phenomena that has been extensively investigated but is not fully understood. Emotions do affect the cardiovascular system and may bring about or facilitate the development of many types of abnormality. Heart disorders also have significant emotional consequences.

These consequences vary with the individual who experiences them. The nature and severity of the disorder are important factors. Other equally important factors are the time and manner in which a person becomes aware of his condition; his personality and prior experience; and the responses of the significant others in his life—his family, his employer, and members of the rehabilitation team that serves him. All have some impact on his interpersonal relations, socialization patterns, and vocational adjustment; and all must be considered in the rehabilitation process. However, as Hagan (1966, p. 62) emphasizes, "In many respects, the most significant stress in the cardiac patient's life is the significance of the disease to *him*."*

HEART DISORDERS IN CHILDHOOD

A heart disorder affects all aspects of a child's life: his physical condition, his personality, and his interaction with the world around him. The rehabilitation worker must consider all of these influences as he tries to help the young cardiac.

---

*Italics the authors'.

37

The physical limitation that a damaged heart imposes may preclude many activities in which most of us routinely engaged as children. Some of these (e.g. skipping rope, playing sandlot baseball) further developed our physical capacities (and, incidentally, our self-confidence) and contributed to our strength and agility. Not only does the young cardiac miss these opportunities, but additional, less obviously physical problems may inhibit a child's development. For example, Rasof, Linde, and Dunn (1967) found that mental retardation may follow the cyanotic episodes that occur in persons with congenital heart disease. And even if frank mental retardation does not result, a more subtle brain damage can arise from reduction of blood flow to the brain caused by the heart condition or by necessary surgical treatment.

In both children and adults, reduced or interrupted blood flow to the brain may also explain why McMahon (1967) found cardiac surgery associated with an increased incidence of serious depression, suicidal attempts, and psychosis. Some of these problems appear in the immediate postsurgical period only; some persist beyond it. Although some may be attributed to the surgery itself, others may be due to the dramatic role shifts which are demanded of the cardiac after successful surgery. Kaplan (1956) suggests that surgical removal of disability does not necessarily evoke universally favorable reactions. Ferguson and Rayport (1965) concur, stating that after successful operations, the cardiac (like the epileptic) is deluged with intrapersonal and interpersonal demands and that he becomes "burdened with normality." In this sense, all of these patients are involved in "an acute maturational phase."

But despite the potential problems already mentioned (including the possibility that surgery may result in death), Reiser and Bakst (1959) discovered that those who are scheduled for cardiac surgery—in contrast to persons scheduled for other operations—appear to welcome, not dread the procedure. This phenomenon is not difficult to understand, since techniques for cardiac surgery are constantly being refined, and the alternative appears to be slow deterioration and eventual death. In fact, the patient who is eager to undergo surgery may be responding in part to a realistic appreciation of the implications of his disability. On the other hand, he may expect a magical intervention producing complete and immediate recovery. Such a person is especially vulnerable to the disappointment that can result when surgery is only partially successful or the recovery process is slow (Nadas and Zaver, 1967).

Regardless of age, candidates for cardiac surgery can be expected to display many fears and ask many questions. All are likely to recognize the critical nature of the event (Fox, Rizzo, and Sanford, 1954). The Mayo Clinic has shown that the postoperative adjustment of general surgery patients is better if they express their fears and questions *before* the operations (McMahon, 1967); thus, some counseling should probably take place prior to surgery. If, during counseling, a child's emotional problems are determined to be severe, Nadas and Zaver (1967) feel the surgery should be postponed and psychiatric help offered. But if the surgery itself is causing the anxiety, postponement would only perpetuate that anxiety. In any case, Nadas and Zaver suggest that the surgery should be undertaken prior to puberty to lessen the possible bad effects of interrupted schooling, pregnancies, major role shifts, and inability to obtain financial assistance through parents' insurance policies.

In addition to major physical consequences, heart disease may affect a child's personality development. If the condition is congenital, the parents may feel responsible. The guilt this engenders may cause them to reject the child overtly and covertly (through overprotection and indulgence)—an attempt to compensate for "wronging" him (Lawrence, 1961; Nadas and Zaver, 1967). In either case, the developing child often responds to the underlying hostility with a negative self-image and low self-esteem, for children with cardiac disease are strongly influenced by parental perceptions or misperceptions. Offord and Aponte (1967) demonstrated that when the mother's view of the disease is distorted, the child is far more likely to have a distorted view of the limitations it imposes on him. He may be passive, dependent, or full of unrealistic fears.

Heart disease also frequently retards or inhibits normal socialization experiences. Lawrence (1961, p. 122) describes a sample of 256 children in New York City who had heart disease or histories of rheumatic fever.

> The case histories showed many school transfers due to illness, with interruption of the normal school program, for which home instruction, classes in hospitals, in convalescent homes and special classes in regular schools were substituted. Frequently, there were periods of no instruction, due to physical condition, or patterns of absence based on this condition, delay in transfer of records, or medical indecision regarding school placement. The children had experienced a sequence of new school adjustments, each one removing them from the normal flow of experience and interfering not only with their educational progress, but also with their general development.

Aware of and sympathetic to the problems that such children face, school personnel are prone to "make allowances" for the child with heart disease and to continue the pattern of overprotection initiated by many parents. Because the child feels "different" from his peers, his experiences become more restricted; consequently, if very little is demanded of him, he may conclude that he is "worthless." He may drop out of school or be in danger of dropping out of life altogether. Lawrence (1961) found that such young people tend not to receive school counseling, not to participate in work training, not to have medical follow-up, and to be unemployed.

Because of the tendency for this group to drop out of school, Lawrence (1961) also stresses the need for early intervention, which includes scholastic remediation and extensive counseling for the cardiac's family as well as the cardiac himself. Such counseling should be made available in the settings where the youngster normally is found—for example, the school or the medical clinic—so that it does not become an additional burden upon his limited physical condition to attend counseling sessions. In addition, placing the service near the potential client makes it easier for the counselor to engage in the aggressive follow-up that is often necessary to overcome the tendency for both parents and child to become discouraged and abandon vocational goals. Even when parents are willing to consider a given vocation, they tend to ". . . influence the child toward the quick, easy solution rather than the more difficult, but more constructive plan" (Lawrence, 1961, p. 134).

One challenge for the rehabilitation worker is to aid the young cardiac to enter the "proper" vocation—that is, one which is not only within his physical limitations but which challenges *him* and will provide a good living. A job which is too strenuous will be harmful in the long run, but a job which is too "easy" is also undesirable. Cardiacs can perform a wide range of jobs (Hellerstein and Hornsten, 1966; Hagan, 1966); too often the counselor (as well as the parent or physician) is guilty of selling these youths short by placing them in overly restrictive environments.

Good evaluation procedures can help the rehabilitation worker to achieve his goal. Yet precise psychometric evaluation of young cardiacs is especially difficult to obtain in the context of typical life experiences such as those described. In the absence of precision, (a) thoroughness, (b) a variety of assessment techniques, and (c) maintenance of a *tentative* attitude toward the findings seem indicated.

Young cardiacs constitute a small percentage of persons with heart disease, yet they are on the threshold of life and usually have many years to live well and contribute to society.

HEART DISORDERS IN THE ADULT YEARS

Unlike childhood cardiacs who usually have either congenitally malformed hearts or scarred valves due to rheumatic fever, the adult cardiac tends to suffer from hypertension or atherosclerosis (Hull, 1972). Although these may progress into heart attacks or congestive heart failure, they are not, in and of themselves, necessarily disabling. For example, Haber (1969) shows that only 2.9 percent of persons between the ages of 18 and 64 are limited in the kind or amount of work (or housework) they can perform because of heart disorders or hypertension, despite the presence of these conditions in 7.6 percent of this population. The incidence of all types of cardiovascular disorder increases with age, as does the proportion of the population disabled by them. For example, the number of persons who had a work-limiting heart disorder increased from 6.2 per 1000 among those 18 to 44 years old to 41.6 per 1000 for those between the ages of 45 and 64 (Haber, 1969). The nature of the rehabilitation problem is clearly modified by the age of the client at the time of onset of the disability.

Moreover, the adult client's personality structure is well developed and presents a framework within which rehabilitation decisions must be made. There has been considerable speculation and controversy about whether a particular constellation of personality characteristics may even predispose some adults to disabling heart disease. Friedman, Rosenman, and their associates, for example, have worked extensively in this area and identify a group of traits summarized as "Pattern Type A" that they believe are associated with increased incidence of coronary heart disease. According to Jenkins, Zyzanski, and Rosenman (1971, p. 194),

> Pattern A is characterized by attributes such as hard driving effort, striving for achievement, competitiveness, uneven bursts of amplitude in speech . . . and hurried motor movement. Individuals with this pattern are usually conscientiously committed to their occupation, and whatever its level, often have achieved success in it.

This description, or at least some part of it, has received support from a number of investigators and studies (e.g. Friedman and Rosenman, 1959; Rosenman, Friedman, Strauss *et al.*, 1964; Keith, Lown, and Stare, 1965; Quinlan, Barrow, Moinuddin *et al.*, 1968; Jenkins *et al.*, 1971; Kemple, 1945; Kaplan, 1956; Lamb, 1969; Gilldea, 1949; Cady, Gertler, Gottach, and Woodbury, 1961; Friedman, 1967; Friedman, Brown, and Rosenman, 1969).

Heart patients have also been characterized as attempting to surpass or subdue authority (Ginsparg and Satten, 1970). Males, who are by far the majority of this group (Cook, 1966), are seen as having strong attachments to father and hostility toward mother (Menninger and Menninger, 1936). Regardless of sex, these patients are described as engaging in total repression of their problems (Ginsparg and Satten, 1970), seeking recognition and advancement, physically and mentally alert, and engaged in multiple activities and unremitting work (Lamb, 1969; Gilldea, 1949). They have even been thought to be unconsciously attempting suicide by means of the heart condition (Ginsparg and Satten, 1970).

However, evidence for the "coronary personality" is equaled by the evidence against it (Mordkoff and Golas, 1968; Brown, 1967), including criticism of the methods of investigation by which such traits were "determined" (Mordkoff and Parsons, 1967; Lebovits, Shekelle, Ostfeld, and Paul, 1967; Peters, 1967; and Kissen, 1968). One significant contradictory study was conducted by Hinkle and his associates (Hinkle, Whitney, Lehman, Dunn, Benjamine *et al.*, 1968) and reviewed by Lamb (1969). In an effort to evaluate the concept that personality factors significantly influence the risk of having a heart attack, Hinkle studied 270,000 men employed by the Bell system operating companies. To determine the role of such traits as "striving," "competitive," "restless," and "mobilized," Hinkle studied people of different occupations, levels of achievement, and education. The study failed to show that men with high levels of responsibility had any greater risk of a heart attack than men with lesser responsibility. Men with college educations and men successful in realizing their goals actually had a lesser number of heart attacks than less educated or less successful men.[*] Although persons with heart disorders or subgroups of such persons may share some personality traits, a specific constellation of predisposing traits cannot be fully supported by the literature.

Reactions to Heart Disease

The perception of the onset of cardiovascular disease, like any disability, evokes some characteristic reactions. Fear, depression, and denial flow directly from the nature of the disorder and are intensified by it. Fear follows the realization that it is life-threatening, while depression arises in contemplation of the profound life changes it portends. The fact that it is a hidden disease

---

[*]Complementing these findings are those of the Framingham study which suggest a greater incidence of heart disease in the lower socioeconomic strata.

process makes denial easier (Gray, Reinhardt, and Ward, 1969). All of these reactions are classically illustrated in the heart attack victim, which is perhaps one reason why the majority of the literature focuses upon this manifestation of cardiovascular disease.

More often than not, a heart attack has suddenly transformed a man at the peak of his career and the height of his powers to a helpless and temporarily passive creature, subject to medical manipulations he may not fully understand, pain which forecasts his death, disintegration in his family and work life, and entirely too much time to think about all of these changes (Heath, 1966). He is encouraged to adopt the sick role, a person in need of help, in order to accept treatment necessary to preserve his life (Parsons and Fox, 1960), and he must direct his attention to internal processes over which he has no control. As a matter of fact, he may become quite bored (McDaniel, 1969) when the usual activities and diversions of his life are forbidden him. His whole world is suddenly narrow, constricted, and self-centered. It is not difficult to understand why the heart attack victim becomes fearful and depressed or wishes to deny his illness.

Nor is it surprising that a heart attack profoundly affects the patient's whole family. The typical responses to such a disability in the family have been described by Parsons and Fox (1960, p. 353).

> Family members may tend to be *more* sympathetic and supportive of the sick person than they ought; bolstering their own defense against a desire to be taken care of by projecting this need onto the sick person. Through their indulgent attitude toward the ill actor . . . the family may invite him to perpetuate his illness. On the other hand, the family may display an excessive intolerance with respect to the debilitating features of illness—regarding them as a sign of weakness—and impose overly harsh sanctions on the sick member. Such hyperseverity, of course, is as unfavorable to full and rapid recovery as over-permissiveness.

When the illness occurs suddenly or is life threatening, these reactions are often more pronounced. Whitehouse (1962) stresses the fear of death which a heart ailment raises in family members, particularly the spouse, who may be sharply reminded of his or her own aging. Financial strains and role shifts are an immediate consequence of illness, and the longer the member is unable to function, the more severe the strain becomes (Hellerstein and Hornsten, 1966; Gelfand, 1967; Whitehouse, 1962). The inability of the breadwinner to earn a living may force other family members to change their roles accordingly. Children may abandon or delay college plans; wives may go to work; homes and possessions may have to be sold.

If the heart patient is the wife, a housekeeper may have to be employed, a nursery found for the children, or other family members drafted to fill these roles. Resentment may well develop with each change, and the family unit may disintegrate altogether as various members decide to abandon it rather than assume some distasteful duty. The greater the change and shift a family is forced to make, the poorer the prognosis for rehabilitation of the cardiac (Hellerstein and Hornsten, 1966; Gelfand, 1967).

Proper intervention by rehabilitation workers early in the process can forestall many of these situations. Such intervention should be initiated by hospital-based personnel, since the family may be at a loss in attempting to thread its way through the maze of agencies that could offer help if contacted (Pohlmann, 1966). Hospital staff should be aware of the proper agencies for financial aid, convalescent homes, homemaker services, nurseries, vocational evaluation and placement, etc. Rapid access to these community supports may prevent families from taking drastic action in response to financial or other crises which with time and/or proper intervention will prove unnecessary. Moreover, early intervention directed towards meeting the immediate practical needs can help to avoid family misunderstandings and to facilitate open and honest dialogue between family members and the patient, as well as among all members of the family and the medical staff (Jefferson, 1966). The hospital-based personnel should also help to bridge the gap between the patient and the community at the time of discharge. Referral to community-based agencies may become necessary if the worker is administratively prohibited from working with discharged patients or if it becomes inconvenient for the family to maintain contact with hospital rehabilitation personnel. Careful handling of the transfer is critical to the continued rehabilitation process.

Assistance to families is extremely important in the rehabilitation process, for the adequately functioning family can provide, in turn, a crucial support for the patient; and the patient is likely to need the help of loved ones as he experiences a host of distressing feelings.

Fear

The direct life threat of a heart disorder can engender exaggerated or persistent fear of impending death in the patient (Miller, 1965). His family, his employer, and perhaps even the rehabilitation workers may come to fear not only his death but their own (Sparkman, 1967). The patient may respond by inhibiting his own rehabilitation efforts, and the significant others in his life may cooperate with such regressive or withdrawal patterns. For example, the patient may interpret the physician's prescription of activity as excluding the work he has always done or might be suited to do. Following a heart attack, his spouse may discourage resumption of sexual relations. An employer may offer the heart patient a job with reduced physical demand—and reduced pay. Even the physician may prescribe an unnecessarily conservative regimen (Whitehouse, 1962, 1967; Hurst and Logue, 1966), and other members of the rehabilitation team may narrowly interpret his prescription and accept the patient's devalued image of himself. In fact, fear of imminent death or the loss of physical capacity is considered by some (Miller, 1965; Sparkman, 1967; Whitehouse, 1967; Hurst and Logue, 1966; and Zohman, 1964) to be the most important factor in the medical management of the cardiac patient; its consequences can be more devastating than the acute physical condition of the individual (Whitehouse, 1962; Schecter, 1967; Cleveland and Johnson, 1962).

Hagan (1966) warns that patients who fail to increase their activities as their doctors suggest may constitute poor candidates for rehabilitation. And this paralysis of the individual because of fear is particularly unfortunate, since many of the other maladjustments seen in the cardiac patient, i.e. immature behavior, social isolation, and negative responses to social and occupational opportunities, may be attributed to the sensory loss or deprivation resulting from enforced inaction during intensive care (Bauman, 1954). If, following the phase of acute care, the patient can be encouraged to "do something" about his condition (or perhaps just to do something!), his "dependency" and "lack of motivation" may disappear (McDaniel, 1969). For example, participation in a graduated exercise program has been shown to benefit cardiac patients not only in physiological terms (Rusk and Gertler, 1960; Fox and Haskell, 1966; Hellerstein and Hornsten, 1966; Hellerstein, 1967; and Zuchlewski, 1957) but also in improved psychological well being. Hellerstein and Hornsten (1966, p. 48) state:

> Following participation in an active reconditioning program these subjects show a significant improvement subjectively and objectively, not only in diminution of angina pectoris . . . but also psychologically. Their depression is much less severe and the depression and psychasthenia scores on the MMPI test improve. Thus group participation in a program of cardiac rehabilitation has a beneficial effect on the attitude of the cardiac patient toward his disease and on his self-image.

Perhaps these improvements also occur partly because the patients' fear of increased activity is significantly reduced by their success.

The natural fear of the new heart patient and of the general public concerning heart attacks is, unfortunately, constantly fed by the popular press, which too often fails to state that the majority of persons recover from their attacks and resume fairly normal lives. The fear is felt so strongly that medical and rehabilitation personnel must be careful how they discuss laboratory and clinical findings around the patient lest they create a cardiac cripple out of a perfectly normal individual (Katz, 1962). Whitehouse (1967) suggests that there may be as many as 20 million of these "cardiacs without disease." Some patients have waited all their lives for an excuse to become disabled and thus seize upon the condition even if the physician denies its existence, using some equivocation or vagueness in his denial as their communication (Whitehouse, 1967). On the other hand, accurate diagnosis of heart disorder is quite difficult, and the physician may choose to err in the conservative direction (Whitehouse, 1962). Whitehouse (1967) found studies that suggested that neither the instruments used nor the symptoms reported for cardiac disease were clearcut in their implications. In one study, a "surprising" number of normal EKG's could be obtained from patients with abnormal readings if the tests were repeated following 15 minutes of rest. Furthermore, there are some 47 extracardiac entities associated with abnormal EKG readings even when they are consistently found. Whitehouse (p. 59) also states that "Over 35 medical conditions cited in the literature can produce pain in the chest simulating to some degree true angina pectoris." White and Sweet (1955) found that such symptoms as angina or dyspnea vary greatly from one individual to another. The same signs have been found by others (Dudley, Martin, and Holmes, 1968; Bakker, 1967; Bakker and Levenson, 1967) *not* to correlate with the severity of the disease and to be strongly influenced by psychological factors. Even murmurs have no limiting effect in 90 percent of the children who have them (Nadas and Zaver, 1967). In fact, one of the chief diseases which must be considered against the diagnosis of heart disorders is anxiety neurosis (Coleman, 1964; Hurst and Logue, 1966; Reiser and Bakst, 1969).

Some of the "cardiacs" the rehabilitation worker encounters, then, could be neurotic or inadvertently misinformed by their physicians. But the patients will experience these disorders as if they were real, and their beliefs will not be waved away by a counselor's assurances to the contrary. Reexaminations and skilled, authoritative interpretation of their significance are certainly indicated. When these appear to substantiate neurosis rather than true heart disease, psychotherapy may be in order. In any case, the rehabilitation worker should be aware of the possible existence of this "disorder" so that he can offer appropriate aid to its victims and so that *he* does not inadvertently contribute to its incidence.

Depression

The depressive reaction has also been called mourning, dejection, despair, or grief; it has been described in chronically ill or disabled persons generally; and it is manifested in such symptoms as hopelessness or self-deprecation; insomnia, loss of appetite, weight loss, and constipation; reduced or absent sexual function; incapacity for physical and mental effort; and increased somatic complaints (Cleghorn and Curtis, 1959). Although the psychological value of such depression or mourning has yet to be demonstrated, many rehabilitation workers (e.g. Wright, 1960) believe that it is equated with "realistic" recognition of loss and facilitates recovery. On the other hand, Moos and Solomon (1965) maintain that the failure of defensive measures against the threat of disability, generation of high levels of anxiety and depression, and increased functional incapacity go hand in hand. This suggests that depression does not facilitate adjustment or acceptance but, if not interrupted, leads to increasing disability. Verwoerdt and Dovenmuehl (1964) consider such depressive reactions, which may persist for years, to be especially significant in cardiac disease. They state (p. 857) that in a group of persons with heart disease, ". . . a cluster of depressive episodes and intensity of unpleasant affect during the depressive period determined the extent of disability for life activities."

Denial

Depression and denial appear to be opposite reactions to the threat of disability. While neither has been proven to facilitate rehabilitation, denial has been shown to be effective in reducing the effects of stress. This pattern of adjustment is not too hard to understand when one realizes the potential consequences of the disorder, e.g. death, loss of income, change in roles. Ludwig (1967) found that farmers, particularly, had an investment in the doctor's being wrong, since the inability to farm meant not only an occupational change but also a complete change in life style. However, Hellerstein and Hornsten (1966, p. 48) note that, "It should be emphasized that this reaction is a normal one, and its absence tends to prognosticate a difficult adjustment to the disease."

There is some evidence that compulsive and pessimistic persons are more apt to utilize the mechanism of denial, and at least one study (Caron, 1959) has shown that those who persist in denial are more likely to be excessively disabled one year after their heart attacks. Denial of the disorder does not necessarily result in refusal to follow the physician's orders, although this tends to occur (Ludwig, 1967; and Rosen and Bibring, 1966). The patient may actually overcomply, while still denying the diagnosis. Either extreme is unlikely to enhance recovery.

Denial, like any other defense mechanism, exists in degrees. Five major types of expressions of denial were noted by Weinstein and Kahn (1955): complete denial of illness, denial of major disability and emphasis upon the least threatening aspects of illness, minimizing of illness, projection of ownership of illness, and temporal displacement.

REHABILITATION OF THE ADULT CARDIAC PATIENT

The rehabilitation professional must be aware of the problems the cardiac faces; he must also have some specific techniques to combat them, including good assessment procedures and counseling skills. In addition, he should be alert to the factors associated with success and those which appear to inhibit success. All of these matters will be discussed in this section.

Assessment of the Cardiac Patient

Because of the complexities of heart disease, many authorities feel that the cardiac can best be evaluated by a team of professionals representing a wide spectrum of disciplines. This idea has been embodied in the more than 40 cardiac work evaluation units which are operating in the United States today (Whitehouse, 1962, 1966; Acker, 1967; Jezer, 1967). The specialists usually included in these centers are a cardiologist, a psychologist, a vocational counselor, and a social worker. Other team members may be added, depending upon client need. For instance, a county agent might be included if a good many farmers are seen, or a home economist, if homemakers are frequently served. The aim of such centers is not only to judge what physical limitations the individual has but also to determine the requirements of the various jobs he might fill.

The reports furnished by these units usually speak of the ability to work in terms of energy expended to perform a given task. Energy is generally expressed in terms of calories per minute since a liter of oxygen is equivalent to five calories. Using this system, a person with a Class I heart should be able to perform tasks which do not require more than 5 calories/min of continuous effort or peak intermittent efforts of more than 6.6 calories/min. A person with a Class II heart should be able to perform tasks which require 2.5 calories/min and 4.0 calories/min, respectively (classification of the American Heart Association). Since many specific industrial jobs as well as activities common to various kinds of work have been calibrated in the same terms (e.g. Rusk and Gertler, 1960; Passmore and Durnin, 1955; Hellerstein and Hornsten, 1966), it is possible to match jobs and persons fairly well. The work of the units has opened a good many jobs to cardiacs. They have demonstrated that the average job in the United States requires less than 6 calories/min (Hagan, 1966) and, according to Hellerstein (1959), most cardiacs with less than Class III limitations can perform that much work or more, safely.

Measurements are made on an *individual* performing a specific task rather than relying upon averages. The cardiac work evaluation unit is particularly suited for making the observational checks that Kline (1967) feels are necessary for accurate judgment of how well the individual cardiac can perform the particular job. Without such an evaluation, the rehabilitation worker can only guess at how fast the client will work and how willing he will be to adjust his pace of work to accommodate his limitations.

Individual assessment is necessary not only because of the differences in pacing among workers but also because the worker brings a number of internal *stresses* with him which may further burden his heart. These include family and financial worries, fears about his adequacy in job performance, etc.

Therefore, in addition to the external demands of the job and the pace of work, the degree of emotional stress under which the worker labors must be considered. According to Whitehouse (1962, p. 92), "emotional excitement can be as taxing as physical exertion; and this is something that the patient needs to remember the rest of his life." Other investigators agree that emotional factors can increase the work of the heart and have harmful consequences (e.g. Hellerstein and Ford, 1957; Sprague, 1961; Hellerstein and Hornsten, 1966; Russek, 1967; Reiser and Bakst, 1959). Chambers and Reiser (1953) found that an acute emotionally stressful experience had immediately preceded the development of congestive failure in 76 percent of those admitted to a general hospital for congestive heart failure. Hellerstein and Hornsten (1966) suggest that in order to fully evaluate the cost of emotional stress, a worker be equipped with a small heart-monitoring device and a tape recorder to wear at work. They point out (p. 52) that ". . . the body of a sedentary worker or executive, under great emotional stress, may be performing the calorie work of a white collar worker while his heart is doing the work of a man shoveling iron in a steel mill."

In evaluating the physical demands of a job, the rehabilitation worker should keep in mind the aggravation of showering, shaving, dressing, and getting to and from work, as well as the adverse effects of certain working conditions (e.g. poor lighting, excessive noise, improper temperature control, dust, etc). All of these have a cardiac cost.

For example, in order to work, the cardiac must have the energy reserves to get to and from his place of employment and to get around on the job once he is there. According to Hellerstein and Hornsten (1966, p. 52), "transportation to and from work may involve more energy expenditure than the job itself." If the cardiac is forbidden to drive an automobile, he will have to expend between 2.9 and 4.5 calories/min walking (depending on whether he is walking slowly on level ground or trying to walk uphill). If his work place has stairs, he will have to expend between 8.4 and 9.3 calories/min to climb them.

Hellerstein and Hornsten (1966) approach these transportation costs by suggesting that the patient be "reconditioned" to perform the tasks of walking and climbing stairs within the limits of his disease. After proper graduated exercise, they urge the patient (p. 51) ". . . to be physically active and vigorous in his everyday life, to climb stairs, to avoid the use of elevators, to walk instead of ride, to run, to skate, etc." Since the evidence is still inconclusive concerning the benefits of physical reconditioning (Fox and Haskell, 1966), the counselor should work closely with the patient's family physician to be sure the extra-job energy costs are not too great.

It should be noted here that assessment is not the only service performed by cardiac work evaluation units, although it is the principal one. They also provide consultation on how to modify a job so that a person can remain in his present vocation. For example, although many household tasks have a higher energy cost than the average job in industry (Katz, Bruce, Plummer, and Hellerstein, 1958), housewives are understandably reluctant to relinquish the role. Therefore, the evaluation is made in terms of how many tasks a housewife can continue to do, how others could be modified so that she could still do them, and how many will have to be performed by other people. Booklets are now widely available on how to modify household tasks (Margolis, 1966), and courses are being offered at the cardiac work evaluation centers and at other locations under the auspices of the American Heart Association and its local affiliates (Fisher, 1966).

Nolan (1966) warns that personality, work habits, attitudes towards employment, overconscientiousness, and reactions to different styles of supervision may be additional sources of stress for a particular individual.

The counselor should be aware of all these potential sources of stress and should attempt to diminish them. For example, he should try to build upon interests, skills, and the past experiences of the cardiac in order to avoid, if possible, the stresses of being in a strange job or having to compete with more skilled individuals for employment. If personal or family disturbances are detected, counseling may well be in order to lessen their impact. The aim of the counselor is to help the cardiac to learn "to do what he must do to take care of himself as a matter of habit and

to otherwise live every day as if he were going to live forever"
(Gardberg, 1957).

Counseling the Cardiac Patient

Counseling the adult cardiac is different from counseling the
child cardiac because adults generally have made some type of
adjustment to life prior to onset. Rehabilitation, rather than habilitation, is required. Thus, for most patients, reconstructive
therapy is not indicated (Bellak and Haselkorn, 1956). The type
of counseling and the member of the rehabilitation team best
qualified to provide it depend upon the nature of the presenting
problems. These, in turn, are often a function of the client's stage
in the rehabilitation process. Interpretation of his present physical limitations and the prognosis for the future is best handled by
the attending physician (Whitehouse, 1962). Diagnosis and trea-
ment of an organic psychosis may be handled by the psychiatrist.
Assessment of hidden fears, psychological overlays, and protracted
pain may be referred to the psychologist. Vocational adjustment
and supportive counseling for return to employment are the role
of the rehabilitation counselor. But in general, the problems encountered in the heart patient are sufficiently complex to require
at least a consultation with all members of the team before proceeding. And in most cases, the sooner the client is reached, the
better the chances of reducing the debilitating effects of disability
and thus the better the chances for eventual success.

Although everyone who experiences a cardiac disability could
probably benefit from some form of counseling, this service seems
particularly indicated for those who show signs of continuing
tension or difficulty in adjusting to their disability. Signs that
counseling is indicated include not only actual solicitation of the
service by the patient but also overt signs of depression, anxiety,
and denial. These can be seen in disturbances in sleep and appetite; fatigue, weakness, and intractable pain; and expressed
feelings of helplessness, hopelessness, and self-criticism (McMahon, 1967). McMahon also describes characteristic patterns of
adjustment to fear and dependency and suggests some ways of
coping with them.

Adjustments

THE CHILD-LIKE REACTION. This type of patient is even more fearful than the realistic dangers he is confronting. By his over-expression of such fears, he is asking for parental protection. Although making no prediction about long-term adjustment, McMahon suggests that rehabilitation workers furnish him this parental protection while he is in the hospital; that they keep his hospital stay as short as possible; and that they allow him as many visitors from home as possible. Under these conditions, the child-like patient will cooperate with professional personnel in doing what is necessary to get him through the rehabilitation process.

THE PASSIVE REACTION. While this type of patient speaks a good deal about his desires to recover quickly and resume his self-sufficient status, his real desire is to prolong the illness and thus legitimize his dependency needs. For him, the illness is a face-saving device, which allows him to withdraw from the competitive world of employment. Since the passive patient is threatened by health, he reacts strongly to the possibility of discontinuing medical care or to any form of "rejection." McMahon believes that the key to success with this type of patient is the trust he develops in his treating physician. Often the issue must be resolved before progress can be made. Early signs of the passive adjustment can be seen in failure to increase an activity schedule during convalescence (Hagan, 1966), a desire for a pension despite the ability to return to work, or fussiness about the nature of the suggested employment (Gelfand, 1967).

THE HOSTILE REACTION. The natural fear which occurs during illness is handled by such a patient in a counterphobic fashion. That is, he is hypercritical, and this can be hard on the rehabilitation workers. However, DeWolf, Barrell, and Cummings (1966) suggest that those who *are* critical of the helping professionals make a better long-term recovery. The provocativeness of these patients must be handled in a firm and quiet manner. The counselor must neither withdraw in the face of the hostility nor be caught up in the polemics. Giving these patients an active role in their rehabilitation seems to help.

THE CONTROLLING REACTION. This reaction is probably a long-standing one. Here the patient attempts to deal with his dependency needs by denying them and making others dependent upon him. Although more common in women than men, it can occur in either sex. The patient expects to be hurt rather than helped and is overly inquisitive about rehabilitation procedures. He wishes to know the purpose of each procedure before submitting to it. Rather than simply asserting authority over him, McMahon suggests that professionals cater to this wish for explanations and also allow him to assist in carrying out as many of the procedures as possible. The same principle might be used in counseling by explaining why the service is needed and what tests he might take and what information they can provide to both client and counselor and then allowing him to choose among alternative measures of the various dimensions. Indeed, this general manner of proceeding has been suggested for all clients (Goldman, 1961).

THE SUPERINDEPENDENT REACTION. In order to overcome feelings of weakness or dependence, the patient has become very strong and decisive. He tends to deny the illness and defy the imposed limitations. He considers any symptom a sign of weakness. Gelfand (1967) found that both the dependent types and the superindependent types tended to undergo more hospitalizations. The challenge to the counselor seems clear. He must convince the superindependent person that it takes strength to accept his disability realistically and to live within its realistically imposed limits. Again, the patient should be actively engaged in the rehabilitation process and he should be told forthrightly what his limitations will be.

The counselor must be aware of the needs of the family as well as of the patient. Signs that intervention are needed include inability of the family to communicate honestly with the patient about the medical facts of his condition, complaints by the patient that the medical personnel are not leveling with him, signs of overprotection or overt hostility by the family towards the patient, or tension regarding financial matters.

Subtler signs of family tension may also be manifested, such as the failure of the partners to resume sexual relations soon after it becomes medically permitted. Whitehouse (1962) stresses that this failure may signal more deep-seated fears or marital discord.

Diet can also be a sign. The patient may show dependency by insisting that the spouse be responsible for his dietary habits. On the other hand, he may punish the spouse by refusing to follow the diet and thus force the partner to watch his self-destruction. However, the most frequent reaction of the males in Ludwig's (1967) study of doctor-patient relations among farmers was an attempt to keep diet restrictions and medication from becoming known in order to protect the wife. This creates problems, since, as Ludwig notes, family members cannot aid the patient if they are unaware of his need for help. He also notes that, in general, the patients cannot be trusted to convey the physicians' recommendations.

Another sign of family discord (as well as other psychological disturbances) is exacerbated heart symptoms.

> For example, some subjects who are 'happy' at home and unhappy at work frequently display tachycardia on the job. On the other hand, a patient whose home life is troubled may develop tachycardia precisely upon entering the driveway of his house, although the heart rate had been normal during the day at work (Hellerstein and Hornsten, 1966, p. 52).

Counselors should keep these symptoms in mind when discussing sensitive subjects, such as how things are going at home. An attack of angina while sitting talking to the counselor probably indicates that he has hit upon a "painful" subject, since the physical demands of talking are minimal.

Factors in Successful Rehabilitation

Successful return to employment following a heart attack is influenced by the previous work history; the personality, age, education, and degree of impairment possessed by the worker; the company attitudes, policies, and types of work available in the area; and a host of nonwork factors. These include the availability of pensions and the economy in general.

Perhaps the most satisfying form of rehabilitation for the client is return to his former employment. With some modifications, this has been suggested as optimal for self-employed persons, such as farmers, housewives, and professionals. Many companies find that the work records of former cardiac patients more than justify their reemployment. According to Rusk and Gertler (1960, p. 109), ". . . it has been demonstrated in a group of industrial cardiac patients in functional classes I and II that over 70 percent returned to their former occupations and maintained an equal work status with their noncardiac colleagues." Similar findings regarding the ability of cardiacs to return to their jobs have been reported by Weaver (1967). However, the problem with this form of rehabilitation is that the employer is often unwilling or unable to make maximum use of the returning worker's residual skills and interests. He is placed at a lower-paying job with demeaning conditions attached to it (Whitehouse, 1962). Increased use of rehabilitation services, including the cardiac work evaluation units, might well reduce this waste of resources and increase the possibility that the cardiac worker will be properly placed.

Gelfand (1959, 1967), in his now-classic study of those who did not return to work following heart attacks, suggests that those who are taken back by their employers tend to be those who have made contributions to their companies. They also tend to be those with stable work histories rather than those who have changed jobs frequently.

Gelfand's study involved some 655 heart patients, mostly from industry, who had been referred to a cardiac work evaluation unit. He found that 92 percent of them were fit to return to employment. However, some 28 percent of those recommended for reemployment either failed to return to work or entered occupations which were too strenuous for them. He found that the differences between those who were successful and those who were not were psychological rather than educational, or in degree or type of disability, former skills, or even the degree of effort required on their new jobs.

The unsuccessful group tended to be characterized by passive dependent adjustment patterns, including acceptance of the feminine role, a high degree of selectivity about the types of work they would consider, and insistence upon claiming pensions despite physical findings which showed that they could return to work. The successful group, on the other hand, tended to possess stable personalities and more realistic reactions to their disabilities. Gray *et al.* (1969) concur that the ability to adopt realistic attitudes towards the disability is critical for success. This includes the ability to accept help when it is needed.

A number of investigators have found that age is another critical factor in rehabilitation of the cardiac. In his review of industrial employment, Whitehouse (1962) found that greater age adversely affected employability. Goldwater and Bronstein (1959) added that it was associated with the presence of multiple disabilities, which make rehabilitation even less likely. Although it is a generally accepted fact that older workers have a more difficult time becoming reemployed, Gertler (1967) warned that the younger workers do not have all of the advantages. For instance, in a large industrial study with which he was associated, one conclusion was that the younger the worker was when he had the first attack, the less likely he was to survive it. Also, younger workers tended to live a shorter time after the first attack than did older workers.

Goldwater and Bronstein (1959) also found that education was a critical factor, determining whether or not a person could be retrained for lighter work. This contradicts the findings of Gelfand (1959) cited earlier and those of Jezer (1967). Jezer noted among workshop clients that the more educated tended to have more problems (such as more severe cardiac conditions or psychological difficulties). The additional problems tended to cancel out their educational advantages.

Severity of disability may well have been the reason that 8 percent of Gelfand's sample were not advised to return to work; however, it did not differentiate between those who followed the work unit's advice and those who did not. It is definitely a factor in reemployment within some occupations. For example, Cook

(1967) feels that heavy lifting and the fast pace of work in the steel industry would severely limit the ability of all but the least handicapped cardiacs to return to this kind of work. Morris (1966, 1967) feels that farmers with handicaps more severe than Class II hearts would have difficulty resuming farm work.

The ability of a cardiac to return to work is not only dependent upon the residual capacities of the worker, but also upon the willingness of the employer to utilize those capacities. The possible legal consequences for employers who hire cardiacs can loom larger than the cardiac's ability to perform the job (Cook, 1967). The reason for this lies in the way cardiovascular disorders are interpreted under the workmen's compensation laws in this country. These laws are built upon two principles. The *first* is that the cost of the product should bear the blood of the employees who contributed to making it. Therefore, employers are required to pay for the insurance, and the number of claims employees make against the insurance policies determines the employer's rates. Although this is a good incentive to provide safe working conditions, it can also be an incentive not to hire cardiacs, particularly when the second principle is also applied (McNiece, 1967).

The *second* principle is that the employer takes the employee as he finds him. As Thornton (1967, p. 242) says ". . . it is no defense to claim for a broken skull that the plaintiff had an exceedingly thin one." Under this principle, an employer becomes responsible for aggravation of any underlying pathological condition—such as hypertension or atherosclerosis. Since the number of persons with various types of chronic health conditions is quite high, employers and insurance companies have tried to limit the number of claims which are processed under these provisions (McNiece, 1966). Despite their efforts, the number of successfully argued cases has actually increased because of the tendency of the compensation boards to see that the employee will be unable to get adequate compensation for his condition under any of the other available systems (McNiece, 1967; Sawyer, 1967; Sprague, 1961). This places an unfair burden upon any employer when he considers hiring a known cardiac.

Employer reluctance has been demonstrated in several surveys of large companies' plant physicians (McNiece, 1967; Cook, 1967; Kline, 1967). If medical expenses are incurred it is the employer who, through increased insurance premiums, will be paying for them. If the worker is unable to resume his employment, the cost of the settlement will be even higher. Sometimes the employer will try to forestall this expense by pensioning the employee or giving him a hidden pension in the form of a nonproductive position within the firm.

The type of work to which the cardiac can return also depends upon the general economy (the disabled fare better when the labor market is tight than when there is high unemployment), and upon the jobs which are available in a given community. Occupations which involve heavy lifting, fast-paced work, and great temperature variations are obviously less able to absorb cardiac workers than jobs which demand lighter work (Whitehouse, 1962). The safety of the public may restrict cardiacs from performing other types of work, such as piloting airplanes (Brandaleone, 1966; Rusk and Gertler, 1960). Heavy lifting and long hours, as well as the public safety, usually exclude them from engaging in commercial trucking (Brandaleone, 1966). These considerations probably explain, in part, why Sigler (1967) found that among elderly cardiacs, a higher percentage of professionals and business men returned to work than did clerks or manual workers. In addition, pensions are more readily available to older workers than younger ones, particularly if they work for large companies. However, de Koning and Meursing (1967) reported that 46 percent of a group of steel workers were able to resume their former jobs within two years of having suffered heart attacks. This shows that heavy industry is not necessarily precluded as a place of employment for the cardiac. Also, in the petroleum industry, enlightened policies have helped many cardiac workers return to work, where their productivity remains as high as that of their noncardiac counterparts (Weaver, 1966, 1967). This example points up the broad range of opportunities which can exist or be created when individualized rehabilitation services and flexible employer attitudes converge.

The Place of Rehabilitation Services
Administration in Cardiac Rehabilitation

In 1966, the Vocational Rehabilitation Administration (now part of the Social and Rehabilitation Service) sponsored a "state of the art" conference at Tufts University entitled "Rehabilitation in Cardiac Disease." Dr. Donald Sparkman (1967), then medical director of the Washington State Division of Vocational Rehabilitation, chose to discuss the "track record" of the federal/state vocational rehabilitation program in his private capacity. For, from 1953 to 1965, an average of only 4 to 5 percent of rehabilitants had heart disease as the primary disability. Dr. Sparkman envisioned a brighter future in vocational rehabilitation of the person with heart disease, based in part upon the potential resources to be provided by President Johnson's initiatives in establishing the Regional Medical Programs in heart disease, cancer, and stroke.

Five thousand, five hundred and fifty-two persons with heart disease were rehabilitated in 1965, and 7,386 were rehabilitated in the year ending June 30, 1970. The percentage of the total rehabilitants actually dropped from 4.1 to 2.9 percent. Thus, the brighter future for cardiacs has not yet been realized. Why? Though important research remains to be done, the problem is not that these persons cannot be rehabilitated but rather that for various reasons they are not finding their way to the agency for assistance. Haber (1969) estimates that 4,408,000 persons between the ages of 18 and 64 are disabled for work because of heart disorders and an additional 2,018,000 are disabled for work because of high blood pressure.

Sparkman's (1967) analysis (paraphrased below) of the reasons for relatively infrequent service to persons disabled by heart disease is still pertinent; several additional reasons could be suggested. Sparkman pointed to (a) inadequate numbers of referrals because medical practitioners lack information about the availability and need for rehabilitation services, (b) insufficient ability to institutionalize services as, e. g. agencies for the blind, special classes, and cooperative arrangements for working with the mentally retarded, etc., (c) the historical roots of the federal/state programs as agencies for the orthopedically disabled, and (d) the discomfort counselors feel in working with cardiac clients because of the changing nature of the problem and the fears of death raised in the counselors themselves. To these reasons could be added the fact that the disability usually occurs late in life and thus the victim is more likely to be eligible for a pension or to be able to "rehabilitate" himself; and the fact that the disability is hidden, which adversely affects case-finding efforts. For instance, schools, which account for a high proportion of VRA referrals, are more likely to be aware of noncardiac clients.

Gray *et al.* (1969) report on their study of heart patients who were part of a cooperative program by the Social Security Administration and the Social and Rehabilitation Service to try to return to work persons who were receiving social security disability benefits. They concluded (p. 354) that ". . . one reason cardiovascular patients are rehabilitated less frequently than other disabled persons is their being less willing or able to accept their impairment realistically . . ." Although all of the participants in the study had been screened for potential to resume employment, these investigators found that the heart patients were less likely than other disabled groups to accept rehabilitation services, to accept their disabilities realistically rather than fatalistically, and to accept the sick role (as measured by Mechanic's test). The cardiac patients, although somewhat less likely to be employed at the time services were terminated, were more likely to be in competitive or self-employed work than the noncardiac patients.

The role of rehabilitation, therefore, is no longer to investigate whether cardiacs can or should go back to work but rather to act as advocate for this disability group in the community in order to facilitate their return to work. It is to counsel with those cardiac patients who have psychological reasons for not wanting to return to employment so that this waste of national resources can be overcome, and it is to do a better job of publicizing its services so that all who need help can obtain it.

REFERENCES

Acker, J. E.: Role of the cardiac work evaluation units in cardiac rehabilitation. In *Rehabilitation in Cardiac Disease.* Boston, Tufts University School of Medicine, 1967.

Bakker, C. B.: Psychological factors in angina pectoris. *Psychosomatics,* 8(1):43, 1967.

Bakker, C. B. and Levenson, R. M.: Determinants of angina pectoris. *Psychosomatic Medicine, 29*(6):621, 1967.

Bauman, M.: *Adjustment to Blindness.* Harrisburg, St. Council Blind, Dept. Welfare, Commonwealth of Pennsylvania, 1954.

Bellak, L. and Haselkorn, F.: Psychological aspects of cardiac illness and rehabilitation. *Social Casework, 37:*483, 1956.

Brandaleone, H.: Driving and the coronary patient. *Journal of Rehabilitation, 32*(2):97, 1966.

Brown, L. B.: A follow-up of young male survivors of myocardial infarction. *Australian Psychologist, 2*(1), 1967.

Cady, L. D., Gertler, M. M., Gottach, L. G., and Woodbury, M. A.: The factor structure of variables concerned with coronary artery disease. *Behavioral Science, 6:*36, 1961.

Caron, H.: The crisis factor in illness and disability. Cleveland Symposium in Behavioral Research in Rehabilitation, 1959 (mimeographed).

Chambers, W. and Reiser, M. F.: Emotional stress in the precipitation of congestive heart failure. *Psychosomatic Medicine, 15:*38, 1953.

Cleghorn, R. and Curtis, G.: *Depression: Mood, Symptom, Syndrome.* Geigy, Basle, 1959.

Cleveland, S. E. and Johnson, D. L.: Personality patterns in young males with coronary disease. *Psychosomatic Medicine, 24*(6):600, 1962.

Coleman, J. C.: *Abnormal Psychology and Modern Life.* Chicago, Scott, Foresman & Co., 1964.

Cook, L. P.: Statistics—magnitude of the problem. *Journal of Rehabilitation, 32*(2): 17, 1966.

Cook, W. L.: Suggestions in cardiac rehabilitation. In *Rehabilitation in Cardiac Disease.* Boston, Tufts University School of Medicine, 1967.

de Koning, N. C. and Meursing, N. A.: Het probleem van het hartinfarct in het bedrijf. *Mens et Ondermeming, 21*(6):390, 1967.

DeWolf, A., Barrell, R. and Cummings, J.: Patient variables in emotional response to hospitalization for physical illness. *Journal of Consulting Psychology, 30*:68, 1966.

Dudley, D. L., Martin, C. J., and Holmes, T. H.: Dyspnea: Psychologic and physiologic observations. *Journal of Psychosomatic Research, 11*(4):325, 1968.

Ferguson, S. and Rayport, M.: The adjustment to living without epilepsy. *Journal of Nervous and Mental Disease, 140*:26, 1965.

Fisher, S. H.: The cardiac homemaker. *Journal of Rehabilitation, 32* (2):74, 1966.

Fox, H. M., Rizzo, N. D., and Sanford, G.: Psychological observations of patients undergoing mitral surgery: A study of stress. *Psychosomatic Medicine, 16*(3):186, 1954.

Fox, S. M. and Haskell, W. L.: Physical activity and health maintenance. *Journal of Rehabilitation, 32*(2):89, 1966.

Friedman, M.: Behavior pattern and its relationship to coronary artery disease. *Psychosomatics, 8*(4, Part 2): 6, 1967.

Friedman, M., Brown, A. E., and Rosenman, R. H.: Voice analysis test for detection of behavior pattern: Responses of normal men and cardiac patients. *Journal of the American Medical Association, 208*:828, 1969.

Friedman, M. and Rosenman, R. H.: Association of specific overt behavior pattern with blood and cardiovascular findings: Blood clotting time, incidence of arcus senilis and clinical coronary artery disease. *Journal of the American Medical Association, 169*:286, 1959.

Gardberg, M.: Remarks on the rehabilitation of the cardiac patient. *Journal of the Louisiana Medical Society, 109*:335, 1957.

Gelfand, D.: Factors related to unsuccessful vocational adjustment of cardiac patients. In *Rehabilitation in Cardiac Disease.* Boston, Tufts University School of Medicine, 1967.

Gelfand, D.: Experience at the cardiac classification unit, Southeastern Pennsylvania. In Rosenbaum, F. F. and Belknap, E. L. (Eds.): *Work and the Heart.* New York, P. B. Hoeber, Inc., 1959.

Gilldea, E. F.: Special features of personality which are common to certain psychosomatic disorders. *Psychosomatic Medicine, 11*:273, 1949.

Ginsparg, S. L. and Satten, J.: Psychiatric aspects of rehabilitation in coronary artery illness. *Proceedings of the American Psychological Annual Convention,* 1970.

Goldman, L.: *Using Tests in Counseling.* New York, Appleton-Century-Crofts, Inc., 1961.

Goldwater, L. J. and Bronstein, L. H.: Fifteen years of cardiac work classification (etiology of heart disease in relation to employment). *Journal of Occupational Medicine, 1:*145, 1959.

Gray, R. M., Reinhardt, A. M., and Ward, J. R.: Psychosocial factors involved in the rehabilitation of persons with cardiovascular diseases. *Rehabilitation Literature, 30:*354, 1969.

Haber, L. D.: Epidemiological factors in disability: I. Major disabling conditions. *Report No. 6 Social Security Survey of the Disabled: 1966.* Washington, D.C.: Office of Research and Statistics, Social Security Administration, February 1969.

Hagan, J.: Vocational counseling in heart disease. *Journal of Rehabilitation, 32*(2):62, 1966.

Heath, M. J.: Myocardial infarction—A personal account. *Journal of Rehabilitation, 32*(2):46, 1966.

Hellerstein, H. K.: Work load and cardiac function. In *Conference on Heart and Industry.* New York, American Heart Association, 1959.

Hellerstein, H. K.: Active physical reconditioning of coronary patients. In *Rehabilitation in Cardiac Disease.* Boston, Tufts University School of Medicine, 1967.

Hellerstein, H. K. and Ford, A. B.: Rehabilitation of the cardiac patients. *Journal of the American Medical Association,* Vol. 164-225, 1957.

Hellerstein, H. K. and Hornsten, T. R.: Assessing and preparing the patient for return to a meaningful, productive life. *Journal of Rehabilitation, 32*(2):48, 1966.

Hinkle, L. E., Whitney, L. H., Lehman, E. W., Dunn, J., Benjamin, B. *et al.*: Occupation, education, and coronary heart disease. *Science, 161:*238, 1968.

Hurst, J. W. and Logue, R. B.: *The Heart Arteries and Veins.* New York, McGraw-Hill, 1966.

Jenkins, C. D., Zyzanski, S. J., and Rosenman, R. H.: Progress toward validation of a computer-scored test for the type A coronary-prone behavior pattern. Psychosomatic Medicine, *Journal of the American Psychosomatic Society, 23*(3):193, 1971.

Jezer, A.: Role of the workshop in ischemic heart disease. In *Rehabilitation in Cardiac Disease.* Boston, Tufts University School of Medicine, 1967.

Kaplan, S.: Psychological aspects of cardiac disease: A study of patients experiencing mitral commissurotomy. *Psychosomatic Medicine, 18:*221, 1956.

Katz, L. N.: Psychological aspects of heart disease. *Psychosomatic Medicine, 26(*4) Part 2:413, 1964.

Katz, L. N., Bruce, R. A., Plummer, N., and Hellerstein, H. K.: Rehabilitation of the cardiac patient: Panel discussion. *Circulation, 17:* 114, 1958.

Keith, R. L., Lown, B., and Stare, F. J.: Coronary heart disease and behavior patterns: An examination of method. *Psychosomatic Medicine, 27:*424, 1965.

Kemple, C.: Rorschach method and psychosomatic diagnosis. *Psychosomatic Medicine, 7:*85, 1945.

Kissen, D. M.: Some methodological problems in clinical psychosomatic research with special reference to chest disease. *Psychosomatic Medicine, 30(*3):324, 1968.

Kline, E. M.: The perspective of the occupational physician. In *Rehabilitation in Cardiac Disease.* Boston, Tufts University School of Medicine, 1967.

Lamb, L. E.: *Your Heart and How to Live with It.* New York, Viking Press, 1969.

Lawrence, E. M.: *Vocational Counseling for Children with Heart Disease or a History of Rheumatic Fever: A Pilot Study.* New York, American Heart Association, 1961.

Lebovits, B. Z., Shekelle, R. B., Ostfeld, A. M., and Paul, O.: Prospective and retrospective psychological studies of coronary heart disease. *Psychosomatic Medicine, 29(*3):265, 1967.

Ludwig, E. G.: Problems of communication between doctor and patient and difficulties with the medical regimen. In *Rehabilitation in Cardiac Disease.* Boston, Tufts University School of Medicine, 1967.

Margolis, D.: Resource material to aid in prevention and treatment. *Journal of Rehabilitation, 32(*2):101, 1966.

Moos, R. and Solomon, G.: Personality correlates to the degree of funtion incapacity of patients with physical disease. *Journal of Chronic Disease, 18:*1019, 1965.

Mordkoff, A. M. and Golas, R. M.: Coronary artery disease and responses to the Rosenzweig Picture-Frustration Study. *Journal of Abnormal Psychology, 73(*4):381, 1968.

Mordkoff, A. M. and Parsons, O. A.: The coronary personality: A critique. *Psychosomatic Medicine, 29*(1):1, 1967.

Morris, W. H. M.: The coronary farmer, *Journal of Rehabilitation, 32*(2):76, 1966.

Morris, W. H. M.: Heart disease in the farmer. In *Rehabilitation in Cardiac Disease.* Boston, Tufts University School of Medicine, 1967.

Nadas, A. and Zaver, A.: Rehabilitation problems in pediatric and adolescent cardiac patients. In *Rehabilitation in Cardiac Disease.* Boston, Tufts University School of Medicine, 1967.

Nolan, J. C.: Vocational assessment. *Journal of Rehabilitation, 32*(2): 61, 1966.

Offord, D. R. and Aponte, J. F.: Distortion of disability and effect on family life. *Journal of the American Academy of Child Psychiatry, 6*(3):499, 1967.

Parsons, T. and Fox, R. C.: Illness, therapy, and the modern urban American family. In Bell, N. W., and Vogel, E. F. (Eds.): *A Modern Introduction to the Family.* Glencoe, Illinois, The Free Press, 1960.

Passmore, R. and Durnin, J. V.: Human energy expenditure. *Physiological Reviews, 35*:801, 1955.

Peters, D.: Het hartinfarct: Een overzicht van de psychologische literatuur. [Myocardial infarction: A review of psychological literature] *Gawein, 15*(4-5):361, 1967.

Pohlmann, K. E.: Labor and the coronary worker. *Journal of Rehabilitation, 32*(2):79, 1966.

Quinlan, C. B., Barrow, J. G., Moinuddin, M. *et al.:* Prevalence of selected coronary heart disease risk factors in Trappist and Benedictine Monks. Paper presented at the Conference on Cardiovascular Disease Epidemiology, American Heart Association, Atlanta, February, 1968.

Rasof, B., Linde, L. M., and Dunn, O. J.: Intellectual development in children with congenital heart disease. *Child Development, 38*(4): 1043, 1967.

Reiser, M. F. and Bakst, H.: Psychology of cardiovascular disorders. In Arieti, S. (Ed.): *American Handbook of Psychiatry,* New York, Basic Books, 1959, Vol. 1.

Rosen, J. L. and Bibring, G. L.: Psychological reactions of hospitalized male patients to a heart attack. *Psychosomatic Medicine, 28*(6): 808, 1966.

Rosenman, R. H., Friedman, M., Strauss, R. *et al.:* A predictive study of coronary heart disease: The Western Collaborative Group Study. *Journal of the American Medical Association, 189:*15, 1964.

Rusk, H. A. and Gertler, M. M.: Rehabilitation in congestive heart failure. In Blumgart, H. L. (Ed.): *Symposium on Congestive Heart Failure. American Heart Association Monograph No. 1.* New York, American Heart Association, 1960.

Russek, H. I.: Emotional stress in the etiology of coronary heart disease. *Geriatrics, 22*(6):84, 1967.

Sawyer, G.: Insurance company view of the problem of cardiac rehabilitation. In *Rehabilitation in Cardiac Disease.* Boston, Tufts University School of Medicine, 1967.

Schecter, N.: Psychological aspects of chronic cardiac disease. *Psychosomatics, 8*(3):166, 1967.

Sigler, L. H.: Emotion and atherosclerotic heart disease: I. Electrocardiographic changes observed on the recall of past emotional disturbances. *British Journal of Medical Psychology, 40*(1):55, 1967.

Sparkman, D. R.: Place of vocational rehabilitation administration in cardiac rehabilitation. In *Rehabilitation in Cardiac Disease.* Boston, Tufts University School of Medicine, 1967.

Sprague, H. B.: Legal aspects of coronary disease. In Blumgart, H. L. (Ed.): *Symposium on Coronary Heart Disease. American Heart Association Monograph No. 2.* New York, American Heart Association, 1961.

Thornton, John: Waiver statute, second injury laws and other compensation law devices as related to rehabilitation. In *Rehabilitation in Cardiac Disease.* Boston, Tufts University School of Medicine, 1967.

Verwoerdt, A. and Dovenmuehle, R.: Heart disease and depression. *Geriatrics, 18:*856, 1964.

Weaver, N. K.: Industry and the coronary worker. *Journal of Rehabilitation, 32*(2):77, 1966.

Weaver, N. K.: Selective placement of the cardiac in industry. In *Rehabilitation in Cardiac Disease.* Boston, Tufts University School of Medicine, 1967.

Weinstein, E. and Kahn, R.: *Denial of Illness.* Springfield, Thomas, 1955.

White, J. and Sweet, W.: *Pain, Its Mechanism and Neurosurgical Control.* Springfield, Thomas, 1955.

Whitehouse, F. A.: "Cardiacs" without heart disease. *Journal of Rehabilitation,* 33(5) Part 14-15:56, 1967.

Whitehouse, F. A.: Cardiovascular disability. In Garrett, J. F., and Levine, E. S. (Eds.): *Psychological Practices with the Physically Disabled.* New York, Columbia University Press, 1962.

Whitehouse, F. A.: The cardiac work evaluation unit as a specialized team approach. *Journal of Rehabilitation,* 32(2):66, 1966.

Wright, B. A.: *Physical Disability—A Psychological Approach.* New York, Harper & Row, 1960.

Zohman, B.: Chest pain of coronary origin. *Psychosomatics,* 2:34, 1964.

Chapter IV

PSYCHOLOGICAL CONSIDERATIONS IN HEMIPLEGIA

Joan L. Bardach

This chapter will discuss psychological factors that can influence the behavior of hemiplegic individuals. Although emotional factors sometimes are of crucial importance, in hemiplegia, additional factors are also of major importance. These factors, though often hidden, are powerful determinants of behavior. Two major perceptual factors that can influence behavior are how a person sees and how he hears the world around him. Sensory changes, which sometimes take place in hemiplegia, also can affect behavior. There may be intellectual changes in memory, judgment, ability to think abstractly, and ability to shift from one task to another. Changes in a person's ideas of his own body often occur. A person's physiological state, his body, and his brain, all affect his behavior. The kind of person he was and his emotional and physical resources to deal with his tragedy all come into play. Although these various factors will be discussed separately, they interact, and the patient's overt behavior is the resultant of that interaction.

PERCEPTUAL DISTURBANCE

A major unseen factor that can affect behavior comes from perceptual distortions. If they are not taken into account, the failure of a patient to learn to walk, for example, may be attributed to poor motivation, when, in reality, the difficulty may be that he does not perceive objects in his environment accurately. An illustration of this difficulty can be seen in the performance of a hemiplegic individual who is asked to copy geometric forms and does so but rotates the designs 90 degrees. Imagine what it would be like to attempt to walk in an environment in which the positions of objects in space are not seen as they really are! Or

71

a patient standing at one end of parallel bars may see the bars not as parallel to the sides of the room but as shooting off at an angle. Since the bars are parallel in fact, the patient may be receiving contradictory cues. The bars look as if they are at an angle, yet, when the patient touches them with his unaffected hand, the sensation he receives tells him that they are straight. Besides the balance problems and the fears, such as the fear of falling, the contradictory cues that the hemiplegic receives from vision and touch confuse him further and may make him even more afraid.

Another visual-perceptual problem present in some brain-damaged individuals, and hence in some hemiplegics, is difficulty in distinguishing foreground from background. These patients cannot always select the most relevant visual cue to which to respond. For this reason, in working with hemiplegic individuals, it is important to keep the environment as visually simple as possible. As an example, one hemiplegic patient was making good progress in ambulation, but he tended to veer off to one side as he walked. The physical therapist, in first evaluating the total problem, marked a line of crosses on the floor with chalk and asked the patient to walk on the crosses. The patient suddenly was unable to walk at all. The physical therapist then spoke to the psychologist. Together they studied the patient's psychological record and found that the patient had visual-perceptual difficulties. After discussion, the physical therapist removed the floor marks as a possible source of the trouble. The patient was then able to walk. In this case the crosses on the floor had added to the visual complexity and had confused the patient to such an extent that he was unable to walk.

Preliminary investigation by Diller and Weinberg (1962) has suggested that some hemiplegic individuals have difficulty in perception of the upright. For instance, in a test in which an individual is seated in a chair in a dark room and is told to look at a line of light and then asked to judge when the light is vertical, hemiplegic patients make more errors in judgment than do non-brain-damaged individuals. A hemiplegic who can walk independently is more accurate in his judgment of the upright than a hemiplegic who is wheelchair-bound. Hemiplegics who make errors in judgment of the vertical also make errors in judgment of the horizontal.

Hemiplegics' difficulty in scanning the environment usually has been associated with occurrence of multiple accidents in a rehabilitation center. Diller and Weinberg (1970) state, ". . . scanning is required . . . in manipulating . . . wheelchairs, and in accurate perception of objects in space, such as location of doors." The nature of the scanning difficulty, especially in left hemiplegics, is neglect of stimuli on the impaired side and "omission of pockets of stimuli" throughout a task requiring the cancellation of a particular digit in rows of randomly distributed digits. With such an impairment, it is easy to imagine how accidents can occur. In an earlier study, Weinberg and Diller (1968) found that such individuals may initially deny having difficulty in performing an everyday visual activity, such as reading a newspaper.

DIFFERENCES BETWEEN RIGHT AND LEFT HEMIPLEGICS

Another factor revealed in the Diller and Weinberg (1962) study of perception of the upright is that right and left hemiplegics differ in a number of ways. Left hemiplegics tend to deviate consistently to the left whereas right hemiplegics deviate to the right. At an Eastern Psychological Association convention, Comalli (1963) reported that amputees also tend to misjudge perception of the vertical. When their bodies are erect, they displace the vertical in the direction opposite to the side of the amputation. The findings from these studies suggest that the difficulty may not result directly from brain damage but may arise from the fact that in both hemiplegics and amputees the two sides of their bodies feel different. It may be that a person's perception of what is straight up and down is derived more by cues from his body than from purely what he sees.

Diller (1963) has pointed out that right and left hemiplegics differ in other ways. For example, damage to the dominant hemisphere in the brain very often is associated with loss of verbal skills, so that there is the common concurrence of right hemiplegia with aphasia. Damage to the nondominant hemisphere appears to be associated with loss of visuomotor skills. More recent findings by Diller (1972) suggest that right and left hemiplegics also differ in their ways of responding. Right hemiplegics tend to be slow and to show anxiety; left hemiplegics tend to be impulsive and to use the defense mechanism of denial. If all these findings are true, then the reasons a person fails to learn a task may differ from one individual to another. A patient learning to transfer from a bed to a wheelchair, for example, may not be able to complete the task because of impairment in verbal skills. He may not understand what the therapist is telling him or he may not be able to tell himself what to do next. Another person may have problems in the perception of space and therefore cannot accurately perceive where his wheelchair is in relation to the bed. Another person does not delay his response until instructions on how to transfer are completed and so he makes a hasty, incorrect move.

Other sensory difficulties may be encountered; vision is not the only modality that may produce difficulties in learning for the hemiplegic. Sounds coming simultaneously from different directions also may confuse some hemiplegics. Some hemiplegic individuals may understand instructions better if the instructor speaks from the patient's unaffected side; for other hemiplegics, the location of the instructor may make no difference. The point here is that if the patient seems to be having difficulty understanding instructions, systematically check out the location of the instructions in relation to the side of impairment of the patient.

Sensory changes also sometimes occur (Ullman, 1962). For example, food does not always taste the same as it did premorbidly. The patient may experience sensations from the involved side of his body that are different from the uninvolved side, again adding confusion and difficulty.

INTELLECTUAL IMPAIRMENT

Hemiplegic patients also may suffer intellectual changes. Memory may be impaired. What is called memory, however, appears to be a complex function. An individual may be able to remember things that he hears but not remember things that he sees, or vice versa. In evaluating a hemiplegic patient, therefore, psychologists should test for both auditory memory and visual memory. The distinction is important as an aid in teaching simple skills to the patient. If a patient has an auditory memory impairment, he should be shown what to do; if a person's primary memory impairment is in the visual area, he should be told, rather than shown, what to do. An individual with a memory impairment has to repeat activities over and over before he can retain what he is supposed to do. If therapists are aware of this particular impairment, they may be more patient and more understanding of the individual.

Repetition Versus Perseveration

Although the repetition of activities to be learned is important in people with memory impairment, it must not be confused with what psychologists call perseveration. Brain-damaged individuals frequently repeat an activity over and over, as if once started they cannot stop unless something outside themselves intervenes. If such an individual is given a row of twelve dots to copy, for example, he will continue to draw dots until he reaches the edge of the paper. Such perseveration may be erroneously interpreted by staff as diligence, that the patient is highly motivated.

Using behavior modification techniques, Goodkin (1966) was able to reduce the number of verbal perseverations of an aphasic patient when positive reinforcers were accompanied by the patient giving himself negative reinforcers for "bad responses," defined as "continuous utterances that contained no new words but consisted of either repeated words or only indistinguishable sounds" (p. 177). When modeling was introduced, with the psychologist reinforcing and punishing himself, the patient made even more improvement. When the psychologist and the patient each kept tabs of the rewards and punishments received during each session, "this treatment resulted in a sharp reduction in the number of bad responses made to non-treated questions, . . ." (p. 179). Goodkin's work suggests that individual prescriptive approaches based on behavior modification techniques can be useful in improving certain kinds of impaired performances of hemiplegic individuals.

Ability to Shift from Task to Task

Some brain-damaged individuals have difficulty in shifting from one task to another or from one aspect of a task to another. If in a particular physical therapy session, for example, a patient has been walking outside the parallel bars, it may be difficult for him in the same session to turn his attention to walking upstairs. With patients who have this kind of difficulty, there probably would be less frustration for both the patient and the therapist if only one activity were taught in each session.

Judgment

Another intellectual factor that often is impaired in brain-damaged individuals is judgment. There are times when poor judgment is easily detected, but individuals who have retained good verbal skills or a good social manner, even when speech is impaired, sometimes give the impression of having better judgment than they actually have. As part of a psychological evaluation, one hemiplegic patient, who had earned over a million dollars as an insurance salesman and who had retained a polished, social manner, was given a simple picture completion test in which he was to select the most appropriate object to insert in the cutout provided. The patient put a clock, rather than a kite, in the sky.

Reasoning

Other kinds of thinking processes sometimes are impaired. Once again, high verbal skills or a good social manner may mask the impairment. A common impairment in thinking is a decrement in abstract reasoning. The brain-damaged patient may be extremely concrete. If such a patient is being taught to ascend and descend stairs, for instance, he gradually may learn to do it, but if he is asked to walk up a different set of stairs, he may not be able to do so. This factor of concrete thinking, rather than such factors as family overprotection, may be the source of the patient's failure to carry over at home, activities he has learned at the rehabilitation center. Because the patient thinks concretely, he has learned to walk up a particular flight of stairs, not to walk up stairs in general. For the same reason, the patient may be able to make progress in a particular area, but if his therapist is changed, he may regress and have to learn all over again.

What can therapists do about these intellectual deficits? Ullman (1962) studied the reactions of 300 patients to their strokes. He found that if a patient is given more tasks to do than he can manage, the patient will react with intense anxiety that leads to disorganized behavior and a fear of the task at hand. What determines whether a patient is motivated to attempt a task depends on whether he can perform that task successfully and what his understanding is of the relevance of the task for his life situation. For many brain-damaged patients, with their limitation in abstract reasoning, the thing that counts most is the immediacy of the result. The therapist should give very simple, concrete instructions with many repetitions. These patients need to be told or shown exactly what to do and when to do it. In addition, the therapist must be patient, understanding, and above all, respectful of his patient.

Remedial techniques for some of the visual-perceptual problems and some of the cognitive difficulties of hemiplegics have begun. Though the techniques are new and therefore have not been fully evaluated as yet, they have enabled some hemiplegics to improve their performance in some areas. These techniques have taken two main thrusts. One, illustrated by the works of Ben-Yishay *et al.* (1970a, 1970b, 1971) involves systematic simplification of the demands of a specific task by giving the patient more and more cues until he is able to pass the item, followed by systematic reduction in cuing until the individual is able to perform the task without the use of cues, or with only minimal cuing. A second approach to remediation has been to study the nature of the defect, devise methods that demonstrate to the patient that he has the defect in question and that its presence is impairing to him, and then teach the patient ways of compensating for the defect. The work of Weinberg and Diller (1968), who have devised ways of teaching hemiplegics to turn their heads when they have a problem in visual neglect of one side, is an illustration of this approach.

BODY IMAGE

Besides perceptual, sensory, and intellectual disturbances, some hemiplegic individuals act as if they have lost familiarity with their body parts. "Body-image problems" is the term used to refer to disturbed notions a person may have about himself and his body. Individuals with body-image problems may have difficulty following instructions related to their bodies. They sometimes cannot localize body parts correctly. Body-image difficulties present major problems in physical rehabilitation where motor learning is so often the focus of the treatment. If the patient is not clearly aware of the parts of his body or of exactly what some part of his body is doing, it is extremely difficult for him to learn the sorts of activities that a physical therapist, for example, may be attempting to teach him. Diller in his chapter "Hemiplegia" in Garrett and Levine's book (1962) gives clear examples of the kinds of difficulties with which a physical therapist may have to contend. A hemiplegic who is not aware when his foot hits the ground may be afraid of falling. A patient may forget to lock his brace, not because of memory impairment, but because he is unaware of the disabled side of his body.

EMOTIONAL FACTORS

Emotional factors following a stroke are varied and complex. The patient often believes he is no longer the person that he was. One aspect of this belief is that he feels far less adequate to deal with his problems and he frequently believes that the problems he has to face are greater than any he has ever experienced. It is not surprising, therefore, that anxiety and depression are typical reactions. The depression is gradually lifted for some patients as they see themselves mastering their rehabilitation tasks. Some other patients, however, continually emphasize their losses. These losses may be connected in their minds with a growing sense of uselessness associated with aging, or the losses may be subjectively equated with previous losses in the persons' lives. Diller (1963) has stated, "these patients represent a serious challenge, for their discouragement and frustration tend to become all pervasive and infect the staff." They pose a serious psychotherapeutic problem, which may be met by an attempt to have the patient delimit the feelings of loss and find some assets that make life worth living. Diller (1963) illustrated this approach by the following case presentation:

> The patient is a 50-year-old depressed woman suffering from right hemiparesis and mild expressive aphasia. Following initial rapport and an attempt to get the patient to describe what troubled her, the therapist met with silence and resistance. The following is a paraphrase of what ensued:
>
> *Therapist:* "I guess you feel sad."
>
> Patient shakes head in agreement.
>
> *Therapist:* "Do you feel sad because of your hand?"
>
> Patient agrees.
>
> *Therapist:* "Your leg?"
>
> Patient agrees.
>
> *Therapist:* "Your speech?"
>
> *Patient:* silence . . . tears . . .
>
> *Therapist:* "Who are you?"
>
> *Patient:* "But I can't do so many things."
>
> *Therapist:* "But who else are you besides an arm, a leg, and a mouth?"

The attempt here is to enlarge the areas the patient thinks about and to focus attention on assets.

Denial

A stroke typically has a sudden onset. A catastrophe that comes out of the blue gives the individual no time to prepare himself for it (Garrett and Levine, 1962). One of the most common reactions to a stroke is what psychologists call denial. Rehabilitation therapists know a great deal about denial (Loomer). There are certain ways everyone protects himself from a truth that he cannot bear to know. Almost everyone is familiar with a situation in which a person telephones and says that someone of whom he is fond has just died. What is the first reaction? "No, I can't believe it." To have a stroke is a terribly distressing thing; it is understandable that the stroke patient will deny it, at least initially. Many degrees and forms of denial have been described in detail by Weinstein and Kahn (1955). An individual may deny that he was ever ill. He may deny that anything is wrong with one side of his body, but complain of a much more minor difficulty such as nausea. He may say that he cannot move his arm because it is "too lazy." He may say that his paralyzed limb is not his, but belongs to his nurse. He may say that he *was* disabled, but he is all right now. For some patients, insofar as the individual is denying his disability, he may see little sense in rehabilitation. After all, if his leg is not paralyzed, why all the fuss to teach him to walk?

The presence of denial can interfere markedly with rehabilitation, yet it is sometimes essential for the patient's emotional stability. Denial has the function of preventing the patient from becoming overwhelmed by his tragedy. Initial gains in functioning encourage patients to participate more wholeheartedly in their rehabilitation. The process of training shows the patient that there are many things he can do despite his disability. This experience increases inner strength. As a result, the patient gradually becomes more realistic about his disability, feeling a sense of worth again as a human being even though at the same time he may feel some depression concerning his residual limitations. As time goes on, then, the degree of denial generally lessens. As it does, there is a more or less corresponding increase in depression. The depression that sets in as denial gradually lifts may, from the short-term view, also hinder rehabilitation precedures, yet the depression, too, is necessary for the patient's psychic economy. It has been found that patients need to go through mourning for the loss of a loved one. Great concern used to be expressed over a rather severe depression in these patients. Now, the psychologist is more concerned if depression is not seen usually in the relatively early stages of the disability, because experience has shown that unless an individual goes through this mourning process, it may well interfere at a later and perhaps more crucial point in his rehabilitation. At the point of active mourning, patients may need psychotherapeutic help. In this whole process, time and patience are important adjuncts to whatever help a psychotherapist can give the patient.

Regression

Another reaction of patients to a hemiplegia is regression. The level of emotional maturity that a person achieves in life is arrived at with difficulty and is maintained with difficulty. If one has a cold in the head and feels sick, he is not apt, when he turns on the television, to want to watch a Shakespearean tragedy. Instead, he will select something light, a western or a vaudeville show or a comedy. In other words, for the moment he does not wish to use his full adult capacities, but instead would rather behave on a more childlike level.

Egocentricity

A third way a patient copes with a hemiplegia is egocentricity. When life is in danger, the natural reaction is to focus attention on saving it. Many hemiplegics feel, and justifiably so, that their life has been threatened. Their tolerance for frustration is low. These patients have difficulty understanding that other patients also need the attention of the staff. The egocentricity that these patients show, of course, can be very trying to the staff, but if they can identify with the patient who sees himself struggling with the enormous problem of life and death, they can be more tolerant of the patient's demandingness.

Disinhibition

Another problem encountered in some hemiplegics is disinhibition, which is related to damage to the cerebral cortex. One of the functions of the cortex is inhibition. When the cortex is damaged, an individual frequently does not have the control over his emotions he once had. He may exhibit a kind of automatic laughing and crying that is not always associated with feeling. He also may be increasingly irritable. If the therapist can remember that the patient's emotional displays are often the result of the brain damage rather than any mishandling of the patient, the therapist will be less threatened by it and will be free to be more understanding of the patient. Damage to the brain is the most humiliating of the disabilities. Low self-esteem, therefore, is a frequent reaction. Because of the individual's derogatory self-concept, he has more need to deny that anything is wrong with him. Moreover, brain-damaged patients have less adequate equipment with which to make evaluations of themselves.

The Effect of Age

Many rehabilitation therapists are young and energetic. They probably have very little idea of what it is like to be old and sick and tired. To many hemiplegics, their stroke signalizes old age, which means not only that they can no longer function so well as before but also that they suffer loss of energy and death may not be far away. Strokes usually happen to people already concerned with growing older. It adds insult to this injury, as if the person has aged ten years overnight. It is not surprising, therefore, that these people are often depressed, concerned with the possibility of having another stroke, and preoccupied with fear of death. If the patient does not cooperate, he may be thinking that the therapist does not know how precarious his life is. He believes that if he is coaxed into activity, it may well kill him.

The Family

In addition to the problems that the patient has concerning his own reactions to his disability, he often has to contend with the reactions of his family. Often, families respond to the patient half as the person he is now and half as the person he was. The result is that families unwittingly hold up a distorting mirror to the patient. Two examples of this kind of distortion illustrate the point. In the first example, a patient, who understood practically nothing, jabbered away using an unintelligible jargon. However, the intonations of his voice, the expression on his face, and his general manner looked appropriate. Family members came to him for business advice. Another example comes from families who occasionally believe the patient is just clowning. These families unwittingly create problems because the patient fails to meet his family's unrealistic expectations.

In an attempt to correct this type of problem, I, along with other members of the rehabilitation team, held group sessions with family members of aphasic patients. The purpose of the sessions was to give information so that members of the family would have a better understanding of the patient, so that they could share experiences, and so they would have a chance to air their feelings, their problems, and their frustrations. Family members often go through a process of adjustment to the disability of one of its members that is similar, though not identical, with that of the patient himself. A flavor of this process can be seen from the description of group sessions with wives of aphasic patients by Bardach (1969).

THE PATIENT IN THE REHABILITATION CENTER

What is the reaction of a patient when he first comes to a rehabilitation center? In some ways it is easier for him to face his disability. For one thing, if he can get about, it helps him to become more self-reliant. He also sees other patients there. This experience is both encouraging and frightening. It is frightening because he sees that some patients do not get better. It is encouraging because he sees that despite all kinds of disabilities, somehow patients and families manage to survive.

Patients seem to experience a progression in rehabilitation. When they first enter the program, they often view themselves in their own minds not as disabled but merely as convalescents. They believe that when they leave the rehabilitation center, they will be the way they were before they had the stroke. As they begin to face the fact that disabling residuals will remain, the period of mourning sets in.

The progression of adjustment to a disability goes on at different rates for different people. In order to determine the rate of adjustment for a particular person, several things must be known. What is the patient's disability costing him in reality? A patient with an expressive aphasia who has little muscular residual and whose job was sewing clothes will have less to lose than an individual with the same type and degree of disability who was a salesman. In the latter individual, loss of speech is crucial to his job. In addition to knowing what the patient is losing in reality, it is necessary to know what the person believes he is losing. For example, a man who has always assured himself of masculinity by means of physical prowess will have lost much more than the man who did not need physical activity to prove his maleness. The individual who in the past has handled anxiety by being very busy is stuck when he becomes disabled. An example is the woman who, when she is anxious, does her spring cleaning no matter what the time of the year. Some of these problems, of course, are not limited specifically to hemiplegics, but are general reactions of patients suffering from a traumatic disability.

If a person has had a stroke, additional strains occur. A variety of adjustments have to be made by those who live with a person who may look peculiarly different and who may act differently. If the patient has aphasia, which is such a bewilderingly inconsistent symptom, the task of adjustment of family members to the patient is all the more difficult. Just how difficult it is for the patient himself was poignantly described by a high-level aphasic patient, who said that people without a speech problem have no idea of the "anguish, torment, and frustration that we suffer."

SUMMARY

Some of the problems encountered in the rehabilitation of hemiplegic patients have been touched upon briefly. They suggest that different skills are needed to accomplish the various tasks in rehabilitation and that the skills that are called upon to master a particular task may be different for different patients. According to Diller and Weinberg (1962),

> It appears that learning in complex situations is related not to the unimpaired skills, but to the residual skills affected by the disability. We would therefore infer that retraining consists in the utilization of residual abilities which remain in the deficit area. Perhaps the patient really learns nothing new but merely to use what he has in a more purposeful manner.

Some of the complexities involved in the retraining of hemiplegics have been mentioned. A great deal is yet to be learned. Out of continued research hopefully will come additional practical techniques for the improvement of rehabilitation procedures. The complexities of the problems are many; rather than being overwhelmed by them, they can furnish a challenge to all.

REFERENCES

Bardach, J. L.: Group sessions with wives of aphasic patients. *International Journal of Group Psychotherapy, 19*(3):361, 1969.

Ben-Yishay, Y., Diller, L., Gerstman, L., and Gordon, W.: Relationship between initial competence and ability to profit from cues in brain damaged individuals. *Journal of Abnormal Psychology, 75*:248, 1970a.

Ben-Yishay, Y., Diller, L., and Mandleberg, I.: Ability to profit from cues as a function of initial competence in normal and brain-injured adults: A replication of previous findings. *Journal of Abnormal Psychology, 76*:378, 1970b.

Ben-Yishay, Y., Diller, L., Mandleberg, I., Gordon, W., and Gerstman, L.: Similarities and differences in block design performance between older normal and brain injured persons: A task analysis. *Journal of Abnormal Psychology, 78*:17, 1971.

Comalli, P.: Effect of unilateral above the knee amputation on perception of verticality. Read at Eastern Psychological Association, New York, 1963.

Diller, L.: Sensorial and psychosocial factors in stroke. Read at "Stroke Conference," Chicago, 1963.

Diller, L.: Cognitive and motor aspects of handicapping conditions. In Neff, W. (Ed.): *Psychological Aspects of Disability*. Washington, D.C., American Psychological Association, 1972.

Diller, L. and Weinberg, J.: Learning in hemiplegia. Read at American Psychological Association, St. Louis, Missouri, 1962.

Diller, L. and Weinberg, J.: Evidence for accident-prone behavior in hemiplegic patients. *Archives of Physical Medicine and Rehabilitation, 51*:358, 1970.

Garrett, J. F. and Levine, E. S.: *Psychological Practices with the Physically Disabled.* New York, Columbia University Press, 1962.

Goodkin, R.: Case studies in behavioral research in rehabilitation. *Perceptual and Motor Skills, 23*:171, 1966.

Loomer, A.: Personal communications.

Ullman, M.: *Behavioral Changes in Patients Following Strokes.* Springfield, Ill., Thomas, 1962.

Weinberg, J. and Diller, L.: On reading newspapers by hemiplegics—Denial of visual disability. Proceedings, 76th Annual Convention, American Psychological Association, San Francisco, September, 1968.

Weinstein, E. A. and Kahn, R. L.: *Denial of Illness.* Springfield, Ill., Thomas, 1955.

Chapter V

STROKE PATIENTS: THEIR SPOUSES, FAMILIES AND THE COMMUNITY

ROBERT P. OVERS AND JOHN R. HEALY

INTRODUCTION

Three different approaches to the social aspects of the stroke impairment will be presented. The first is primarily a sociological approach and at a somewhat abstract level describes the societal and family setting within which the coping with the stroke problem occurs. The second approach presents selected data from a four-year research and demonstration study (Overs and Healy, 1971) on the effectiveness of rehabilitation counseling in helping families with stroke patients. The third approach describes concrete things the counselor can do to help. These helping suggestions are inferred from the first (sociological) and the second (empirical field data) approaches.

SOCIOLOGICAL APPROACH: THE FAMILY AS A SYSTEM OF RECIPROCAL ROLES

Considerable sociological and counseling theory supports the view that the family, rather than the individual patient, should be the focus of attention in the effort to rehabilitate stroke victims. Stein (1969) presents an historical overview of the development of this concept. Increasingly, the family has come to be seen as an integrated system of reciprocal roles. Under this approach, the family as a unit functions adequately or inadequately accord-

NOTE: Much of this chapter is based on "Educating Stroke Families," *Milwaukee Media for Rehabilitation Research Reports No. 12,* July, 1971, which presented the final report of Research and Demonstration Grant No. RD-2537P (new numbering system 15-P-55211/5-03), supported in part by the Division of Research and Demonstration Grants, Social and Rehabilitation Service, Department of Health, Education and Welfare. A free copy of the three-volume report may be obtained by writing the Research Department, Curative Workshop of Milwaukee, 750 N. 18th Street, Milwaukee, Wisconsin 53233.

ing to the degree of integration among the role perceptions and performances of the various members.

By definition, roles are reciprocal in nature. A person's self-concept is based both upon his perception of the roles he can and should perform vis-à-vis the others in his environment and his estimation of the roles those others will wish to play towards him. His mental health and adjustment will depend upon how accurately he has gauged his own ability and the expectations of the others. Maladjustment occurs when the individual's own perceptions of his own or the other's roles do not coincide with the other's view of respective roles.

Under this theoretical framework, it does not make sense to talk of "individual" pathology. So-called "sick" or "maladjusted" members of the family system interact with "well" or "adjusted" members and it is this system of interaction that has produced the pathology. Thus, it is the system itself which must be investigated. Friedman (1964), Hurvitz (1967), and Tharp (1966) have all elaborated on this concept in detail.

Some marital counselors and family theorists have come to define marital success or adjustment in terms of the congruence between husband and wife perceptions of their respective roles. Dyer (1962) points out that the problem facing newlyweds is exactly one of defining their role expectations and performances. Hurvitz (1961) has developed a whole counseling approach based on the agreement between husband and wife perceptions of roles. Tharp (1963, 1966) and Kotler (1965) have found relationships between congruence of role perceptions and marital adjustment. Heer (1962) and Stuckert (1963) have indicated that there are differences in the degree of disparity according to the social class of the couples. While it is difficult to come up with a precise definition of exactly what marital or family adjustment consists of, an operational definition comes easier. If a family is still together as a family—that is, not divorced or separated—we can assume that some accommodation with the environment has been established, however marginal or minimal. The patterns of interaction and task performance are sufficiently well integrated to keep the system surviving, if just barely.

Family Crisis Situations

A crisis is that kind of event or situation that would make the established pattern of role performance inappropriate. A reevaluation of the performances expected of each member of the family system is necessary. Roles must be reshuffled, at least temporarily. Kosa (1965) distinguishes between a crisis situation and a chronic stress situation in that the latter requires a permanent changing of roles. Adjustment to the crisis is related to the degree to which the realignment of roles is satisfactory to each of the family members. This, in turn, is dependent on their ability to perceive what roles have been changed and how.

Chronic illness or disability would be an example of a chronic stress situation. Even nonchronic illness would require a temporary adjustment. Being disabled or sick is itself a role with its own set of self- and other-expectations of performance. Thus, the concept of "sick-role" has been developed. All the best efforts of rehabilitation personnel are for naught if the family encourages the patient in his sick-role performance.

Thomas (1966) in his "Problems of Disability from the Perspective of Role Theory" and Kassebaum (1965) in "Dimensions of the Sick-Role in Chronic Illness" both provide theoretical support for the importance of the sick-role as a factor in rehabilitation. Starkey (1967) provided empirical evidence to support the theory. Subjects matched for extent of cardiac impairment were found to differ in success of rehabilitation according to the extent to which they saw themselves as disabled. Bell (1966) and Deutsch (1960) showed the influence of family member and co-worker expectations on the adjustment of the patient. If others expected the patient to contribute to the proper functioning of the family unit, then he was more likely to improve.

A stroke presents a full crisis to the family system. Whether it occurred to the husband or wife, an almost lifelong pattern of performance with its corresponding self-concept is brought to a halt. The victim is at least temporarily rendered incapable of performing any roles (crisis stage) and permanently hindered in the performance of many of them (chronic stress stage). Other family members have to take up the slack. The patient and others have to be aware of what changes have been made and by whom. Olsen and May (1966), Straus *et al.* (1967), Barrow *et al.* (1962), Derman (1967), and Overs (1967) have all suggested the need for family education in stroke care.

The medical professions as well as the counseling professions, have also come to see the family as the unit of rehabilitation, although as Brodsky (1967) points out, the differing professions themselves require different approaches towards the family. She outlined some of the differences between the role relationships in the physician-family and the psychotherapist-family dyads. The approach of the research upon which this chapter is based, is to focus on the family as a system, educate the members with respect to what a stroke is and its effects are, and through counseling, to facilitate and encourage necessary role changes. Such changes would be considered as evidence of good adjustment to the stroke.

Changes in Family Roles During Crisis

At least logically, the possibility of role-changing or role reversal presents itself in the crisis produced by stroke. Christopherson (1960, 1963) developed an elaborate theoretical schema of the potential for role changes by the disabled man or the disabled woman. The disabled man could take over the housework while the wife goes to work; the disabled woman could concentrate on the affective, emotive aspects of her wifely role and serve as "enabler" or "setter of mood" for the husband or children. The implications for counseling are many.

Probably the single most important influence on a person's action or decision is the person's attitudes, beliefs, and values. As structuring and ordering devices, attitudes, beliefs, and values precede logical thinking and do not derive from logic or rationality. Therefore, the influence of basic attitudes, beliefs, and values on actions or decisions is primarily of an emotional, not an intellectual nature. The lower the educational development of the person concerned, the more evident this becomes. Therefore, to expect cognitive or factual data to greatly influence the decision-making process of a group at the educational level of most stroke patient families is not realistic! One value or attitude a person could have that would definitely affect his willingness to change roles would be a feeling that change itself is bad, that things should stay the same. This rigidity is a compulsive seeking of permanence, of stability.

The United States Department of Health, Education, and Welfare (1970) reports that "rigidity in an individual is associated with the extent of schooling and the number of years that have passed since school was attended."

A major theoretical assumption of Overs' project was that families must make decisions about patient care and safety, and these decisions can lead to maladjustment if the different family members have different perceptions of the extent of the patient's ability. Therapists, spouses and the patients themselves were asked to make separate evaluations of the patient's ability to perform nine activities of daily living. These separate ratings were then compared to see what differences there were. Brown *et al.* (1968) and New (1968) did similar studies and came up with similar findings. Patients, spouses, and therapists are not always in agreement as to what the patient can do. When the patient describes himself as dependent, the others usually agree; but when the patient describes himself as independent, there is less agreement. Spouses tend to be more conservative than the therapists. In some cases, the patient may lack the judgment to make competent ratings; in other cases, it could be that both spouses and therapists are perpetuating patient dependency.

Blood (1960) and Centers (1971) interviewed more than 700 families each, in Detroit and Los Angeles respectively. The purpose of both studies was to ascertain the relative power of the husband and wife in the contemporary American family. They did this by asking a random sample of husbands or wives (not couples) to describe who had the final say in making certain decisions, or performing certain tasks. Their respondents were of all ages, were not disabled, and did not have their spouses present. The stroke respondents (Overs and Healy, 1971) were old, disabled, and half the time had a spouse present during the interview. However, all three studies revealed a pattern of marked sex specialization in terms of division of household labor. Family decision-making tended to be more equalitarian. This would seem to indicate that the stroke families were not unique in their perception of the usual division of household tasks.

All three studies also found that companionship was the most important aspect or role of marriage for the respondents. (Romanticists take heart!) This has implications for counseling in an era when work, in or out of the home, takes up less and less of the day.

Ballweg (1967) interviewed 52 urban housewives whose husbands ranged in age from 65 to 82. Some of the husbands were still working; others had retired. The two groups were compared as to the division of labor between husband and wife on 12 household tasks. Differences between the two groups were slight, the retired husbands performing only slightly more of the housework than their still-working counterparts. Those jobs they did take over were usually the more "masculine" in nature. Blood (1960) also found that nonworking husbands usually "puttered" around the house rather than sharing the housework.

Overs and Healy's (1971) findings agree with these and further suggest that the reason is not so much laziness on the part of the husbands as rigidity on the part of the wives! The stroke study findings show that disabled husbands said they were willing to take over some of the household tasks but that the wife did not want this intrusion into her sphere of responsibility. Perhaps new roles outside the home could be found for the retired or nonworking husband.

Artes (1967) interviewed the wives of 65 former stroke patients in their homes. These families were preselected from an original sample of 345 former patients. The families were all from the Iowa City area of Iowa and median time from onset of stroke to interview with wife was 19 to 24 months. Husbands were not present for the interview which consisted of 271 items (mostly yes/no or multiple choice items, but there were a few open-ended questions).

Haese *et al.* (1970) interviewed 20 former patients from metropolitan Milwaukee in their homes on a 60-item yes/no questionnaire about three years after discharge from the hospital.

In the stroke research (Overs and Healy, 1971) upon which this chapter is based, 88 former patients were interviewed in their homes in metropolitan Milwaukee and half of the time their spouses were present. Average time since admission for rehabilitation was 22 months and the interview schedule consisted of 92 items, worded to elicit short answers.

All three studies (Artes, 1967; Haese *et al.*, 1970; Overs and Healy, 1971) concluded that stroke families are not given sufficient information regarding strokes and their effects. In all three studies, 40 to 50 percent of the respondents indicated that their doctors had not adequately described a stroke to them. In the Artes and Overs studies, finances were not mentioned as an overwhelming problem, although almost all families had cut into their savings and had been forced to change their spending habits. Neither group of families had undergone much change in their living situation, most still living in their own or a child's home. Few of the men patients returned to work, started new avocational activities, or helped much with the housework. Few of the spouses had started working to supplement the family income. Physical changes were most frequently mentioned as being the chief problem since the stroke and as the main reason for the drop in activity level. However, in both groups, the majority of patients were rated by their spouses as independent in most activities of daily living.

In both the Haese (1970) and Overs and Healy (1971) studies, the majority of patients felt therapy had helped them, and all three studies found that the support of family and friends was a great help to the recovery from the stroke.

Christopherson's studies (1960, 1963) suggest that counseling should be aimed at fostering changes in the family role structures that are more in line with the changed physical and mental capacities of the family members. However, Overs and Healy's population did not respond with many such changes and neither did Christopherson's. Only 22 percent of the men in his sample assumed more than 25 percent of the housework, and Christopherson's sample was considerably younger than Overs and Healy's. Overs and Healy, like Christopherson, found differences between the patient's self-description and the spouse's patient-description. Again, in both studies, there was a general tendency for the spouses to be harder on the patient than he was on himself.

Summary

On all the variables selected as possible areas for role change, the families were noticcably reluctant to make any fundamental changes. There did not seem to be any greater degree of role changing in those 21 families exposed to "intensive" counseling than in the other families. Whether such role changes are indeed indicative of adjustment to a stroke remains an unanswered question. Families do not operate in a sociological vacuum, and changes in family role assignment must be acceptable to the community at large. Family members must perceive that society will allow them to act in a certain way, and in fact *expects* them to act in that way, before they can decide on their appropriate roles. To expect persons of advanced age, low education, and impaired physical and mental functioning to reallocate their family roles in a manner directly contradictory to the norms of the society at large is presumptuous. Whether younger families, brought up under different conditions, will be more amenable to role switching is still to be seen.

The findings of Overs and Healy (1971) served to support and extend the theoretical implications of earlier studies. There were differences in the size, scope, design, purpose, and findings between this project and the other studies, as well as among the others themselves, but these differences serve only to make the similarities more significant.

EFFECTIVENESS OF REHABILITATION COUNSELING WITH FAMILIES OF STROKE PATIENTS

This section seeks to describe data drawn from the Overs and Healy (1971) and other reports as a survey of the effectiveness of and problems related to counseling with stroke patients and their families. The roles of the family versus the neighborhood in the rehabilitation process of stroke clients will be reviewed. Helping patterns within stroke families will be described. Neighborhood helping patterns will be surveyed. Finally, patient social contacts will be presented.

The Family Versus the Neighborhood

There has been a lot said about the death of the extended family and the implications for urban living. It has been assumed that interaction among relatives has decreased as the trend towards nuclear household units has developed. However, the project of Overs and Healy showed, and some other recent studies have also found, that *it is not so much the family that is dying as the neighborhood.* Eighty percent of the interaction the Overs and Healy patients had was with family or relatives. Less than 10 percent of the interaction was with neighbors. This corresponds to Rosenberg's (1970) findings in Philadelphia, where nearly 90 percent of his sample of older workers saw at least one relative a week. Other estimates of the elderly's contact with their children show that few of the older people are out of touch with their children (United States Department of Health, Education and Welfare, 1970; Rodman, 1965; Youmans, 1967). From one third to one fourth are estimated to live with an adult child. The sample which Overs and Healy studied found 28 percent living with an adult child. Another half of the patients are supposed to live within walking or a short ride's distance from a child.

Nor do the children merely visit. Help is usually available if needed, more often supplied by a daughter than a son and usually by one child of the family more than the others. The difficulty arises from the fact that as our cities decay, the children no longer live in geographical proximity to the patients. Visiting, even when it involves a walk or a short ride, can be a major expedition in some of our cities. Thus the demands made on the helper can be disproportionate to the actual help itself. Neighbors would be in a better position to give some types of help, but it is the neighborhood interaction that is missing. When children, relatives, and neighbors were all the same set of people, there was no problem. As the proportion of children and relatives in the neighborhood or nearby area declines, the demand on each one of those remaining increases. What might have been an easy task when spread over three or four nearby relatives can be a severe drain on the emotional resources of the one child remaining in the area. Christopherson describes the danger of "locked" relationships (Donahue, 1969). He suggests more thought be given to how patients can help their helpers.

The Helping Patterns Within Families of Stroke Victims

The spouse, if there is one, is obviously the central helping figure in most families of stroke victims. Among the patients Overs and Healy (1971) studied, the sex of the patient influenced who helped the patient. Excluding the spouse, the distribution of who helped whom is shown in Table V-1. As you can see, the burden usually fell most heavily on one person.

TABLE V-1

WHO HELPED THE PATIENT? (IN RANK ORDER)

When the Patient was a Man			When the Patient was a Woman		
Helper			*Helper*		
One son	62	31%	One daughter	66	43%
One daughter	62	31%	One sister	21	14%
Two daughters	18	9%	One son	18	12%
One sister	14	7%	Neighbor	12	8%
Neighbor	13	7%	Friend	11	7%
Friend	6	3%	Parents	8	5%
One brother	5	3%	Two daughters	5	3%
Two sons	4	2%	Two sons	4	3%
Parents	4	2%	One brother	3	2%
Three or more daughters	3	2%	Two sisters	2	1%
Cousins	3	2%	Two brothers	2	1%
Two sisters	2	1%	Co-worker	1	1%
Co-worker	1	1%	Niece/nephew	1	1%
Total	197	101%	Total	154	101%

In those cases where help was not forthcoming from children of the patients, the primary reason for the lack of help was judged

by the rehabilitation counselor working on our project to fall
in categories described in Table V-2 (in rank order).

TABLE V-2
CHILDREN UNABLE TO HELP BECAUSE:

		% of 40	% of 66
Children moved away	12	30%	18%
Children's work	11	28%	17%
Deficient role definitions for sons	8	20%	12%
Alienated from parents	6	15%	9%
Parent's inability to accept help	3	8%	5%
Total	40	101%	61%

The forms of help given also varied according to the sex of
the patient. Table V-3 shows the distribution of the forms of
help given, both when the patient was a man and when the
patient was a woman. Transportation topped the list for men
patients and accounted for 25 percent of the help given. Patient
care tops the list of help given women patients. Shopping help
ranks second for both men and women patients.

TABLE V-3
WHAT FORMS OF HELP WERE GIVEN TO THE PATIENT*

When the Patient was a Man			*When the Patient was a Woman*		
Type of Help			*Type of Help*		
Transportation	49	25%	Patient care	25	16%
Shopping	35	18%	Shopping	24	16%
Patient care	27	14%	Transportation	24	16%
Chores	26	13%	Chores	20	13%
Maintenance	23	12%	Financial	16	10%
Financial	13	7%	Living accommodations	13	8%
Advice	11	6%	Advice	12	8%
Supplies	7	4%	Supplies	11	7%
Living accommodations	5	3%	Maintenance	7	5%
Care of children	1	1%	Care of children	1	1%
			Other	1	1%
Total	197	103%	Total	154	101%

*In rank order

The Neighborhood Helping Pattern

In the Overs and Healy (1971) sample of stroke patients' families, help given by someone outside of the family (neighbor, friend, or co-worker) amounted to only 11 percent for men patients and 16 percent for women patients.

Help given to neighbors closely approximated the amount of help received from them. Thus, men patients gave 8 percent of their help to neighbors and received 7 percent from them. Women patients gave 6 percent of their help to neighbors and received 8 percent from them. Neighbors made up 9 percent of the types of people seen once a week or more by patients.

Attitudes toward neighbors as judged by the project rehabilitation counselor are shown in Table V-4. These are overlapping categories; some families expressed feelings in several categories.

TABLE V-4

THE NEGATIVE FEELINGS OF PATIENTS AND THEIR FAMILIES
ABOUT THEIR NEIGHBORHOODS

		% of 51	% of 66
Complained of neighborhood changing	9	18%	14%
Neighbors unfriendly and don't care	12	24%	18%
Patients did not want to get involved	21	41%	32%
Patients were proud of not wanting to get involved .	9	18%	14%
Total	51	101%	77%

On the positive side, from the counseling records we are able to present at least two positive examples of good neighborhood relationships:

> The patient apparently has a good relationship with the upstairs neighbor and with a cousin who visits often. The neighbor escorts her around the neighborhood and the cousin has promised to take her out in the car "when the weather turns nice."
>
> The patient has obtained permission of her landlord to work on the grounds of her apartment building, primarily planting shrubs and other plants.

Patient Social Contacts

Families were classified by the project rehabilitation counselor according to type and degree of neighborhood isolation (in rank order from least to most) as indicated in Table V-5.

TABLE V-5

DEGREE OF ISOLATION OF PATIENTS AND FAMILIES

		% of 61	% of 66
Not isolated (had interdependent contact with more than one family in neighborhood)	6	10%	9%
Marginally isolated (had interdependent contact with one family in neighborhood)	3	5%	5%
Isolated from neighbors but maintained social contacts outside neighborhood, including institutional ties, such as churches and lodges	16	26%	24%
Isolated from neighbors with no other contacts other than family and work group	36	59%	55%
Total	61	100%	93%

Information secured at the time of the home visit follow-up interview showed that men average only 2.86 people seen a week and women only 2.20. Even more important, though, is the type of people seen. For both men and women, about 80 percent of the people seen were family members, of whom 65 percent were a spouse or child. Clearly, the patients were not interacting very often with their community. (See Tables V-6 and V-7.)

Of the twelve patients who were seeing fellow stroke victims at least once a week, seven were still receiving therapy at the agency and the other five were in nursing homes. In reality, only about 10 percent of the clients maintain any close relationships with other stroke patients once they leave the agency. This would seem to highlight the need for programs to ease the client's transition from the status of a dependent patient to that of a peer in social relationships. There were twenty clients (23 percent) who reported having contact with other stroke patients in their house or someone else's home, but the frequency of such

TABLE V-6

NUMBER OF PEOPLE SEEN ONCE A WEEK OR MORE BY PATIENTS*

	Men Patients		Women Patients		All Patients	
0 persons seen	2	4%	1	3%	3	3%
1 person seen	10	20%	12	31%	22	25%
2 persons seen	10	20%	11	28%	21	24%
3 persons seen	12	25%	9	23%	21	24%
4 persons seen	5	10%	5	13%	10	11%
5 persons seen	7	14%	1	3%	8	9%
6 persons seen	2	4%	0		2	2%
7 persons seen	1	2%	0		1	1%
Total patients	49	99%	39	101%	88	99%
Total persons seen	140		86		226	
Average per patient	2.86		2.20		2.57	

*Includes spouse.

TABLE V-7

TYPES OF PEOPLE SEEN ONCE A WEEK OR MORE BY PATIENTS

	Men Patients		Women Patients		All Patients	
Spouse	40	29%	20	23%	60	26%
Daughter	32	23%	26	30%	58	26%
Son	19	14%	10	12%	29	13%
Friend	13	9%	10	12%	23	10%
Neighbor	12	9%	9	10%	21	9%
Sister	7	5%	6	7%	13	6%
Brother	7	5%	2	2%	9	4%
Parent	6	4%	3	3%	9	4%
Other relative	2	1%	0		2	1%
Co-worker	2	1%	0		2	1%
Total people seen	140	100%	86	99%	226	100%
Average per patient	2.86		2.20		2.57	

social contact was very low. Patients did not seem to carry their relationships with fellow clients out of the physical setting of the agency. Also, there was only one reported case of clients exchanging services with one another—in this case, transportation. (See Table V-8.)

TABLE V-8

FREQUENCY OF CONTACT WITH OTHER STROKE VICTIMS

At least once a week	12	14%
1-3 times monthly	8	9%
Less than monthly	5	6%

THE COUNSELOR'S CHALLENGE

In trying to make highly specific suggestions as to what the rehabilitation counselor can do, it is realized that what worked with one sample of patients (Overs and Healy study) may not be applicable to the total population of stroke patient families. The assumption is made that the stroke population with which most counselors will be working will be somewhat like the one reported from Milwaukee. First, in light of the counselor's responsibility, family coping limits will be discussed. Second, the question of probability of value change in a stroke population is explored. Third, the impact of psychological therapy on stroke patients is reviewed. Fourth, encouraging community action resulting in satellite centers will be described. Finally, specific implications for rehabilitation counselors will be developed.

The Family Coping Limits

It is unrealistic to expect a counselor to effect major changes in the life style of families after a catastrophe like a stroke. The basic instinct of people under stress is to hold to previously proven patterns of action, whether these are effective in the situation or not. The whole life style of the population is that of a traditional, conservative, sex-typed, inflexible division of roles and a fairly limited array of roles at that. If just one or two items in the repertoire are eliminated, the whole show collapses. In Goffman's (1959) terms, most of these people have never been encouraged to develop a wide range of "selfs" to present. Since longevity, enforced retirement, and shorter working hours are a fact of present-day life, the problems faced by stroke families today are only a prototype of the ones all families will eventually have to confront.

One cannot overestimate the trauma of a stroke. It is a frightening and shattering experience for all those affected, spouses and children as well as patients. However, it is concluded that a stroke does not change the basic approach to life and the problems of life that the individual and the family have been using the previous 50 or more years of life, and 20 or so years of marriage. The fact is that most people and families do not have a well-defined or well-developed philosophy of life or approach to problems. More fundamentally, they do not have well-developed self or family concepts. The society, its schools, its institutions, its values, have never encouraged people to develop such a concept.

The HEW publication (1970, p. 62) referred to above states that at the present time "if retirement income is adequate, a period of two years is about the usual length of time for personal adjustment to retirement to be achieved." This is a sad commentary on a society that prides itself on its ability to extend the life span and increase the percentage of leisure time. If two years are required for couples with "adequate income" and in good health, one hesitates to make an estimate of the time required for those families with a disabled member and strained financial resources.

Overs and Healy's findings seem to indicate that by two years after the stroke, most families have reached some sort of an equilibrium with their surroundings. After the immediate crisis period ends and it becomes clear that no miracle to restore the lost function is about to occur, the family members pick up the pieces that remain and continue about as they did before but at a reduced level. If their adjustment was marginal before the stroke, it is likely that the stroke will be the proverbial last straw. It is worth speculating that perhaps therapy merely prolongs the wishful thinking stage and does not encourage patients to face the fact that new roles and new patterns of interaction with the surroundings are necessary.

Can Patient Values Be Changed?

To develop the argument further, a stroke is an impairment suffered primarily by the middle-aged and elderly. The age of the Overs and Healy group at admission for rehabilitation was as described in Table V-9.

TABLE V-9

PATIENT AGE DISTRIBUTION

Age	N	%
65 and over	54	41%
62-64	15	11%
40-61	58	44%
39 and under	5	4%
Total	132	100%

Certain values held by patients which prior to the stroke may have been adaptive or at least minimally impairing became maladaptive after the stroke.

The following values are inferred from a knowledge of commonly held values in our society, together with attitude inventory responses from patients and their spouses. Client behavior which appears to be congruent with these inferred values was also observed. It is suggested that the following values guided the behavior of most of the stroke patients and their spouses and are maladaptive when continued unchanged after the stroke crisis. Some of these points have been illustrated with excerpts from case records.

1. Maintaining the rigidity of one's values as a virtue.
2. Keeping up appearances as more important than solving problems.

3. For men, holding a job is necessary to maintain self-respect, until after retirement age is reached.

Case excerpt:

The patient has made great advances since his stroke. He does quite a bit of the housework while his wife works. This, however, is not what the patient wants. He does not like being dependent on his wife for the income she brings home, and he feels that he has lost much of his manhood as a result.

4. For women, self-respect is earned only by doing the housework.

Case excerpt:

The patient's only function in the family at this time seems to be that of housewife, and while the counselor was at home, she seemed to stress this function, cleaning somewhat compulsively.

5. Dependence on people outside the family is undesirable, even in a reciprocal arrangement where something is contributed by the stroke victim's family.

Values are instilled in children at an early age, which for currently middle-aged patients is likely to have been during the 1900 to 1925 period. Values instilled early in life change less with individuals of limited education, so that the rigidity of values is more apt to be seen among working-class and lower-middle–class individuals. These are the social classes with whom rehabilitation counselors are most likely to be working.

Counseling theory in general implies that the most productive use of counseling time and skills is usually attributed to helping the client gain insight so that he will change his attitudes and achieve personal growth which will enable him to solve future problems on his own. Based on the counseling experience with the Overs and Healy sample of stroke patients, it is projected that this goal of counseling cannot be achieved with stroke patients. Their experience points out that it is not possible, through counseling, to help these middle-aged people to change from maladaptive to adaptive values and that counseling time is better spent on rehabilitation counseling goals which can be achieved. These may usually be performed by the rehabilitation counselor, but some do not require technical counseling skills and may be performed by other professionals, paraprofessionals, and in some cases, aides.

Although values may not be changed, counseling may aid decision-making when a particular attitude is not strongly held by the client or there is evidence in the past history that patient-spouse reciprocal roles have been somewhat flexible, as for instance when the wife has occasionally worked outside the home or the husband has occasionally done some of the housework. Counseling can also help the patient or spouse to alleviate the distress caused by emotionally charged negative feelings by telling the counselor how they feel and why. This sometimes improves the ability of the patient or the spouse to deal more comfortably with one another and to make better decisions. As a result of counseling, problems may be faced with less anxiety and emotional ambivalence, although the problems are still resolved within the fundamental value system of the family.

The Impact of Therapy

Gains made in therapy are frequently not carried over to or maintained in the home. Sometimes these gains, although important from an objective point of view, are not compatible with the self-concept of the patient or the patient's spouse. Thus, when the patient's unrealistic expectations of being able to return to work or of using his impaired arm are not met, he rejects the significant lesser gains the rehabilitation therapies are able to accomplish. How to motivate patients to work for, and appreciate, important and useful gains which do not meet their level of aspiration continues to be an unsolved problem.

Therapy given shortly after the cerebral vascular accident occurs, obviously has to be prescribed, as does therapy for patients who continue to be unable to make rational decisions. However, for those patients capable of rational decision-making, experiments in greater patient involvement in getting the patient to think through what he wants out of therapy before he participates in it seems a possible way out of this dilemma.

Getting patients who are capable of rational decision-making more involved in planning personal goals to be achieved by therapy would require a reevaluation of the medical concept that therapy should be prescribed for every patient. The need for greater pre-therapy planning involvement by the patient is supported by the general tendency of community helping programs in our society to encourage those being helped to participate more in the process of deciding how they should be helped.

The Satellite Center: A New Sense of Community?

One encouraging result of the Overs and Healy project was the success of an Agency Activities Program and the enthusiastic community response to preliminary efforts to extend it. It seems that small groups, perhaps located near or in the patient's own neighborhood, might be the most productive means of encouraging patient activity, especially for men patients who expressed a greater need to get out of the house. If nothing else, it would provide a setting where those unwilling pioneers of the leisure-time frontier might work out new patterns and values that could serve as models for those of us who must surely follow.

Specific Implications for Rehabilitation Counselors

In the preceding pages of this chapter, the nature of the society in which stroke families work out the tragic drama of family life, programmed, as it were, by the cerebral vascular accident which occurred, has been described. Some of these themes will be repeated in more detail. Specific dimensions of the problem in which the rehabilitation counselor may or may not become usefully involved will be developed.

Additional data from the Overs and Healy (1971) study on normative patterns in the stroke victims' families' behavior will be presented so that the beginning counselor will have some idea of what to expect to encounter. Specific ways in which the counselor may be useful and offer support for Overs and Healy's recommendations based on the counseling with a sample of stroke families will be suggested.

Giving Information About the Stroke Condition

The Overs and Healy (1971) study documented that giving more information about the nature of the stroke disability is necessary. After the stroke, it was usually the family doctor who described what had happened, but fully half the clients either did not remember their doctor describing the stroke or felt the description was inadequate. Another 20 percent could not recall anyone explaining their illness to them. The report of the clients in the Overs and Healy study on who gave information about strokes after the stroke occurred is given in Table V-10.

TABLE V-10

SOURCES OF INFORMATION ABOUT STROKES

	N	%
Doctor	45	51%
Therapists	13	15%
News media	11	13%
Visiting nurse	5	6%
Relatives	5	6%
Friends and neighbors	3	3%
Caseworker-Counselor	2	2%
Total	84	96%

Preferably, it would seem that giving information about the physical aspects of the stroke syndrome should be done by a physician, nurse, physical therapist, occupational therapist, or speech therapist, all of whom know more about it than the rehabilitation counselor. However, the evidence shows that it is frequently not done by anyone, and in this case, the counselor may well undertake it himself if he cannot arrange for medical personnel to undertake it. This means becoming knowledgeable about the facts and limiting his explanation to what he knows for sure.*

---

*If it is desired to use 16 mm sound films as educational aids, the following films are recommended. They were chosen from among a total of 26 films reviewed. (See next page.)

The following incident extracted from counseling records illustrates how coping with the psychological changes in a stroke patient were successfully explained by the counselor and acted upon by a bewildered wife.

> Mr. X, the patient, found the subject of money an especially sensitive one. He refused to believe that they were short of funds and interpreted his wife's efforts to get him to help her make financial decisions as harassment and her complaints of the difficulties of living within their income as a direct attack on his ability as a provider. Financial discussions usually ended with a tearful wife and a highly agitated patient.
>
> The counselor discussed the situation with the wife and explained how a stroke can affect psychological functioning, decrease powers of memory and concentration, make working with figures difficult, and cause a lack of self-esteem due to loss of employment and feelings of helplessness. This was suggested as a part of the origin of Mr. X's unrealistic attitude and erratic behavior. The counselor suggested that Mrs. X discuss financial matters with her adult son or daughter.
>
> *Outcome:* Mrs. X no longer tried to discuss money with her husband. He kept his small check from the Agency Education and Adjustment Program and that satisfied him.

Giving Information About Community Resources

The financial resources of the typical lower-middle-class and working-class family are usually severely depleted by the stroke crisis, and the family needs to avail itself of every possible community resource to meet its needs at the least possible expense. In the Overs and Healy sample, at the time of the followup (1970 to 1971), a little more than half of the families were living

1. *Strokes:* American Heart Association, 1957, Produced by Churchill Wexler; time: 6 minutes.
2. *Cerebral Vascular Disease:* Challenge of Management; time: 39 minutes.
3. *Second Chance:* time: 28 minutes. Both 2 and 3 are American Heart Association films, produced by George C. Stoney Associates, 1969.
4. *Inner World of Aphasia:* Psychology Exploration Films, 1600 LaLanna Ave., Berkeley, California 94709; Produced by Leonard Pearson, 1968.

on an income less than 4000 dollars yearly and had less than 1000 dollars in savings against a future emergency.

The follow-up study also showed that the education provided by the rehabilitation counselor was effective in the experimental group knowing more about and using more community resources than the control group. Even the beginning counselor can be very effective in obtaining, organizing, and disseminating this type of information in his local community. Information known about and used by this sample of experimental and control groups combined is indicated in the following table. Obviously, resources vary from community to community; each counselor or rehabilitation agency will have to independently develop information about what is available on the local scene. (See Table V-11.)

TABLE V-11

MILWAUKEE COUNTY COMMUNITY RESOURCES

Service or Program	Patients Knew About		Patients Have Used	
Visiting Nurse Association	54	82%	29	44%
Washington Park Senior Center	48	73%	5	8%
Local senior citizen centers	48	73%	2	3%
Federal food stamp program	41	62%	2	3%
Bookmobile	36	55%	2	3%
Golden Age clubs	35	53%	1	2%
Marquette University Dental Clinic	35	53%	6	9%
Tuberculosis Clinic	34	52%	8	12%
Union Drug Stores	33	50%	11	17%
Immunization Clinic	28	42%	6	9%
Talking Books	27	41%	6	9%
Wisconsin Homestead Tax Credit	25	38%	3	5%
Project Involve	19	29%	1	2%
Mail-order drug service	18	27%	1	2%
Multiphasic physical exam	17	26%	1	2%
Project involve telephone service	14	21%		

Clients completing questions: 66

The following excerpts from the case records show the counselor at work informing patients about available community resources.

Case excerpt:

The counselor informed the patient of activities at Washington Park and told her about the bookmobile that stops in her neighborhood. Counselor tried to ascertain what activities local church groups might sponsor in the neighborhood.

Case excerpt:

For some time, the L's were worried about the rising cost of medical services for their three grandchildren. They investigated the possibility of Title 19 and found that the three boys were eligible for the program. This has made it possible for the boys to obtain needed glasses and other medical help without putting the L's in any financial debt.

Advising Patients About Adaptive Devices in the Home

Ideally, advising patients about adaptive devices in the home is better done by the occupational and/or physical therapist who is more expert than the rehabilitation counselor. In the Overs and Healy (1971) study, the services of these specialists were available to the patients. Unfortunately, in many instances the occupational and/or physical therapists do not make regular calls to the home, and the rehabilitation counselor, if he is not able to arrange for expert consultation, can be helpful to the extent of his knowledge.

In the Overs and Healy (1971) study, about 70 percent of all patients interviewed had made some household changes. About one third of the total changes were simple rearrangement of furniture or removal of rugs, which involved no expense or equipment. About 15 percent of the adaptations mentioned, usually grab bars or kitchen devices, had been suggested by medical or paramedical professionals.

To give the counselor a specific idea of what adaptations have been made and the frequency of their use, detailed findings from the Overs and Healy (1971) study are included in Table V-12.

TABLE V-12

HOUSEHOLD OR BUILDING ADAPTATIONS FOR PATIENTS

Type of Adaptation	Adaptations were Made	
Removed throw rugs, small carpets	22	28%
Grab bars in bathroom	16	20%
Railings on stairways, along wall	12	15%
Stool, rubber mat for bathtub	11	14%
Special furniture: beds, chairs, etc.	9	11%
Commode, raised seat for toilet	8	10%
Ramps for stairways, split level, car	6	8%
One-handed kitchen devices	6	8%
Additional telephone jacks	5	6%
Rearrangement of furniture	4	5%
Not waxing linoleum	2	3%
Removed door or threshold	2	3%
Steering knob for car	1	1%
Weaving loom	1	1%
Pulley in bedroom	1	1%
Total number of adaptations	106	Range 0 to 8
Mean for all clients completing question	1.33	N=80
Mean for those clients making adaptations	1.93	N=55

Counseling About Transportation Possibilities

Nearly all of the various studies which have been done on the problems of the severely disabled cite transportation as a major problem for effective living, and it will come as no surprise that this is true of stroke patients. As a minimum, transportation elements are the type of vehicle, the method of payment, the social role of the driver, and the social role of the attendant, if one is required.

It is the impression that stroke patients and their families and probably other severely disabled people are not using the social techniques for meeting transportation needs used by the typical nondisabled worker. Typical nondisabled persons trade off rides to work when necessary. They form car pools or pay for rides with fellow employees. The disabled seem remiss in using these social solutions.

The comprehensive schema presented in Figures V-1 and V-2 covers most of the possible ways to arrange transportation. Counselors may find this schema helpful in systematically going over with patients and their families the many ways by which the patients may be transported. It is the impression that the social relationships involved require as much attention as the actual mechanical means of conveyance, and the counselor can help the patient and family in working through their feelings about these relationships.

Method of Payment	Self	Spouse	Rela- tive	Friend	Neigh- bor	Co- worker	Fellow client	Paid at- tendant	Car pool
Free									
Drive alternately									
Pay own share of expenses									
Pay more than own share of expenses									
Hire driver									
Hire attendant									
Hire car plus driver plus attendant									
Agency pays									
DVR trans- portation allowance									

Figure V-1. Private transportation: driver and type of assistant required.

Type of Public Transportation	Self	Spouse	Rela-tive	Friend	Neigh-bor	Co-worker	Paid at-tendant	Paid driver	Fellow client
Bus									
Train									
Subway									
Taxi									
Handicab, Proprietory									
Handicab, Cooperatively Owned									

Figure V-2. Public transportation: type of assistant required.

The Use of Subprofessional Personnel

In the Overs and Healy (1971) project, research clerks and secretaries were utilized in a variety of ways to save the counselor's time and assist the client. The diverse talents of this college-level clerical staff were fitted to the special demands of the situations. Some of the services provided by these subprofessional personnel to the counselor and/or client were as follows:

1. Gathering purely factual data for Agency reports.
2. Helping clients fill out forms (medicare, Blue Cross, etc.).
3. Telephoning agencies to check on progress of client's applications.
4. Contacting business associations and service companies to see what special programs they might offer to disabled people.
5. Notifying families of, and referring them to, special services available to them (library loans, talking books, tax credits, food stamps, etc.).
6. Making daily telephone contact with isolated clients in poor health.
7. Patient-sitting for spouse of severely disabled client so he could go shopping.

8. Transporting clients to doctor's, dentist's, or other urgent appointments when no other alternative was available.
9. Visiting homes to see if assistive devices could be installed.
10. Teaching games to clients.
11. Finding factual information. If a question requiring factual information arose while the counselor was conducting a home interview, the counselor telephoned the office, a research clerk or secretary would find out the information about community resources available or whatever the problem was, and telephone the information to the counselor while the counselor was still at the patient's home.
12. Finding information on community resources. In the same way, when a question of fact about the availability of community resources or related problems arose during a staff conference, a research clerk or secretary was asked to find out the information by telephone, and report it immediately to the conference. In this way, the information became available upon which to make a decision without either interrupting the conference or postponing the decision.

All of these techniques have great possibilities for further development and significant improvement in the efficiency of counseling. The Overs and Healy study was not able to demonstrate the efficiency of the subprofessional personnel because they were used only incidentally on a pilot basis. It was found that the project counselor, during the latter part of the demonstration when these techniques had been developed, only occasionally used the support provided. At one point she quipped, "You have provided me with so much back-up support that I no longer have any excuse for being inefficient and this makes me nervous!"

It is possible that rehabilitation counselors are not taught how to function with this kind of back-up support; it is a major work role adjustment, therefore, for them to meet the higher demands that it makes of them.

SUMMARY

In one chapter it is obviously not possible to describe all of the various complex relationships among patient-family-neighborhood-society and how the counselor, as a catalyst, can go about helping patient and family cope with the adverse psychosocial situation precipitated by a stroke.

Three different approaches to the problem have been presented. First, the sociological approach has described the societal setting, emphasizing the family as a system of reciprocal roles, the stroke as the crisis event, the sick-role as a factor in rehabilitation, the problem of change or lack of it in family member roles, and the current status of family and neighborhood help.

In the second approach, selected data from a four-year research and demonstration project in counseling with families of stroke patients was presented. The third and final approach, based on inferences drawn from the first two, presented rather concrete suggestions as to ways in which counselors and other related professionals working with stroke patients and their families may help.

REFERENCES

Artes, R. H.: A study of family problems as identified and evaluated by the wives of stroke patients. The University of Iowa Speech Pathology, 1967.

Ballweg, J. A.: Resolution of conjugal adjustment after retirement. *Journal of Marriage and the Family, 29*:277, 1967.

Barrow, J. G. *et al.*: Development of a stroke program in Georgia. *American Journal of Public Health, 52*(4):627, 1962.

Bell, G. D. and Derek, L. P.: Playing the sick role and avoidance of responsibility. *Research Preview, 13*:41, 1966. Paper presented at the Sixth World Congress of Sociology.

Blood, R. O.: *Husbands and Wives: The Dynamics of Married Living.* New York, Free Press, 1960.

Brodsky, C. M.: Medical roles in family treatment. *Psychosomatics, 8*(4) Part 1:227, 1967.

Brown, T. S. *et al.*: Physical activities, attitudes and therapeutic classification of coronary heart patients. Institute of Behavioral Research, Texas Christian University, August, 1968.

Centers, R., Raven, B. H., and Rodrigues, A.: Conjugal power structure: A re-examination. *American Sociological Review, 36*(2):264, 1971.

Christopherson, V. A.: Role modifications of the handicapped home-maker. *Rehabilitation Literature, 21*(4):110, 1960.

Christopherson, V. A.: *Role Modifications of the Disabled Male with Implications for Counseling.* Final report of VRA Project No. 755, University of Arizona, November, 1963.

Derman, S.: Family counseling with relatives of patients at Schwab Rehabilitation Hospital. *Rehabilitation Literature,* Abstract—June, 1967.

Deutsch, C. P.: Family factors in home adjustment of the severely disabled. *Journal of Marriage and the Family, 22*(4):312, 1960.

Donahue, W., Kornbluh, J., and Power, L. (Ed.): *Living in the Multigeneration Family.* Occasional Papers in Gerontology, No. 3, Institute of Gerontology, University of Michigan, Wayne State University, January, 1969.

Dyer, W.: Analyzing marital adjustment using role theory. *Marriage and Family Living, 24*(4):371, 1962.

Friedman, A. S.: The "well" sibling in the "sick" family: A contradiction. *International Journal of Social Psychiatry,* Congress Issue, 47-53, 1964.

Goffman, E.: *The Presentation of the Self in Everyday Life.* Garden City, New York, Doubleday-Anchor, 1959.

Haese, J. B. *et al.*: Attitudes of stroke patients toward rehabilitation and recovery. *American Journal of Occupational Therapy, 24*(4), May-June, 1970.

Heer, D.: Husband and wife perceptions of family power structure. *Marriage and Family Living, 24*(1): 65, 1962 (Annotated).

Hurvitz, N.: *Marital Roles Inventory Manual.* Western Psychology Services, Beverly Hills, California, 1961.

Hurvitz, N.: Marital problems following psychotherapy with one spouse. *Journal of Consulting Psychology, 31*(1):38, 1967.

Kassebaum, G. and Baumann, B. O.: Dimensions of the sick role in chronic illness. *Journal of Health and Human Behavior, 6*:16, 1965.

Kosa, J. L. *et al.*: Crisis and stress in family life: A re-evaluation of concepts. *Wisconsin Sociology, 4*(2): 1965.

Kotlar, S. L.: Middle class marital role-perceptions and role adjustment. *Sociological Social Research, 49*:283, 1965.

New, P. K.: The support structure of heart and stroke patients: A study of the role of significant others in patient rehabilitation. *Social Science and Medicine, 2*:185, 1968.

Olsen, J. Z. and May, B. J.: Family education: Necessary adjunct to total stroke rehabilitation. *American Journal of Occupational Therapy, 20:*88, 1966.

Overs, R. P. and Belknap, E. L.: Educating stroke patient families. *Journal of Chronic Disease, 20:*45, 1967.

Overs, R. P. and Healy, J.: Educating stroke patient families. *Milwaukee Media for Rehabilitation Research Reports No. 12,* July, 1971.

Rodman, H.: *Marriage, Family and Society.* New York, Random House, 1965.

Rosenberg, G. S.: *The Worker Grows Old.* San Francisco, Jossey-Bass, 1970.

Starkey, P. D.: Sick-role retention as a factor in non-rehabilitation. *Journal of Counseling Psychology, 15*(1):75, 1967.

Stein, J. W.: *The Family as a Unit of Study and Treatment.* Monograph one, Region IX, Rehabilitation Research Institute, University of Washington, 1969.

Straus, A. B. *et al.:* Groupwork with stroke patients. *Rehabilitation Record,* November-December 1967, 30-32.

Stuckert, R. P.: Role perception and marital satisfaction—A configurational approach. *Marriage and Family Living, 25:*415, 1963.

Tharp, R. G.: Psychological patterning in marriage. *Psychology Bulletin, 60:*97, 1963.

Tharp, R. G. and Otis, G.: Toward a theory for therapeutic intervention in families. *Journal of Consulting Psychology, 30:*426, 1966.

Thomas, E.: Problems of disability from the perspective of role theory. *Journal of Health and Human Behavior, 7:*2, 1966.

U. S. Department of Health, Education and Welfare Publications: *Working with Older People: Biological, Psychological and Sociological Aspects of Aging.* 2, 1970.

Youmans, E. G. (Ed.): *Older Rural Americans: A Sociological Perspective.* Lexington, University of Kentucky Press, 1967.

Chapter VI

THE MULTIPLE DYSFUNCTIONS CALLED CEREBRAL PALSY

ISABEL P. ROBINAULT AND ERIC DENHOFF

Every 53 minutes a child is born in the United States with multiple neurological difficulties. He is labeled "cerebral palsied." In fact, by the time you finish this chapter, one more CP will have been born. It is estimated that throughout the nation there are now about 750,000 such persons, one third of whom are under 21 years of age (National Health Education Committee, 1971). Today these people are being identified by careful medical diagnosis and being treated earlier and earlier. Consequently they are finding their way into special and regular schools, and some of them are working in the competitive world (although others are in institutions). Rehabilitation professionals are coming into contact with them more and more in a variety of situations (Publications List, United Cerebral Palsy, Inc.). Thus, such workers have more reason than ever to ask "What is CP—what is being done about it, and what can I do for them?"

DEFINITION OF CEREBRAL PALSY

Cerebral palsy is a general term applied to a group of disabilities resulting directly or indirectly from damage to the developing brain which may occur before, during or after birth (United Cerebral Palsy Research and Educational Foundation, 1960). Its primary characteristic is loss or impairment of control over voluntary muscles, such as found in arms, legs, tongue, eyes or over body movements. The impairment may be in isolated parts, but more generally a variety of combinations is found. Vision, speech, gait, balance, and coordination may be impaired in a range from very mild to severe. In addition to motor dysfunction, CP may include convulsive and behavior disorders of organic origin, psychological problems, perceptual problems, and sensory defects which lead to learning difficulty.

CAUSES OF CEREBRAL PALSY

There are many reasons for cerebral palsy (Denhoff and Robinault, 1960; Denhoff, 1967). Virtually any factor or combination of factors that can alter brain function can be a contributing entity to cerebral palsy. Among the common causes are (a) insufficient oxygen during pregnancy and around delivery, (b) long-standing intrauterine viral infections, or chemical and metabolic imbalances producing congenital malformations, (c) incompatibility of blood factors producing kernicterus (pigmentation and damage of vital brain centers), (d) brain hemorrhage with resulting birth injury, (e) prematurity, especially under four pounds, (f) severe illnesses in the early years, such as encephalitis, meningitis, measles, and other viral diseases, and (g) toxic causes such as lead poisoning, arsenic, and coal tar derivatives.

PHYSICAL CHARACTERISTICS OF
THE CEREBRAL PALSIED

While one may be intellectually aware of the causes and the findings which make the diagnosis, it is possible to go through life without actually recognizing cerebral palsied persons. Let us take a closer look at them. First there is a wide variation between types of cases and individual cases. For instance, there is one out of seven persons with cerebral palsy who never comes to a clinic because his disabilities are so mild that he fits into normal society. At the other extreme are those who lie in institutions helplessly contorted by rigidly contracting muscles. Their intellectual powers also may be "paralyzed" because of associated disabilities such as deafness or blindness. However, the majority of cases may be recognized by either awkward or involuntary movements with or without lack of balance, irregular gait, gutteral speech, facial grimacing, and/or drooling. All of these stem from lack of voluntary muscle control. There is nothing wrong with the muscle architecture; but dysfunction occurs because muscles are not getting proper signals from the controlling brain. For this reason, CP is known as a "neuromuscular disorder" that takes five characteristic forms. There may be combinations the informed layman can spot (Denhoff and Robinault, 1960). These are as follows:

1. Spasticity, the most frequently occurring form, found in over half of the cases. It is the motor symptom of cerebral palsy wherein the voluntary muscles overcontract, causing awkward postures when flexor muscles of the limb are involved.

2. Athetosis, marked by a constant recurring series of slow, wormlike involuntary movements of hands, feet and trunk. It occurs in about 25% of the cases.

3. Ataxia, lack of balance from failure of coordination, occurring in about 7% of cases.

4. Tremor (1-5%), coarser movements than in athetosis.

5. Rigidity (7%), recognized by resistance to a limb being moved. It is characteristically called "lead pipe" movement.

Actual case histories illustrate that we are more concerned with people who happen to have characteristic types of disability, than with merely diagnostic labels (Denhoff and Robinault, 1960).

1. *Diagnosis:* cerebral palsy; spastic hemiplegia, right severe; intelligence, borderline; convulsive disorder; generalized behavior; hyperkinetic-impulse disorder, severe; form perception disturbance, mild.

A 7 lb. male infant was delivered one month prematurely by Caesarian section. Cyanosis, respiratory distress with chest retraction persisted for 6 days after birth. Feeding difficulty was manifested as gagging, choking, reversed swallowing, and vomiting. Irritability and hypertonic muscle spasms stimulated by mild degree of noise characterized the first year of life. At 4 months inability to use right hand properly or to kick right leg adequately was noted. Motor development was delayed with tonic neck reflex persisting until the age of 7 months, inability to reach for or transfer objects until 9 months, unable to sit unsupported until 16 months, and inability to walk independently until 28 months. However, speech development was normal.

At 17 months markedly increased reflexes in the right upper and right lower extremities were noted. A positive Babinski reflex and ankle clonus were also noted in the right lower limb. In addition to the spastic right leg, a moderate internal rotation of the left lower extremity was noted as well as a mild metatarsus adductus of the left foot. When walking was attempted, the child fell repeatedly because of lack of balance. The right hand seemed tighter than the left and there was deformity of internal rotation and pronation of the right hand on reaching. At 30 months he could walk unsupported but with typical stiff-legged gait on the toes and ball of his right foot, with heel up. His right hand was somewhat flexed to the side, and he used his left hand to feed or dress himself. He drooled considerably and was hyperactive. He had his first generalized convulsion at 36 months and had three such episodes until anticonvulsive drug therapy effected control.

At 7 years, gait improved following bracing, and he used his right hand as a helping hand. Now 10 years old, he can oppose poorly with the right hand, but can grasp and release objects adequately. He is completely independent in self-care. He attends public school but has difficulty keeping pace with the class because of poor attention span, hyperactive behavior, and lack of interest. In his last evaluation he was found to have poor eye-hand coordination, diminished sensation in the right hand, and difficulties in form perception which contributed to his learning problems. Thus he does not have the "mechanics" to support likely dull-normal intellectual potential.

2. *Diagnosis:* cerebral palsy; spastic paraplegia, moderate; intelligence, normal; behavior, anxiety state.

A 1¼ lb. premature female infant propelled herself into the world in a taxicab enroute to the hospital. She required hospital care for 3 months, but did well. There were no feeding or sleeping problems during the early months, and she gained weight normally. However, her development was delayed beyond expectancy so that head control was achieved at 6 months, sitting without support at 3 years, and standing and walking at 5 years, following orthopedic surgery. Hypertonicity of the lower limbs was noted at 5 to 6 months and there was no attempt at making reciprocal walking motions when held in upright position. Rhythmic activities were absent. No attempt was made to kick in the prone position and scissoring of the lower limbs was noted when she was held upright at 11 months. At 3 years, deep tendon reflexes were markedly increased in the lower extremities as compared to the upper extremities, in which they were mildly increased. A bilateral Babinski sign with ankle clonus was noted on the right. Passive examination of the lower extremities revealed increased bilateral tightness in adductor and gastrocnemius muscle groups and bilateral equinus at the ankles. There was very little limitation of motion in the upper extremities, with good reach, grasp, and release patterns present bilaterally. At 5 years, orthopedic surgery was performed to help overcome inability to walk because of bilateral adductor-muscle spasticity. When walking was attempted in the correct position, the knees could not flex and scissoring of the legs resulted in a poor base, making balance impossible. After surgery the patient developed a wide base, rather stiff-legged gait with poor reciprocal pattern and very little flexion at the hip and knee joints. The stiff-legged gait tended to keep her heels slightly off the floor, but the extent of toe-walking was decreased. She is now, at the age of 9, able to walk holding on to furniture or pushing a chair. She has not yet been able to learn crutch walking because of excessive fear and anxiety which developed perhaps as a result of prolonged over-protection. She has not yet had complications such as convulsions, visual, perceptual, speech, or hearing problems.

3. *Diagnosis:* cerebral palsy; spastic quadriplegia, moderate; convulsions; generalized behavior; hyperkinetic impulse disorder; visual perceptual dysfunction.

First seen at age 2, mother reports having had diabetes during pregnancy and child delivered by Caesarian section at 8½ months' gestation. Appeared normal until 9 months when poor ability to use left hand was noted. Walking delayed.

When seen at age 2 for lobar pneumonia with associated febrile convulsions, left hemiplegia and equivocal right-sided hyperreflexia were noted. Diagnostic-prognostic assessment revealed right cerebral dilitation; EEG abnormality in right occipital and frontal regions; psychological evaluation normal.

From age 6, generalized convulsions resisted drug control; hyperactive behavior affected school adjustment; gait became worse; progressive deformity of left hand.

At age 9, surgery was done to improve gait and mobility; an active physical therapy program was followed; boy became seizure-free under drug control. By the age of 12, he walked normally, but left hand and awkwardness interfered with baseball. Attended regular day camp and kept up with playmates after 4 months on a muscle relaxant. Upon recheck, anticonvulsant medication could be reduced and perceptual difficulties formerly noted were much improved. After 10 years of many-faceted therapy, he is considered normal by playmates, teachers, and neighbors.

4. *Diagnosis:* cerebral dysfunction; athetosis, mild; perceptual dysfunction; overanxious behavior disorder.

Born at 8½ months' gestation, one of twins required 3 weeks of hospitalization. Lethargic; slow development; head support at 3 months, walked at 15 months, spoke single word at 2 years, sentences after 2½ years. Seen first at age 6 with complaints of poor coordination and difficulty adjusting at school, where he was unable to write well, sit quietly, or to coordinate. Examination revealed hyperactive boy unable to follow direction well; borderline EEG; psychological testing showed normal IQ with evidence of organic brain dysfunction. Over the next year, primary problem was assessed the result of environmental pressure, not independent of the primary disability. A program of parent counseling, psychotherapy, medication, and perceptual retraining continued through elementary school.

During therapy, he was able to attend camp and summer school without medication and his parents reported no difficulties at home. By age 12, he had been promoted into regular grade of junior high school. He did well in most subjects, although arithmetic and writing grades were poor. However, his social adjustment was up to normal expectancy.

This illustrates how parent guidance and behavioral medication with supportive therapy can facilitate the adjustment of a handicapped youngster.

These abbreviated histories illustrate the wide range of dysfunctions which characterize cerebral palsy. Until about 20 years ago, cerebral palsy was considered an almost hopeless problem. The obstetrician was blamed for the cause, and the orthopedist tried to correct physical deformities. Often cases were left untreated. Bronson Crothers (1959) was one of the first to correlate the intellectual with the physical and social factors and to suggest this as a broad prognostic base for the individual's eventual place in society. Arnold Gessell also looked beyond the physical defects, calling attention to the impact on personality and social adjustment of a chronic disorder such as cerebral palsy. This medical-psychological-social approach remained theoretic for many years during which recreational facilities, educational opportunities and vocational exploration were largely lacking.

Slowly the team approach broadened the therapeutic horizon. Psychological evaluations were added to the diagnostic procedures, and social workers were brought in to link community facilities to individual needs. Trials of various methods and modalities were attempted in scattered clinics. However, a truly continuous comprehensive developmental approach, such as recommended by Denhoff and Robinault (1960), to the individual's physical, mental, emotional, social, and vocational needs from birth to maturity still remains in the blueprint stage (Denhoff, 1967).

Historically, orthopedics played the initial role in cerebral palsy. An English orthopedist, W. J. Little, wrote a monograph in 1861 wherein he described a disorder that he called "spastic paralysis." Later this became known as "Little's Disease." In true interdisciplinary sense, he wrote about a relatively small segment of persons with spastic paralysis who are "cross-legged, can't walk, have no use of arms, no speech, drool and are often feebleminded." This hardly characterizes all individuals with spastic paralysis, much less those with other neuromuscular disorders which are included under cerebral palsy today.

Developmentally, the medically oriented team initiates all efforts on behalf of the cerebral palsied individual, starting with prenatal care of the mother (National Health Education Committee, 1971; Denhoff and Robinault, 1960; Crothers and Paine, 1959). Medical research has made many valuable contributions toward better understanding of pregnancy "at-risk" factors. Among the recent strides are the following:

1. Discovering a method of multiple-exchange blood transfusions to modify hyperbilirubinemia and prevent kernicterus, a leading cause of infant death and of cerebral palsy athetosis (National Health Education Committee, 1971).

2. Establishing that overdosage of oxygen to premature babies caused retrolental fibroplasia and blindness in infants.

3. Establishing the correlation between excessive smoking by mothers and increase in premature births (Denhoff and Robinault, 1960).

4. Discovering that infants with certain metabolic defects may be treated with special diets, as in galactosemia and phenylketonuria, has led to the development of blood and urine tests that may be applied during the first few days of

life. If corrective diets are given in the earliest weeks to those babies who have positive blood and urine tests, significant brain damage may be avoided altogether (Chamberlin, 1964).

IDENTIFICATION AND MEDICAL TREATMENT OF THE CEREBRAL PALSIED

Surveys of incidence, prevalence, medical factors, treatment, and care have increased our knowledge about cerebral palsy. Perhaps the most exhaustive and generally useful survey is the comprehensive review and study done in Austin, Texas (Wolfe and Reid, 1958).

Medical research in cerebral palsy emphasizes prevention, while medical treatment of the child starts with detection. When the physician knows that the mother's prenatal history contains factors that may threaten the well-being of the baby, he will maintain a high index of suspicion, even through the preschool years. He will watch to see whether the function of the child deviates from normal development (Peiper, 1963). However, there may be no suspicious history and only vague difficulties of feeding and sleeping in the early months. Babies may leave the hospital with no deviation detected until signs such as seizures, squint eyes, lagging development, or muscle imbalances bring the mother back to the doctor or are picked up and referred to a doctor by alert nurses, relatives, or friends. If his problems are not obvious, a child's difficulty may be detected only at school age when he is too slow, physically or mentally, to succeed in a normal class. Some children who get through the first few grades start to experience trouble in the fourth and fifth grades when concept formation, rather than memory, becomes the modality for learning. A Texas survey corroborates these clinical impressions and alerts us to the fact that as many as 20 percent of the total caseload are not diagnosed or reported to any medical agency during the first five years of life (Wolfe and Reid, 1958).

Too often the sole criterion for improvement in a given case of CP is lessening the degree of neuromuscular involvement.

Experience indicates that the other factors play equal, if not at times more important roles. These factors include:

1. Attention to feeding, sleeping, bowel, bladder, and behavior variations.

2. Supportive counseling of parents during the necessary uncertain years when the balance between the natural maturity of the nervous system and the extent of the brain injury makes the outward pattern of the disability change with growth.

3. Medication for seizure control and for behavioral controls starting in infancy.

4. Continuous reevaluation of vision, hearing, perception, and speech to take advantage of the child's ability to respond to tests in these areas from the first year on.

5. Neuromuscular reeducation (PT, OT), starting in infancy. Bracing and surgery on the lower extremities may be started during the first three years *if* indicated.

6. Preschool therapy related to stages of development: poorly coordinated, semicoordinated, evolving body control, early skills. Correlation of the therapy evaluations during this period with psychological tests since *rate of development* or the particular *sequence* of the development is far more important than the result of any individual summary test battery from therapy and/or from psychology.

7. Neuromuscular modalities, bracing, splinting, orthopedic aids, muscle reeducation, proprioceptive facilitation, ultrasonic therapy, dynamic relaxation, patterns of control via inhibitory control after analysis to conservative therapy. Choice of method will depend upon the nature of the lesion, capacity of the child to cooperate, and philosophy of the medical leadership. Denhoff and Robinault believe that during the school years, neuromuscular reeducation should be secondary to educational and social experiences of that child who has potential for remaining in society. This philosophy is corroborated by Roth and Eddy, who state that "Therapy is a double-edged sword; the social control

necessary to ameliorate physical ills may bring in its wake the deterioration or destruction of the natural interaction of man with his environment" (Roth and Eddy, 1963; Robinault, 1961).

8. At adolescence, a general review of all tests (sensory, motor, and intellectual) and of therapy given to date. Therapeutic measures should be geared to the possibility that remaining remedial procedures may lead to the independence required for maturity: ADL for independent grooming and travel; group experiences and counseling toward social interaction at whatever level the individual is capable of beyond his family contacts; medical procedures, if indicated, for cosmetic or functional social acceptance; review of drug control, since a few adolescents experience their first seizures at this time of body readjustment, and others require re-evaluation of convulsants or relaxants. Prevocational testing upon entering high school so that courses may be selected to ameliorate deficits, counseling may be available to promote attitudes compatible with approaching maturity, and summers may be used for developmental experiences.

9. Any advances in drug, surgery or mechanical aids which may help the individual to function at his optimum. Psychotherapy, if indicated, may help the maturing individual to cope with those remaining disabilities that must be tolerated for life and to find those emotional capabilities that will be his own strengths and satisfactions in mature years.

Comprehensive medical care initiates early management of the interdisciplinary team. However, during a lifetime of chronic disability,

Health teams form and reform. Members of the team assume different levels of authority which are pertinent to a patient's needs at successive stages of his rehabilitation. During the stage of physical rehabilitation, the physician is the unquestioned leader of many ancillary health services. As the patient moves out of the dependency of the hospital (or clinic) situation toward his place in society, the teacher, social worker, vocational counselor, or psychologist may lead the team, calling upon medical specialists as

consultants for establishing health precautions. Ideally, the patient
becomes the final team leader—and then we call him our "client"—
as he approaches his place in society and selects support from
health, education, or welfare personnel on an "as needed" basis, or
even on an "as wanted" basis, in our free society (Robinault, 1964,
pp. 226-230).

Before leaving the purely medical aspects of these related
dysfunctions known as cerebral palsy, it is pertinent to emphasize
that one is dealing with long-term, nonfatal, but nevertheless
noncurable, disorders. Sometimes they have also been referred
to as "nonprogressive." Indeed they are when one compares
them with the type of progression associated with a malignant
tumor. Rehabilitation personnel who are new to the field may
interpret "nonprogressive" to mean that the condition of the
client cannot get worse. Consequently, they are confused when
they watch some mildly disabled children become less able to
cope with the demands of adult living. In such instances, the
lesion in the brain may not change substantially. Rather brain
growth and maturation cause changes in the balance of functions.
To complicate the picture, convulsions may appear at adolescence
or an uncorrected cross-eye may lead to loss of vision (ambly-
opia) with subsequent loss of depth perception. Sensory losses
may go undetected because of professional ignorance (many still
believe that CP is essentially a motor problem). While these
may be tolerable within the gross activities of childhood, they
may eliminate a man from study or possible vocations.

Although we are dealing with a noncurable group of disorders,
there is much that can be constructively done to alleviate initial
disabilities and later complications. Among the important preventive techniques are early eye correction, early training for
hearing disorders; carefully timed surgery or series of surgical
procedures for gait irregularity, drug control for seizures and
for behavioral aberrations, ancillary visual perceptual and language therapy according to developmental capacity to profit
from it, and family-centered counseling and support. Since the
function of the CP is not fixed or static, all the remedial factors
that stand a chance of favorably influencing the outcome should

be brought to bear upon the disabilities at developmentally pertinent times (Denhoff and Robinault, 1960).

PSYCHOLOGICAL ASPECTS OF CEREBRAL PALSY

Just as the medical picture has potential for change, so too does the psychological picture. Historically, the psychological picture has been confusing. Incorrect views ranged from Little's estimate that most "spastics" were mentally deficient to overoptimistic evaluations which resulted from inappropriate testing methods. Now more realistic appraisal of mental abilities, personality strengths, learning processes, and modes of communication can be provided at all stages of growth and development.

Whatever the test or tests selected, it is imperative that they be given individually and be *repeated at meaningful intervals,* to determine not only the developmental *rate* and *direction* of intellectual capacities but also their *character.* For example, there is a transition from concrete and memorized items of learning, which predominate in preschool development, to increased abstract reasoning required of the school child from third grade up. This cannot be anticipated by one isolated test given prior to, or upon entering, school. Counselors reading case histories should be wary of such test reports. Rembolt (1963) has pointed out that the reliability of psychological appraisals and the predictive value of eventual intellectual potentials become enhanced by retesting the child recurrently after six- to eight-month intervals in the early years. Thereafter, minimum retesting might be geared to elementary school, pre-junior high and pre-high school years. Allen and Jefferson (1962) have contributed a practical guide to general test selection. For individuals who understand oral instructions and have difficulty with manipulation, he suggests the Ammons Full-Range Picture Vocabulary Test, the Peabody Picture Vocabulary Test, the Columbia Mental Maturity Scale, Raven's Progressive Matrices, and the Leiter International Performance Scale. A useful test battery for prevocational *or* precollege purposes is the following:

Wechsler Adult Intelligence Scale
Draw-A-Person

Bender Gestalt
S. California Perceptual Motor Battery
Vineland Social Maturity Scale
Kudor or California Picture Interest Inventory
Standard Aptitude Tests for Reading and Arithmetic

Parts of these tests, plus the Vineland Social Maturity Scale, the Gessell Preliminary Behavior Inventory, and the adaptations used by Haussermann to detect ascending reasoning give valuable insights into the mental processes and development of severely handicapped youngsters. When it is possible to administer the Revised Stanford-Binet Scale or the Wechsler Adult Intelligence Scale, the IQ derived is less important than analysis of the subtests which give valuable cues to adaptive behavior and strengths in various intellectual capacities. A good educator or counselor who confers with the psychologist about these subtests can direct his remedial education or prevocational training around these foci.

Other fruitful diagnostic and remedial approaches to mental capacities have been reached through analyses of specific perceptual, integrative, and expressive capabilities. Among others, Strauss, Werner, and Cruickshank researched various perceptual disorders which laid groundwork for the Frostig, Kephart, and Ayres instruments of assessment. New methods for diagnosis of learning disabilities have been developed by Kirk and Myklebust. Special programs and techniques of remediation have been proposed by Kephart, Gallagher, Barsch, and Strothers. As Birch points out in his studies of the biologic and social aspects of brain damage, this field is wide open for research and research utilization since its causes and effects are not yet clarified (Birch, 1964).

It is important for counselors to realize that there are some very intelligent individuals among the cerebral palsied. Some of them are wheelchair-bound and show no correlation between severity of motor disability and intellectual capacity. However, in general, the mean IQ of CP populations varies from 70 to 75, as compared to 100 for the normal population (Denhoff and Robinault, 1960). Mental deficiency and mental retardation of about 50 percent of the CP population pose problems for the therapist, educator, and counselor. Approximately 25 percent are dull-normal and about 25 percent test at normal, above-average, and superior.

No matter what the tested level of intelligence, no one can make the most of his innate capacities if he is emotionally fragile. Many retarded persons are working in the competitive world in unskilled jobs, and many a dull-normal individual is fully employed in a routine job because he is well-adjusted. Conversely, in the normal population, the greatest factor in loss of jobs is interpersonal problems. Therefore, a personality assessment, followed by remedial interpersonal and social experiences and counseling, is a basic service for the palsied (Allen and Jefferson, 1962; Allen, 1962). The premise that there is any correlation between types of CP and types of personality is unfounded. There is no special psychology for specific physical disabilities and no reason for devising unique personality theories or special personality tests. There are, however, psychological aspects of what impact any disability has upon any individual and the society in which he lives. These may determine whether he sees them as a frustration, a challenge, or a nuisance to be borne (Wright, 1960).

Individuals with cerebral palsy have a wide variety of disabilities and intelligence, and come from all socioeconomic levels, races, and creeds. They are met with a variety of reactions—from appreciation to sentimental smothering, from bare tolerance to actual avoidance and ostracism by thoughtless people in their families, clinics, schools, and neighborhoods. Some of them, irrespective of diagnostic label, are responsive and charming people. Some of them are outwardly holding their own while fighting emotional storms. Others are holding on to normality by a thread. Still others are recognizably disturbed yet manage to function, while the remainder are swamped by unresolved obstructions. Personality assessment, early parent counseling, and early developmental experiences, bolstered by supportive or dynamic counseling, will shift the responsiveness of these disabled toward positive attitudes.

REHABILITATION OF THE CEREBRAL PALSIED

So far, the discussion has been concerned with separate overviews of medical and psychological evaluation and treatment. To gauge how these and other aspects of living influence the individual as a person, we turn to rehabilitation. The International Labor Organization (ILO) definition of rehabilitation (International Society for Rehabilitation, 1963) states that it is the "restoration to the fullest possible physical, mental, social, vocational, economic usefulness of which a person is capable." Using this as a base, one sees that rehabilitation is concerned with the multiply handicapped individual's evolution from the total dependency of infancy to the independence of maturity. Crothers and Paine (1959) pointed out that the early pattern of their total protection must give way to experimentation during school years and ease its way, with or without friction, during adolescence, by gradually transferring authority to the young adult. Objectives of rehabilitation thus conceived are developmentally anchored as follows.

Body homeostasis at all ages must provide a modicum of comfort, yet be functional. Stimuli must be brought to the baby who cannot reach or crawl out toward it. Sensory experiences must be provided for the restricted toddler, and motor reeducation must be a heavy part of the preschool child's learning. However, during school age, the body needs must play second place to those of the mind and the personality while maturity seeks psychosocial movement, although physically curtailed, and concedes to live with what cannot be changed.

Communication of thoughts must evolve from receiving ideas to sending them in some form recognizable to a stranger, be it through code speech, typing, or writing. These thoughts must have content that can be exchanged with one's peers in formal education, recreation, or creative activities.

Communication of feelings must evolve from the cries and guffaws of childhood and the desperate attempts of awkward adolescence. Just as braces are worn temporarily or permanently for uncoordinated muscles, so may methods of emotional support be provided through guidance, counseling and psychotherapy to coordinate the many conflicting feelings of self-awareness and self-contentment. Eventually the mature individual communicates with the more subtle demands of group interests, friendships, and love.

Progressive independence and responsibility must have its start in an experience of trust, evolving through experimentation accompanied by growing awareness of values that are meaningful in one's own life and the life of others. No one wakes up a "sharer" and a "giver" at any appointed age. It comes only after holding one's weight, as far as possible, within the family, the school or play group and finally the group that one has to make and remake during adult years.

To illustrate the pertinence of developmental factors in the rehabilitation of young adults, Denhoff and Robinault (1960) devised a Capacity Analysis. It is a functional balance sheet giving an evaluator an idea of what one can draw upon and what one has to remedy or substitute.

For example, here is Jimmy at 21:

Area	Assets	Liabilities
Physical.	One good hand, no seizures, clear speech.	Assisting hand capable only of gross activities.
Activities of daily living.	Independent, good on public transportation.	
Mental and emotional.	Dull-normal intelligence (higher potential initiative, tractability).	Anxiety.
Parents.		Unrealistic goals.
Educational.	High school graduate reads slowly but well, uses library.	Failed standardized vocational tests.
Recreational and social.	Attends regularly; good assistant with children.	No close friends; rarely visited outside of home; never went to camp.

Jimmy is typical of hundreds of young men and women who had been exemplary "patients," who had been labeled "Prognosis: Good" in the several clinics through which they passed. Yet these same young adults consistently failed most *standard* written vocational tests. Their prognosis was "good" so far as survival and getting through the requirements of high school education. However, few had anticipated the social, communication, and skill demands of the working world. When a boy or girl such as Jimmy fails to pass vocational aptitude tests, parents or professionals may suggest college. They may hope to delay the issue and also hope that some vocational skill at a higher level will develop. Since this attitude is held by a large percentage of the normal population, it is not an unusual solution for some parents of the disabled to seek. Clinic personnel, too, take emotional sides on whether they believe that college is the vocational answer for that disabled person or whether he should start to "face reality." Actually, the very adults who try to make last-minute decisions from an emotional perspective are the ones who have compounded the task of facing reality by not having consulted a counselor from the earliest time that this may have been helpful. Going to college should not be an isolated prevocational hope. If a person gains satisfactions thereby and is able to get through college physically, financially, and intellectually, that is a personal growth decision.

A comprehensive study of the education and employment of cerebral palsied college students is available. Muthard and Hutchinson (1968) designed this to provide guidelines for counseling college students and to assist CP youth in making sound decisions concerning the rehabilitative value of higher education. Based on data regarding the physical and intellectual capabilities, they estimate that about 50,000 persons with cerebral palsy have the potential for college work. At present, only hundreds of CP's are attending college, but this number is expected to increase. One of the realities encouraging higher enrollment is the increased number of community colleges and universities modifying campuses to accommodate severely physically impaired students with capacity to benefit from higher education (Hall and

Lehman, 1967). Therefore, it is important to be aware of the major findings and implication of the Muthard and Hutchinson (1968) study.

1. Individual differences among college-going CP's are great.
2. As a group college CP's differed in some ways from the non-impaired—started elementary school later—more likely to have a hiatus between high school and college—previous education lagged at all points—required more time to complete both undergraduate and graduate study programs—appeared to progress more slowly in his career—enrolled in every major field of study, more of this group majored in the humanities or social studies—curricula followed were limited only by the individual's skills and mobility.
3. CP's need to develop a wide range of novel techniques for coping with required basic college skills such as note taking, preparing for and taking examinations, preparing reports and doing laboratory work.
4. CP college students make greater use of counseling and guidance services—consider most helpful traits of counselors to be interest in the student as a person and ability to provide information. They need substantial help also in personal and physical adjustment problems.
5. About half of the CP college students expressed the attitudes and uncertainties of classmates who "think I can do things I can't or think I can't do things I can." This can be modified "If the CP student will gracefully accept help when needed and gracefully refuse help when not needed . . . try to help others, by their own interests, actions and attitudes, to interact freely and graciously with impaired persons including themselves."

College is not a guaranteed vocational solution, any more than high school was for the person who is not aware of his general vocational trends. When can these vocational trends be determined? After years of testing young cerebral palsied adults, Moed urges that prevocational evaluation be made available *before high school,* not after (Moed and Interagency Project Staff, 1955-1960).

This would provide recommendations that would augment high school academics and make the summers in between building blocks for the future. Moed's suggestion is on the conservative side. If one goes back to an important but long-forgotten teachers' conference in 1956, recommendations about the best time to start prevocational activities suggest (Reports of Teachers Conference, 1956):

1. By age of six, determine potentialities if possible.
   Pick a broad field.
   Screen early to allow for intellectual training.
   Stress appearance in regard to handicap.
   Get precautions from the physicians.
   Discuss realistic goals with the parents with an open-mind for possible changes which development and experience may bring.
2. Prevocational experiences should be provided in primary grades.
   Explore environment; work toward social adjustment.
3. Prevocational experience in higher grades, such as occupational information and job requirements.
   Social development and responsibility.
   Occupational experience (activity clubs, school, store, field trips to factories, etc., courses for work skills).
   At this time a residential summer camp may provide the interpersonal and group experiences which are independent of family influences and in this sense may be considered "prevocational."

The age of six may seem premature to many who realize the changing demands in an adult world of new requirements coming through technology and automation. However, there are factors—not necessarily skills—that are neglected in the experiences offered the disabled child which cripple him further on his eventual labor market. Therefore, it is not important to quibble over the sacredness of the age of six but to do something about the woefully lacking interpersonal work attitudes and the work adjustment skills that led the Moed report to state: "Among the essentially ambulatory CP's, physical disability is not a sufficient cause of vocational disability." In other words, jobs existed that people could cope with mentally and physically, but they were completely unprepared for the demands, the responsibilities, the impersonal attitudes, the amount of perseverance, etc. that goes into getting and holding a job. Nor were they aware of the place that even the humblest job holds in the hierarchy of eventually getting ahead. Many wished to start at the top or despaired of the meaninglessness of starting jobs. This could be circumvented by early guidance and counseling. In fact, Kramer (1962) at the Fort Worth Society for Crippled Children and Adults started one of the now more frequent programs for the disabled that attempt to put theory into practice. He organized a summer prevocational program for disabled youngsters between the ages of nine and sixteen. They attended this workshop program for 2½ hours a day, three times a week. A factory assembly line was instituted for a woodwork product, time cards were used, work and rest periods as well as "coffee breaks" were established, and production goals were set. This teenage work experience program has been accepted by the Special Education School System and the Texas Rehabilitation Commission as a part of the regular school semester. It aids the school in providing normal development experiences not readily available to the handicapped and will help the vocational rehabilitation office by laying a basis for future definitive vocational tests.

Are special vocational tests needed by the cerebral palsied? Yes, many of the CP's, as well as persons with multiple handicaps, cannot find their way to the working world without selected testing to help them. Furthermore, many cannot be definitely considered unable to work until they have had the benefit of special tryouts based upon test information. True, there are some CP's who do enter the work world before or after college, without special assistance. Another small percentage are able to find their vocational niches from standardized tests. Others reveal potential through work samples such as TOWER and workshop experiences (Institute for the Crippled and Disabled, 1963). However, the great majority who are presently receiving no prevocational preparation sit at home until they reach the legal age eligible for state vocational services. Often by then it is too late for them to be helped by these special services. In fact, regression may occur. For example, it was found necessary to test former high school graduates for *actual* achievement in arithmetic and spelling and reading prior to starting vocational tests at the ICD Rehabilitation and Research Center. Work samples had to be demonstrated over and over again for the client who could not read, but no test was eliminated until given a fair trial. Conversely, it was often surprising to see how well-coordinated an athetoid could be on a mechanical task test that might never have been offered to him had his general incoordination alone been made the decisive factor in offering the test. This is best seen in a vocational film made by ICD under VRA sponsorship (film).

Of the CP's who were evaluated during a seven-week period using work sample tasks, there were those who showed definite skills and conversely those who definitely could be termed employable only at the unskilled level even if they had adequate work habits (Moed and Litwin, 1963). For these, ICD, in cooperation with the United Cerebral Palsy of New York City, established a training sheltered workshop. Of 95 young people who went through this workshop for eighteen months, 25 found employment as messengers and floorboys in a factory. While the jobs were unskilled, they depended upon newly learned work attitudes and habits. Another 20 persons left the workshop voluntarily and are on their own. There now remains the question of what is the best way of life for the fifty others who have had workshop experience but show no ability to get beyond the stage of shelter employment. As a result of over eight years of research and comparing the results of other work adjustment programs, Moed has estimated that at least 50 percent of the national CP population need some form of sheltered employment, or some meaningful substitute for a satisfying adult way of life (Moed and Litwin, 1963). Garrett (1963) corroborates this, stating that perhaps 10 percent of CP's are ready for work. Probably 50 to 60 percent of those who present themselves for vocational rehabilitation need some type of sheltered workshop experience. He estimates that about half of these will remain in the workshop for the rest of their lives. Those who are ready to enter the job market need early intensive job placement help, since it takes considerable time and effort to make the first placement. However, Garrett does point out that once the individual with CP is employed, he usually makes a fairly consistent employment record. Cohen (1966) would attribute this good placement record to six factors: a personality capable of adult interpersonal relationships, oral and written communication, evaluation of true function or potential, mobility, and an education related to basic needs or to the CP's ultimate vocational goal. The Muthard and Hutchinson (1968) study relates education and vocational goals as follows:

1. College CP's would find it desirable to seek and secure more interim and part-time experience—to provide a more realistic understanding of career fields and the demands of evenual employment.
2. More nonimpaired college grads than graduate CP's are employed in jobs related to their education.
3. Of eight personal characteristics examined by the Employment Relatedness scale, the CP's good academic score indicated that he could compete well in jobs related to his educational background.
4. Although this study does not categorically prove that a vocationally oriented college education is the most useful course for a CP to pursue, it does indicate that CP's who followed such a course were more often employed in work related to their training, liked the work more than those who completed nonvocational curricula, and had generally fewer adjustment problems and accounted for higher salaries.

Important as work may be to the adult in our society, it may not be the ultimate answer to life as a whole. The attention given by our society to retirement problems, shorter work hours encouraged by automation, and increased population illustrates the increasing importance that will be assumed by nonworking aspects of our life. Rehabilitation has several roles to play here. In the long-

term care of the CP who may live to an old age, there are many
unanswered questions addressed to rehabilitation.

1. Can institutions be improved to handle emergency short-
   term care or can homemaker services be provided to the
   family whose mother is ill?
2. Can boarding homes or foster homes be arranged for the
   young adult who can no longer stay in a home that he has
   outgrown or that has dissolved due to illness or death of
   other members?
3. Can activity-oriented day-care and developmental centers
   be made available for those unable to go to school or have
   graduated such as the nonworking disabled young adult?
   (Helsel-Messner and Reid, 1965).
4. Can rehabilitation facilities provide the homebound CP
   with techniques to teach activities of daily living that will
   equip him to take over some of the home responsibilities
   and free an able-bodied member of his family from those
   chores?
5. Can remedial education and socialization be made available to the adult CP who is above the intellectual capacity
   of those attending daycare and developmental centers but
   at the same time is not productive in a sheltered workshop?
6. Can vocational activities be developed in the community
   wherein the CP adult might make a contribution as a
   volunteer . . . where can he get training toward this?
7. Can churches, the "Y," or other groups accept the adult CP
   into their normal youth groups? Who will prepare him for
   such participation?

To fulfill these inquiries will require the rehabilitation team
to put forth its fullest efforts, especially in educating the population at large. The public will have to be told that CP is here to
stay in the foreseeable future. The disease will not disappear in
the next few generations. While it is true that prevention lessens
the number so afflicted, it is equally true that fewer of the remaining afflicted persons will die in the early years, as in previous
generations. Ours is the first generation to see medical and
therapeutic care wipe out the static pneumonias and other in-

fectious diseases that plagued CP's during the winters of former generations. Although the life span statistically has been computed as somewhat shorter for the CP than for the average citizen, improved conditions combined with antibiotics, even in overcrowded institutions, augers well for a full life span for the majority of CP's born today. Therefore, a citizenry that prides itself in the physical well-being of its youth has a strong responsibility toward those CP and other disabled individuals who may be less gifted in the productive roles of life. To achieve comprehensive well-being for youths and young adults, this citizenry must insist that (a) education for all children be based on functional limits rather than on the archaic system of advancement by chronological age, (b) functional work opportunities, via permanent community sheltered workshops or sheltered work situations, be provided for those earnest producers who cannot attain the minimum wage level, and (c) functional use of leisure time be provided in conjunction with public education and rehabilitation.

It is obvious that rehabilitation will best serve the nation by gearing itself not to isolate the cerebral palsied and his problems but toward fitting him into normal society at proper functional level. At his level of optimal function, he will join others who also need meaningful ways of life. Together they can explore ways to develop how to live together productively. To do this will require the initiative and concerted efforts of all rehabilitation personnel.

REFERENCES

Allen, R.: Cerebral palsy. In Garrett, J. F. and Levine, E. S. (Eds.): *Psychological Practices with Physically Handicapped.* New York, Columbia University Press, 1962.

Allen, R. M. and Jefferson, T. W.: *Psychological Evaluation of the C.P.: Person-Intellectual Personality & Vocational Applications.* Springfield, Thomas, 1962.

Birch, H. G.: *Brain Damage in Children—Biologic and Social Aspects.* Baltimore, Williams & Wilkins, 1964.

Chamberlin, H.: *Current Research Potential in Mental Retardation and Its Significance for the Problem of Cerebral Palsy.* Address given at UCP Fourteenth Annual Conference, Dallas, Texas, March 7, 1964.

Cohen, J.: Employment: A goal of rehabilitation. In Cruickshank, William (Ed.): *Cerebral Palsy—Its Individual and Community Problems.* New York, Syracuse University Press, 1966.

Crothers, B. and Paine, R.: *The Natural History of Cerebral Palsy.* Cambridge, Harvard University Press, 1959.

Denhoff, E.: *Cerebral Palsy—The Preschool Years: Diagnosis and Treatment.* Springfield, Thomas, 1967.

Denhoff, E. and Robinault, I. P.: *Cerebral Palsy and Related Disorders—A Developmental Approach to Dysfunction.* New York, Mc-Graw-Hill, 1960.

Film: "Work Evaluation for the Cerebral Palsied Client." Obtainable on loan from the Institute for the Crippled and Disabled, 400 First Avenue, New York, N. Y. 10010.

Garrett, J.: The CP adult. In O'Brien, X. (Ed.): *Total Life Planning for the CP: New Concepts of Vocational Rehabilitation.* East Lansing, Michigan Proceedings of Professional Training Institute, Kellogg Center for Continuing Education, Michigan State University, June, 1963.

Hall, R. E. and Lehman, E. F.: Some colleges and universities with special facilities to accommodate handicapped students. Office of Education, HEW, Washington, D. C., March 1967 (mimeographed).

Helsel-Messner, E. S. and Reid, L. O.: Opening new doors: Through daycare and developmental centers. Booklet issued by United Cerebral Palsy Associations, 321 West 44 Street, New York, New York, 1965.

Institute for the Crippled and Disabled: TOWER text of work sample philosophy and practice. New York, 1963.

International Society for Rehabilitation of Disabled: Training and Planning. Proceedings of International Seminar on Vocational Rehabilitation, Copenhagen, June 30-July 3, 1963.

Kramer, J.: Work experience for the teenager. In *Work Adjustment as a Function of Occupational Therapy.* New York, American Occupational Therapy Association, 1962.

Moed, M. and Interagency Project Staff: CP Work Classification and Evaluation Project Report. New York, Institute for the Crippled and Disabled, 1955-1960, Vols. I, II.

Moed, M. and Litwin, E. S.: The employability of the cerebral palsied, A summary of two related studies. *Rehabilitation Literature,* September, 1963.

Muthard, J. and Hutchinson, J.: *Cerebral Palsied College Students— Their Education and Employment.* Gainesville, University of Florida, 1968.

National Health Education Committee: What Are the Facts About Cerebral Palsy. New York, 1971.

Peiper, A.: *Cerebral Function in Infancy and Childhood.* New York, International Behavioral Sciences Series, 1963.

Publications List, United Cerebral Palsy, Inc., 66 East 34 Street, New York.

Rembolt, R. R.: Comments in Progress Report of November 6, 1963, on revisions of Alpha Guide on Services for Children with Cerebral Palsy, National Society for Crippled Children & Adults, Chicago.

Reports of Teachers Conference at University of Georgia and University of Kentucky in the "Cerebral Palsy Review," September, 1956.

Robinault, I. P.: How Interpersonal Relations Affect Patient Care. *Rehabilitation Literature,* 1964.

Robinault, I. P.: Using "Latest Techniques" for Therapy. In *A Look at the Future,* pamphlet, United Cerebral Palsy, New York, 1961.

Roth, J. and Eddy, D.: *Rehabilitation for the Unwanted.* Report to VRA for Grant RD 577, Research Center, Columbia School of Social Work, N. Y., 1963.

United Cerebral Palsy Research & Educational Foundation: Annual Report for Calendar Year, 1960, New York.

Wolfe, W. G. and Reid, L. I.: A Survey of Cerebral Palsy in Texas, May, 1958. Sponsored by the United Cerebral Palsy of Texas, Austin, Texas.

Wright, B.: *Physical Disability—A Psychological Approach.* New York, Harper, 1960.

Chapter VII

AMPUTATIONS AND AMPUTEES

Royce C. Lewis, Jr.

There are many things that cause a person to lose an extremity or a portion of an extremity. The person who has lost a major portion of one of his extremities has undergone a physical alteration that will not only cause him to alter his functional capacity and many times his way of life, but also in many instances, cause rather profound psychological changes in the acceptance of, and the adaptation to, his disability. In the past, too often, the emphasis has been placed upon the medical approach to these patients with the amputation being performed according to certain described techniques. The patient was then watched as he proceeded through his post-operative stage until the wound had healed. He was then merely "turned loose" and allowed to fend for himself rather than being given the very necessary assistance in adapting to his loss both functionally and psychologically. It is the purpose of this section to indicate the various medical aspects of amputations that are considered important from a rehabilitation standpoint and to indicate the specific areas of amputations that are encountered, along with the specific problems that may arise from each of these levels. It is important to remember, however, that while the aim of rehabilitation is to restore function to as nearly a normal level as possible that this actually is an unobtainable goal. It must be remembered that no matter how good the prosthesis that is manufactured, no matter how well the patient accepts his amputation and learns to use his prosthesis, the prosthesis can never be as good as the normal extremity. The prosthesis has no sensation, so that the artificial hand, for example, cannot be used to feel. There are no proprioceptive sensations, so that the wearer never knows where the extremity is in space without looking at it. The prosthesis is never able to completely fulfill the function of the normal limb. Be that as it may, however, great strides have occurred in the improvement of the prosthesis from a cosmetic and functional standpoint and the modern amputee certainly has a much brighter outlook than did his predecessor fifty years ago.

REASONS FOR AMPUTATION

In order to learn something about dealing with amputees, it is first wise to learn some of the most common causes for the loss of an extremity. An examination of the list of most common causes will quickly reveal that there is a tremendous difference in the causes for amputation in different age groups. Whereas, the younger individual is much more likely to lose an extremity because of trauma or because of a malignant tumor, the older individual is much more likely to lose an extremity because of vascular disease or infections, particularly associated with diabetes. In the average center the frequency of occurrence of the various conditions necessitating amputation are roughly as follows: Trauma, vascular disorders, neoplasms, infections, and useless extremities.

Trauma

Trauma, of course, is a much more common cause in younger people because individuals in a younger age group are much more likely to be involved in automobile accidents. Younger individuals are much more prone to have jobs in industry which require hazardous conditions which may result in severe injuries to their extremities. Inexperience in the use of machinery will also make the younger worker more liable to injury than his older, more experienced, co-worker. Injuries may occasionally result in amputation of an extremity at the time. This is termed a "traumatic amputation." In these instances the extremity is completely severed by the original accident, so that the surgical procedure is a plastic repair of the amputation stump usually at the highest optimum level. On other occasions, an extremity will be so badly mangled at the time of an injury that it is irreparable, and amputation offers the only choice of treatment. In these instances, there is usually a combined severe damage to bone, nerve, blood vessel, and soft tissue, so that no hope of function is left even if the extremity survives, and amputation is therefore done at the time. It should be pointed out, however, that most surgeons make every effort to save a mangled extremity even though at a later date amputation becomes necessary because of failure to restore adequate blood supply or failure to restore proper function to the extremity. Amputations resulting from trauma usually heal quite rapidly, and usually the stump is of high quality so that a prosthesis can be worn very nicely.

Vascular

The loss of adequate blood supply to an extremity is the second most common cause of amputation, and in the older age group it probably is the most common of all causes. In individuals in the higher age group, the generalized narrowing of the arterial bed by arteriosclerosis (the so-called *hardening of the arteries*) often results in diminution of the blood supply below levels consistant with life of the tissue and a condition called gangrene results. The particular type of condition which results in occlusion of the blood vessels, or diminution of the lumen of the blood vessel, is called *arteriosclerosis obliterans;* and while the condition may be generally progressive over a long period of time, a sudden complete occlusion of the vessel by clotting in an already narrowed lumen will result in acute loss of blood supply to the extremity and subsequent gangrene. Gangrene occurring with arteriosclerosis is seldom associated with infection and is therefore called a *dry gangrene*. On the other hand, gangrene associated with infections is usually accompanied by considerable drainage and is therefore called *wet gangrene*. This type of gangrene is seen most often in diabetes and occurs because of the unusual lack of resistance that diabetics exhibit to infection. Amputations from diabetes either occur on the basis of a *presenile arteriosclerosis* which occurs many times in a younger age group with narrowing of the blood vessel lumen due to advanced atheromatous deposits occurring in the vessel wall because of the diabetic condition; or they occur from this overwhelming infection with wet gangrene which results from the unusual susceptibility that these individuals have to infection.

A third cause of vascular amputations, once again, is that of trauma. In this instance, however, the trauma occurs to blood vessels proximal to the extremity. In these cases, an extremity that is not otherwise injured may have a complete loss of blood supply from irreparable damage to the blood vessel serving this area. For example, a severe mutilating injury to the shoulder such as that caused by heavy weight falling upon it will, many times, cause irreparable damage to the arterial supply to the arm without the arm being otherwise injured. In these instances, therefore, amputation of the arm itself is necessitated only by this vascular insufficiency.

Neoplasms

Amputations of extremities occur from either one of the two large general classes of neoplasms, namely malignant and benign types of tumors. In the case of malignant tumors, amputation is usually accomplished at a site proximal to the tumor itself in an effort to remove the tumor and any local spread that may have occurred. In these cases it is necessary to amputate considerably higher than the site of the tumor in order to be certain that all tumor tissue is removed. For instance, in patients with malignant tumors involving the tibia, or shin bone, the amputation is usually carried out above the knee at the mid-thigh level. In the case of benign tumors, amputation is sometimes necessary because of repeated local recurrences of the tumor with subsequent destruction of vital structures; or occasionally it is necessitated because of the tumor's attaining tremendous size. This is particularly true in the cartilaginous tumors which many times will grow to tremendous sizes without actually becoming malignant. In these instances, removal of the extremity is necessary because of loss of function due to the size of the tumor mass itself.

Infections

Infections of an extremity occasionally necessitate its removal. This, of course, is particularly true, as mentioned above in the diabetic. It may also occur, however, following injuries with entrance of the infecting organism into a badly mangled extremity and subsequent amputation being necessary because of the over-whelming and extensive nature of the infection. On the other hand, a more chronic type of infection usually does not result in amputation except in cases where a chronic indolent ulcer results in systemic or generalized changes which endanger the individual's health. Other patients may have large ulcers with very foul drainage that defy conservative management, and occasionally these patients are willing to sacrifice an extremity for hygienic reasons.

Useless Extremity

In some instances, an extremity that has become completely useless is amputated, particularly when its presence is a liability. This occurs most usually in flail extremities which have lost their nerve supply either as a result of damage to the major nerve serving the extremity or in some instances from severe poliomyelitis residuals. If an extremity has no motor function whatsoever and is therefore completely, totally, and permanently useless, the individual is many times better off to have this extremity amputated and a usable prosthesis substituted. Flail extremities, particularly in the arm, are often dangerous because the patient cannot control this extremity and it may become entangled in car doors, machinery, or other such dangerous situations. In other instances, severe deformities of an extremity will necessitate removal of the extremity for strictly cosmetic reasons. When a deformity is particularly grotesque, and particularly when the deformity is associated with almost total loss of function, the individual is once again markedly improved by removal of the ugly, useless extremity and the substitution of a usable prosthesis.

TECHNIQUE OF AMPUTATION

In order to understand fully the problems associated with amputations, it might be well to understand the actual surgical technique involved in the amputation of an extremity. For this reason, the surgical technique in a general manner is described in the amputation of a leg through the mid-thigh area.

The amputation is done in most instances under a general anesthetic, though a spinal anesthetic can sometimes be substituted. Usually a pneumatic tourniquet is used to control bleeding, though in cases of vascular insufficiency requiring amputation, the tourniquet it not used because it may further injure or cause damage to the blood vessel as it passes deep into it. The usual incision for an amputation through the thigh is made in the form of two flaps which extend in front and back and which meet in deep V-shaped depressions on either side. The skin and subcutaneous tissue are then dissected back and the muscles are exposed.

In most instances, dissection is carried out over the area where major vessels are known to lie, and these vessels are isolated, then clamped and severed early in the course of the operation. Once this has been done, one is less likely to encounter serious bleeding during the remainder of the procedure. In the case of major arteries, it is usually necessary to tie the artery with some type of nonabsorbable suture. It is the custom of most surgeons to apply several separate ligatures around the vessel to be certain that the tie will not come off. In the case of the veins, the pressure is much less and a single tie with either an absorbable suture such as catgut or a nonabsorbable suture is used. Major nerves are isolated and the soft tissue is stripped away from them. They are usually sectioned relatively high and allowed to retract up in the muscle tissue. It is the custom of many surgeons to inject these nerves with a local anesthetic solution prior to severing them in order to prevent shocking the patient, even though he is anesthetized, by the sudden severe stimulation of severing a major nerve. It is also the custom of many surgeons to inject absolute alcohol into the cut end of the nerve in order to cause tissue death of the nerve cells and possibly prevent the formation of a neuroma, or small nerve tumor, at the end of the cut nerve. After vessels have been tied and sectioned, the muscles are next cut in a manner so that they can be pulled forward to adequately cover the severed bone. The bone itself, once it has been isolated, is cut, usually with a hand saw, and is cut far enough back so that the surrounding muscles can be pulled forward to form a cushion for the end of the severed bone. Bleeding points are all controlled, the muscles are sutured down in their proper places usually with absorbable catgut suture; finally, the skin is sutured down with nonabsorbable sutures such as nylon. Following completion of the closure, a large compression dressing is applied to the stump. Many surgeons prefer to glue a dressing over the stump to which traction can be attached, and they prefer to maintain continuous gentle traction with two or three pounds of weight on the stump for several days in order to keep the skin relaxed over the tip of the stump. This step is not completely necessary and is many times eliminated.

POSTOPERATIVE CARE

The postoperative care of amputees is also quite important during the first several days. Rather severe pain is experienced which requires the administration of narcotics for relief. The patient can usually be gotten out of bed on the second or third postoperative day and allowed up in a wheelchair. After the elapse of ten or twelve days, he can usually be ambulated on crutches and probably dismissed from the hospital. As soon as the soreness has diminished in the stump and the wound has healed, the patient is started on active physical therapy which is aimed at strengthening the propelling musculature of the stump preparatory to fitting with a prosthesis at a later date. In the case of the lower extremity amputations, the prosthesis can usually be fitted in a matter of ten or twelve weeks. There is, of course, a current fad that has gained widespread popularity of applying a socket at the operating table immediately following surgery. It is felt that further evaluation of this rather drastic procedure will be necessary before it can be universally accepted.

As soon as the stump has lost its swelling and the tenderness has subsided, the patient is fitted with a preliminary socket, realizing that as the months go by, the stump will shrink further and it will be necessary to alter the socket rather often during these first few months in order to maintain the proper fit. Even then it will usually be necessary to manufacture a new socket after approximately one year, since by this time the stump will have shrunk down to its permanent size and a proper fit can be obtained.

SPECIFIC SITES OF AMPUTATION

Since there is considerable difference in the problems that are faced by amputees with loss of different portions of their extremities, the various prominent sites of amputation of the lower and upper extremity are enumerated with the various specific problems that are characteristic of amputation at each of these specific levels.

Lower Extremity

The difficulties encountered in loss of portions of the lower extermity are those encountered in locomotion or the alteration of locomotion occasioned by the loss of a portion of the supporting structure of the body. Persons with amputations involving portions of the lower extremity will face difficulties that are quite different from those of upper-extremity amputees because of the alteration of their locomotion mechanism. This alteration, of course, is more pronounced the higher the level of amputation in the extremity.

Foot

TOES. Amputations through various portions of the foot constitute the group of lower extremity amputations which have least disability. The loss of one or more of the small toes usually does not cause any disability at all, since locomotion is not dependent upon function in these small members.

There are complications from the standpoint of deformity of the foot with development of callosities and the like, but these can usually be cared for by proper padding and minor alterations of the shoes.

HALLUX. The loss of the great toe itself does constitute some disability since the great toe is responsible for much of the spring in the average gait. It is the pushoff with the great toe that accomplishes much of the rhythm of a normal gait; and loss of the great toe will usually cause considerable limp and awkwardness in walking. The prosthesis that is used following loss of a great toe is primarily fitted into a regular shoe. It includes a heavy piece of spring metal incorporated in the sole of the shoe that substitutes for the loss of spring in the gait when the great toe is amputated.

TRANSMETATARSAL. Amputations through the transmetatarsal area are usually the result of trauma, since vascular amputations do not heal well through this particular level. Most individuals with this problem can get by with a minimal prosthetic appliance. Prosthetic appliances following transmetatarsal amputations must, of necessity, fit onto the lower leg in order to improve stability and to give better spring in the gait.

However, this type of patient can, of course, walk reasonably well barefooted since he has a good supporting device. This is a considerable advantage, particularly for walking around in the bedroom prior to retiring, for walking on the beach, for swimming, and the like where the prosthesis may be left off without serious alteration of function.

HEEL. Amputations through the area of the heel were popular in previous years, but in more recent times have been less popular as they require the wearing of a short leg prosthesis which fits onto the lower leg itself. They, however, have the same advantage as the transmetatarsal amputations in that weight-bearing without the prosthesis is possible without undue difficulty.

Amputations Below the Knee Joint

After the level of amputation which provides for a weight-bearing stump with the retention of a portion of the foot, the next site of optimum level for amputation is approximately six inches below the knee. It has been learned that leaving stumps longer than this not only fails to improve function but is actually undesirable. The addition of two or three inches of stump to the optimum six-inch level is often a temptation to surgeons who have the false impression that this will improve stability and function. This, however, is not true and the longer *below-knee* amputation stumps actually present a real difficulty when it comes to the fitting of a prosthesis. The prosthetist is not able to fashion the socket nearly as well either from the standpoint of fit or from the standpoint of the cosmetic appearance of the artificial leg. The prosthetic extremities for fitting these longer stumps are likely to be bulky, unwieldy, and unsightly. While stumps longer than six inches are not desirable, it is possible to obtain very good function with stumps that are sometimes considerably shorter than six inches below the knee.

Individuals with extremely short stumps are not able to walk with as normal a gait because of the lack of strength in kicking the leg forward in walking. However, the development in recent years of the so-called *patellar tendon weight-bearing prosthesis* allows for reasonably good walking on stumps which have only three inches or so of tibia (shin bone) remaining.

Amputations Above the Knee

The main reason for the extreme desirability of amputations through the lower leg as compared with amputations through the higher level is the retention of the normally functioning knee joint. The presence of a knee joint with good voluntary function and with voluntary control of strength in various degrees of motion is of paramount importance if one is to maintain a normal gait. The fact that a patient with his own knee joint is able to maintain stability in varying degrees of flexion gives him considerable advantage over the patient who must depend upon an artificial knee joint for stability. The latter must be careful to keep the knee in a position of near full extension when complete weight bearing is done, since the attempt to flex the knee to any extent while bearing full weight will result in *buckling* of the knee and falling.

However, when the pathologic process that necessitates the amputation involves the knee joint or is so high in location as to render a below-the-knee amputation not feasible, one has no alternative but to amputate the extremity through the thigh area. Once again, extremely long thigh stumps are found to be ill advised, and the site of optimum level for amputations through the upper leg is at the mid-thigh region. This is of even more importance in above-the-knee stumps, since the bulkiness of the knee-supporting mechanisms present in modern-day prosthetic devices make it necessary to leave room for these devices in the normal knee joint region. Also it has been found that amputation through the mid-portion of the thigh will leave a long enough stump to provide good strength in propelling the prosthesis; therefore, when possible, amputations are done through this level.

Extremely high amputations in the thigh result in stumps that have little strength in propelling the prosthetic device and also give less surface area for the suction-type socket, which makes the wearing of harnesses to support the prosthesis and hold it to the body a necessity. The prosthetic device that is used in most cases of above-the-knee amputations includes a knee joint that passes through a full range of motion up to a point of reasonable acute flexion of the knee. As pointed out above, however, the patient has very little control of the function of the knee joint on a voluntary basis when he has passed five to ten degrees of flexion. The prosthesis is, in effect, propelled forward by raising it so that the foot clears the ground in extension and actually swings the prosthesis forward, propelling it with the flexor strength of the stump. The lower portion of the prosthesis must come into full extension at the knee joint before engaging the heel on the floor and locking the knee in full extension so that full weight bearing may be accomplished. Amputees who have had experience walking with a prosthesis of this nature develop skills whereby this procedure can be accomplished with very little concentration, and their walking gradually becomes automatic.

However, the newer amputee finds that he must be constantly on guard to be certain that the prosthesis does not strike the ground at its point of *pass through* in full extension which will cause him to fall. On the other hand, he must be certain that full weight bearing is not placed on the extremity until it has been locked in full extension and has thereby become stable. To help overcome the difficulty presented by this second portion of the gait mechanism, modern prosthetic devices include a safety hydraulic valve which gives the patient a measure of support during the first five to ten degrees of flexion and prevents the knee from buckling under him when he inadvertently places his full weight on the prosthesis before the knee has been fully extended. The modern lower-extremity prosthesis for above-the-knee amputations has been developed to a point wherein the patient with training and practice can enjoy an essentially normal gait. However, the loss of his own knee joint prohibits his accomplishing many things such as climbing ladders, walking on extremely uneven ground, climbing up and down stairs rapidly, and similar feats which are quite easily done by the below-the-knee amputee who has had some practice. The advent of the total-contact socket which keeps its position on the stump by suction and obviates the necessity of wearing a special harness to transport it has been a tremendous boon to the amputee and has markedly increased the degree of agility possible for these individuals.

Hip Disarticulations

The patient who has had a disarticulation of his hip has lost one of the most important factors which makes walking possible, that is, a lever arm to propel his prosthesis in walking. The disarticulated hip leaves the patient with a stump which provides a measure of support on the pelvis itself, but the prosthesis must, of necessity, be rather bulky with the pelvis being encased in a type of *bucket* which includes much of the pelvis to give him a measure of stability. It also must include various amounts of harness to hold it in place. The patient usually propels this prosthesis by violently flexing his pelvis with it tilted slightly so that the foot will clear the ground. In doing this he is able to gain a measure of reasonable ambulation with it. However, most individuals with hip disarticulations eventually decide that they are able to maneuver better and have much greater agility walking on crutches. Except for the cosmetic appearance of having another extremity most of them prefer to go without a prosthesis. Certainly, even when the prosthesis is worn, some type of supporting mechanism such as crutches, or possibly a cane for the more agile, is necessary.

Hemipelvectomy

Amputation of the lower extremity including the half of the pelvis is usually done for extremely high tumors which involve tissue high enough so that adequate stump cannot be left or which involve portions of the pelvic structures themselves, so that adequate removal necessitates removal of the hemipelvis as well as the extremity. Occasionally, mutilating injuries will occur high within the extremity which will necessitate amputation through this level; but for the most part a simple disarticulation will suffice in these cases. There have been cases reported of amputation through the pelvis for cases of severe infection which involved the pelvic bones. However, the most common cause of amputation including the half of one's pelvis is removal of malignant tumors. This is a relatively infrequent operation and one that, as recent as 20 years ago, was still fraught with considerable mortality during the operative procedure itself or during the immediate preoperative course. As better surgical techniques evolved and as better supporting techniques such as the massive transfusion of whole blood, the use of drugs to support the circulatory system, and the use of antibiotics in preventing infection have come into popular use, this operation has become more widespread, and more amputees who have had a *hindquarter* amputation are now seen.

These individuals almost never satisfactorily wear a prosthetic device for the reasons listed above for hip disarticulations. In their particular case, there is the added feature that with most of the pelvis on this side absent, there is little supporting structure. Hence, the amount of straps and harness necessary to hold the prosthesis to their body is increased. Most of these individuals prefer to use crutches for ambulation, and while many have a prosthesis made at one time or another, most do not end up wearing it to any great extent. Many of these individuals do find it necessary to have a leveling pad made to help them sit straight, since with the loss of the buttocks musculature and the pelvic bones on the involved side, they find it difficult to balance on the opposite buttocks when sitting down. Many of these individuals find it much more comfortable to have a type of harness made which includes a padding to equalize their body when sitting, and most amputees with this type of amputation wear one of these devices more or less continuously.

Upper Extremity

Since the function of the upper extremity in humans concerns reach, pinch, grasp, carrying procedures, and the like, as distinguished from stability and locomotion in the lower extremity, the implications when an upper extremity is lost are quite different from those previously discussed in the section on lower extremity amputations. The psychological effect is sometimes not as great, since the patient does not have interference with his locomotion and can be up and about during his convalescence. He is not subject to the marked emotional depressions that sometimes occur in the chairbound or crutch-limited individual. On the other hand, there is a much greater tendency to learn skills with partial amputation of the upper extremity, and since there is a greater voluntary control of the musculature of the upper extremity, the use of such a prosthesis is many times much more easily learned than that of a lower-extremity prosthesis. On the other hand, the loss of sensation from an amputation of the hand is much more of a functional loss than the loss of sensation in the lower extremity. The amputee with a lower-extremity prosthesis soon learns to make allowances for the lack of sensation in his foot while walking, and since he still has a pressure sensation on the stump itself, he regains many of the senses of position and gait habit through experience and training. Conversely, the upper-extremity amputee may become very skilled in the use of a hand prosthesis, but no matter how well he can use the apparatus from a functional standpoint, he still must operate within his field of vision, since he is not able to use the tactile sensation which most individuals take for granted when handling objects that are out of their field of vision. Fortunately, however, many of the upper-extremity amputees have only partial loss of their digits, and their rehabilitation is largely one of substitution rather than actual learning of new skills.

Hand

Since the hand is so all important from the standpoint of function, every effort is made to save as much of it as possible when an amputation of a portion of it is necessary. However, through the years, various principles concerning amputations within the hand have been developed, aimed at restoration of more nearly normal function in pinch and grasp.

FINGERS. When the index finger is amputated, it is much better to amputate the majority of the metacarpal bone attached to it in order to remove the bulge that will occur in the web-space between the thumb and the middle finger after the index finger is gone. The same is true when either the middle or ring finger is amputated. In those instances, if the amputation occurs proximal to the middle joint of the finger, it is usually much more acceptable to remove not only the entire finger but the bone in the hand called the metacarpal which coincides with that particular finger. By removing the entire ray, it is then possible to bring the remaining fingers on either side together and obliterate entirely the space occupied by the amputated finger. This makes for a more narrow hand which, of course, is not as strong in grasp, but it allows for greater dexterity. It closes up an opening between these fingers through which water falls when washing the face and through which change falls when bringing it from the trousers pocket and the like. Furthermore, the loss of an entire finger when the two adjacent fingers are brought together and the space obliterated is much more acceptable cosmetically. When amputations are possible distal to the middle joint so that flexion of the middle joint of the finger can occur voluntarily, it is naturally more desirable to leave the stump, since it will have some function in cooperating with the remainder of the hand. Amputation of the little finger occurring at the middle joint or proximal to it should likewise include at least the head of the fifth metacarpal bone in order to give a better cosmetic effect.

THUMB. When the thumb or a portion of it is lost, a much greater amount of disability arises, since the thumb constitutes the post against which the remainder of the fingers work in pinch or grasp. For this reason, it is of utmost importance to leave as much of the thumb as possible. Thus many surgical procedures have been developed to reestablish the thumb as a member or to make a relatively longer thumb that has been markedly shortened by amputation of the distal portion of it. As an example, it is possible to make the thumb that is amputated between its two joints longer by deepening the thumb web. The resulting thumb has its base much further down into the hand, but the relative length has been increased so that larger articles can be grasped without difficulty.

Loss of All Fingers

When all of the fingers are lost, it is sometimes possible to establish some type of post in the region of the absent little finger against which the thumb can work for some semblance of pinch and grasp. This can be done many times by removing all of the distal portions of the metacarpal bones to the index, middle, and ring fingers, thereby removing tissue that is in the way when the opposing member to the thumb is greatly shortened. It has also occasionally been possible to do pedicle skin grafts and incorporate a bone graft in the central portion of this to reestablish some type of digit against which the thumb may work. When the site of amputation is in the most proximal portion of the hand so that the thumb and all fingers are lost, it is quite difficult to establish much function. However, occasionally if enough tissue is left to warrant it, a large cleft can be established surgically in the remaining portion of the hand in order to give a certain amount of ability to hold objects when helping the opposite hand.

FOREARM. When the amputation level is at least at the wrist, then the amputation should be carried out several inches above the wrist in order to allow for the fitting of a suitable prosthesis. This is much the same principal that was discussed in relation to the amputations below the knee. It is possible to get by with a relatively short forearm and still maintain a functional elbow with various types of devices which increase the mechanical advantage of flexion in the elbow and thereby allow for some use of the prosthesis in the patient's field of vision, even when the forearm stump is quite short and has very little leverage. As in the case of the lower extremity, the retention of the patient's own elbow joint is of paramount importance in maintaining good function in the upper extremity, and the patient who has his own elbow has a tremendous functional advantage over the individual whose amputation site is above the elbow. The most effective hand mechanism for an upper-extremity amputee is the so-called "hook." This constitutes a large pinching mechanism which is formed in the shape of a hook. This has the advantage of allowing pinch to occur as well as use of the hook.

ARM. Amputations that occur above the elbow may be done at almost any level, with the optimum site being two or three inches above the elbow joint. The extremely short stump without much bone left below the shoulder joint is a distinct disadvantage, since the leverage is diminished and strength is greatly impaired. Prostheses made for amputees with levels above the elbow have an elbow joint containing a lock which automatically fixes the elbow at various degrees of flexion. By activating a small trigger mechanism to lock the elbow in these various degrees, the elbow joint is stabilized and the pincher mechanism is effective.

SHOULDER DISARTICULATIONS. Disarticulation of the shoulder leaves the patient without any way in which to move a prosthesis to get it into position for activating the hand mechanism. Prosthetic appliances for the shoulder disarticulation are therefore of very limited value. Occasionally an individual with this type of amputation can be fitted with an extremity whose function is primarily that of cosmetic appearance, but from the standpoint of actually functioning, the shoulder disarticulation prosthesis has very little to offer.

FOREQUARTER AMPUTATIONS. This type of amputation, which includes not only the extremity itself but also the clavicle or collar bone and the scapula or shoulder blade, leaves only the side of the rib cage, covered by soft tissue. As in the shoulder disarticulation, a prosthesis for forequarter amputations has no chance of function and is usually not indicated. Occasionally some type of padding is desirable to fill out the contour of the shoulder and make the patient's clothes fit better, but usually this type of padding can be made without including the extremity itself.

SPECIFIC PROBLEMS

There are a few specific problems that are common to most amputees who have lost a major portion of one or more extremities that affect their rehabilitation. Since these specific problems are of a generalized nature and have no predilection for any particular extremity, they will be discussed as a general group.

Persistent Pain

Many individuals with amputations involving major extremities have a persistence of pain that exceeds the amount expected from the trauma of injury or the surgical trauma that accompanied the actual operative procedure itself.

Neuroma

In some of these individuals, the sectioned nerve ending may form a small growth which is called a neuroma and which becomes the site of rather intense pain, particularly when pressure is applied to the neuroma. In these instances, patients localize the pain to the area but many times experience some sensation of pain into the absent portion of the extremity, making differentiation of this type of pain from true phantom pain very difficult. However, in most instances, the physician can inject the suspected neuroma with some type of local anesthetic and completely relieve the symptoms; whereas, an individual with phantom pain experiences no relief. Many times, also, the neuroma can be actually felt by the examiner. The finding of a localized discrete area of tenderness points toward the formation of a neuroma as being the cause of the patient's pain.

Phantom Pain

Phantom pain, or the pain that one experiences in the absent extremity, is a phenomenon that has long puzzled both physicians and psychologists. During the early postoperative periods, almost all patients experience a certain amount of phantom pain. This is usually described as either a deep aching type of pain, a burning sensation, or a sensation that the absent extremity is being twisted into a grotesque position. For example, an individual who has lost a lower extremity may experience the sensation that his toes are being bent backward on the foot, with severe pain resulting from the abnormal stretch. This pain is often excruciating and the patient will often describe it as being unbearable. It is interesting to note that this type of pain is not relieved by the usual narcotic medications which relieve actual organic pain. In fact, many of these patients can be given an injection of some type of narcotic that will actually cause them to lose consciousness without relieving the pain. It is because of persistence of this type of pain and the attempts of the physicians to relieve it with narcotic medications that some amputees become addicted to narcotics during their postoperative period.

The phantom pain that most all patients experience early in the postoperative course is undoubtedly due to irritation of the severed nerve endings which were cut at the time of amputation. However, the persistence of this pain over a period of several months becomes more abnormal as this pain is not felt to be associated with any type of organic lesion. Most investigators believe that this type of true phantom pain is based entirely upon the psychological reaction that this patient has to alteration of his body image; for this reason patients with severe excruciating phantom pain which persists over a period of many months usually require psychiatric treatment.

It is usually best during the early postoperative period to warn patients that they will experience phantom pain and to assure them that it is normal for them to have it and it will gradually disappear with time. It is usually better to assure them that the pain should not last and that they should do their best to try to ignore it as much as possible. Many times it is beneficial for the patient, if possible, to attempt to "exercise the phantom limb" or attempt to voluntarily move the cramped toes or foot or hand that seems to be the site of pain. For some reason if the patient can in his own mind feel that the phantom extremity is being voluntarily moved, his phantom pain will be greatly diminished. The description of treatment of persistent phantom pain is not within the scope of this writing.

PSYCHOLOGICAL PROBLEMS

All too often, individuals whose extremities are intact fail to realize the tremendous emotional impact that occurs when a patient loses a major portion of one or more of his extremities. Many times he is faced not only with the problem of having to learn to get along without the use of this extremity or to use some type of prosthesis which is never as good as the extremity that he lost, but with other profound psychological problems as well.

Among the psychological problems is the fear that accompanies removal of an extremity for a malignant-type tumor, the actual pain following the injury or operation, and occasionally the other associated injuries that occur at the time that an injury necessitates amputation of an extremity. Therefore, it is important for individuals dealing with rehabilitation of amputees to take all of these factors into consideration rather than dealing with the amputee entirely on the basis of his being an individual who has only lost the use of an extremity. The amputee should be treated as a whole individual, and the counselor should attempt to gain some insight into the possibility of his having other emotional problems associated with the amputation in order to more satisfactorily help him in the long course of rehabilitation that is necessary.

SUGGESTED READINGS

Aitken, G. P. and Frantz, C. H.: The juvenile amputee. *Journal of Bone and Joint Surgeons,* 35-A:659, 1953.

Alldredge, R. H.: Artificial limbs: A consideration of aids employed in the practice of orthopedic surgery. In American Academy of Orthopedic Surgeons, Inc.: *Artificial Limbs,* Orthopedic Appliance Atlas, vol. 2. Ann Arbor, J. W. Edwards, 1960.

Lewis, R. C., Jr., and Bickel, William H.: Hemipelvectomy for malignant disease. *Journal of the American Medical Association, 165:8,* 1957.

Thomas, A.: Anatomical and physical consideration in the alignment and setting of amputation prosthesis for the lower extremities. *Journal of Bone and Joint Surgeons, 26:645,* 1944.

Chapter VIII

RESPIRATORY DISEASES

JOHN H. SELBY

In considering the rehabilitation of patients who have suffered, or are still suffering, from respiratory ailments, it is essential that the counselor have a reasonable understanding of the underlying pathology and physiology involved. In general, rehabilitation of the respiratory patient is based upon four factors. First, priority must be given to overcoming pain and discomfort arising from thoracic incisions and pleuritic type pain. Second, the patient must have reached some level of adjustment to the changes in respiratory function, such as moderate dyspnea or shortness of breath requiring change in occupation, changes in the work situation, or even circumstances of employment. Third, a special challenge is entailed in the rehabilitation of the patient left with a severe chronic cough. Often, this patient cannot be exposed to the public because of a foul sputum or difficulty in controlling the cough. Fourth, the patient who must readjust his life to a more sedentary activity because of the dangers of reactivation of an underlying disease, or overexertion, or putting too much strain on the general body structures poses unique problems for the counselor.

The first factor is principally medical in nature. The last three are specific problems to be coped with jointly by the patient and the rehabilitation counselor with guidance from the physician when needed.

The medical aspects of the respiratory diseases will be presented under three major headings. First, the anatomy of the lungs will be described in order that the counselor may understand the effect of disease upon the respiratory functions. Second, the most common respiratory conditions which produce inability to work will be presented. These diseases are pulmonary tuberculosis, bronchiectasis emphysema, asthma, fungus infections, and cancer of the lungs. Finally, the problem of rehabilitation of the respiratory patient is briefly discussed.

ANATOMY OF THE LUNGS

The normal physiology of the lungs can be compared with a box which contains a balloon. The bottom of the box is like a leather or rubber mat which moves up and down and the balloon is thrust through a hole, extending to the outside into the atmospheric pressure. It is obvious that when the diaphragm is pulled downward, the volume of the box is increased. This, in effect, increases the negative pressure between the balloon and the

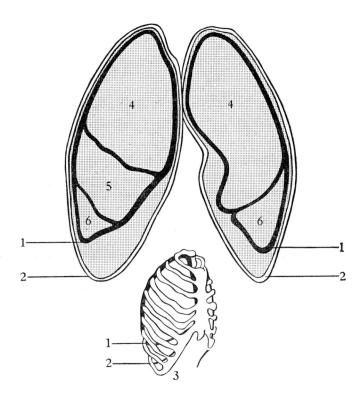

1 LOWER MARGIN OF LUNGS	2 LOWER MARGIN OF PLEURA
3 LOWER RIB MARGIN	4 UPPER LOBES
5 MIDDLE LOBE	6 LOWER LOBES

Figure VIII-1. The lungs. (Courtesy of U. S. Department of Health, Education, and Welfare. *Descriptions of Common Impairments.* Washington, D.C., U. S. Govt. Printing Office, 1959.)

box. In response to this, the balloon expands and draws air in through the opening which is in the atmosphere. If one keeps this analogy in mind, one can understand the various pathological processes which may affect the lungs. This, then, is a mechanism of inflating the lungs and drawing air into the pulmonary passages. As the air is drawn in, it goes down to the alveoli or air sacs where it is transferred into the circulatory system. Oxygen then passes to the red cells and thus travels to the various parts of the body. Thus it is obvious that respiration of the body depends on two systems functioning properly: the respiratory system which brings air into the alveoli and the circulatory system which carries blood to the alveoli to pick up oxygen and distribute it to the cells of the body.

Disability in respiratory conditions results from interference with the process by which oxygen is taken into the lungs and transferred to the blood and by which carbon dioxide and other waste gases are then taken from the blood cells, transferred to the lungs, and exhaled. The ability of the lungs to do this is called respiration. Types of damage to the breathing apparatus are varied and depend upon the disease involved.

In order to understand the effect of diseases upon the respiratory functions, it is necessary to understand the function of the lungs in supplying oxygen to the bloodstream and carrying away carbon dioxide. In this activity the lungs perform two basic services: (a) *ventilation*, the displacement of air into and out of the lung spaces and (b) *diffusion*, the passage of gases across lung membranes into the bloodstream. The alveoli are small air sacs at the ends of the bronchial tubes. It is in these tiny sacs that diffusion of necessary gases into and out of the blood occurs. The oxygen passes into the blood and carbon dioxide out through the walls of the sacs.

Ventilation

Effective ventilation depends on clear airways and air ducts, expandable lungs, and adequate chest wall and diaphragmatic apparatus.

Abnormal constrictions of the air passages tend to decrease the total amount of air that can enter and leave the lung in the required amount of time. Expiration is particularly susceptible to airway constriction so that persons with constricted airways usually have most of their difficulty in expelling the air that has been taken in. This is the basis for changes in vital capacity or timed vital capacity. Other ways of expressing timed vital capacity are maximum expiratory flow rate, or maximum breathing capacity. Any constriction of the air passages will usually be reflected by a decrease of the timed measurements. The ventilatory functions are more commonly impaired than the diffusion functions. The vital capacity is the maximum volume of air that can be expelled after a full inspiration.

The normal vital capacity in humans ranges from about 3,000 to 6,000 cc. The normal vital capacity is surprisingly variable between individuals of differing ages and body build, tending to decrease as the individual becomes older. Thus a vital capacity must be compared to the normal for the specific age and body build. Such norms for age and body build are called *predicted vital capacity*.

Diffusion

The air passes down the trachea (windpipe), bronchi (air tubes), and bronchioles (smaller air tubes) into the alveolar duct and air sac, and finally to the alveoli where gas exchange occurs. As air goes down the passages, it normally is being distributed equally to the many functioning air sacs. Good equal distribution to the air sacs is essential for optimal passage across the alveolar membranes into the blood. If the air passages are either constricted or abnormally dilated, this normal distribution to alveoli and over the alveolar membrane does not occur. The passage of gases into the blood or out with the expelled air is reduced. This occurs most frequently in emphysema and bronchiectasis, but may also occur in other diseases.

DISEASES OF RESPIRATORY SYSTEM

Diseases that will be considered involve conditions which interfere with the processes of ventilation and diffusion. They are usually characterized by an infection which damages a portion of the pulmonary tree. Tuberculosis, bronchiectasis, emphysema, asthma, fungus infections, and cancer of the lungs will be presented.

Tuberculosis

Tuberculosis is caused by *Mycobacterium tuberculosis.* This is a small organism which is quite sturdy because it is covered with a waxy type of capsule. This coating makes it able to survive under unusual circumstances of changes in environment.

When the disease involves the lungs, we call the condition pulmonary tuberculosis. It is widespread among man and animals and no nation has escaped its touch. The severity, however, varies among different societies. Recent studies indicate that there has been no significant decline in the incidence of the infection in the United States. However, there has been significant decrease in the mortality of the disease over the past 25 years and even more over the past decade. This may be because people in the United States are becoming less exposed to the disease and are developing immunity, because methods of treatment have been considerably improved as the result of the discovery of antibiotics, and because of the development of new surgical techniques.

One can only get tuberculosis from someone else who has it. This is one of the most important points in the eventual control of this disease. Epidemiologically, it can be seen that if all of the sources of infection could be found—that is, all the patients who harbor the tuberculosis organism—and then isolated until they are cured, the disease could be completely eradicated. It is this formula that is being attempted in the present battle against the disease.

Diagnostic Symptoms and Classifications

In general, tuberculosis may be considered active whether it is progressing, stationary, or healing. Unless the patient has been free from cavitation, bacilli in the sputum, and x-ray changes for at least six months, the condition is said to be active. It is classified according to the extent of the lung damage it has caused and whether it is active or inactive. The classifications of the National Tuberculosis Association in terms of extent are *minimal, moderately advanced,* and *far advanced.* To illustrate, tuberculosis of the lungs which has resulted in a cavity greater than 4 cm or which has involved an area greater than that of one lung is classified as far-advanced tuberculosis. Conditions are classified as moderately advanced tuberculosis and minimal tuberculosis where the involvement is less extensive. There can be no cavity in minimal disease. If tests have been made repeatedly over a period of at least six months and laboratory findings do not disclose the presence of tuberculosis germs, if the x-ray films show that there is no cavitation and that the condition has not changed during this entire period, and if no symptoms are present, the disease is called inactive.

This does not necessarily mean that a cure has been achieved. It means that the body has, for a substantial period of time, succeeded in overcoming the effects of the germ and is starting a process of healing. So long as the wound has not been completely healed, there is the danger of reactivation at the site of the original infection.

The existence of pulmonary tuberculosis may be demonstrated by a number of laboratory procedures. The sputum of the patient is tested, and in cases of active disease the test will generally show the presence of what are called *acid-fast bacilli,* i.e. bacilli of the type to which the tuberculosis germ belongs. Another means of demonstrating whether there is an active tuberculosis condition is by inoculating animals with sputum or other matter taken from the bronchial tubes, lungs, stomach, or other body cavities. If the animal is infected with tuberculosis, this can be recognized and it can be concluded that the patient has active disease in his body. The matter which is taken from the patient may also be prepared in the form of a culture, i.e. the organisms may be grown in the laboratory test tube. Usually tuberculosis germs in the sputum are swallowed into the stomach, from which they may be conveniently collected by rinsing out the stomach through a rubber tube inserted briefly down the esophagus. This is the basis for the frequently used *gastric washing* test which is used to show when tuberculosis is still actively present in persons who have negative sputum. A *positive gastric washing test*, then, does not indicate any tuberculosis of the stomach but is just another method of showing that the patient has active tuberculosis of the lungs when a positive sputum is not present.

Other tests for determining the existence and extent of tuberculosis are *biopsy, aspiration* of lung area which is suspected, *blood tests,* and *x-ray.* Under conditions of modern treatment in hospitals and clinics, favorable outcome occurs in most cases with minimal disease and in many cases with far-advanced disease.

Other portions of the body may be involved. However, pulmonary tuberculosis (tuberculosis in the lungs) is numerically far in the lead over other forms as the cause of death, and it is usually the source from which infection is spread through the community.

The initial infection is called a *primary lesion.* Early in the disease, a small area of lung is usually involved. The disease may progress and destroy variable amounts of lung tissue. The tissue may die and slough through the breathing tubes leaving holes or cavities in the lungs. Tissue death is referred to as *caseation,* and sloughing of caseated material produces cavities or ulcerated areas. The healing of these ulcerations or cavities is by means of replacing the damaged tissue by fibrous (scar) tissue, the process by which wounds generally are healed. The smaller caseated areas may become chalky or calcified. The disease process may spread through both lung areas or it may be confined to a small portion of one lung. The disease can be detected earliest by tuberculin testing, next by bacteriologic study, and next by routine x-ray.

The tissues react with inflammation to the tuberculin. Many methods and strengths of injection are used, and interpretations are varied accordingly. A positive reaction means that at some time there was exposure and tuberculous infection. It does not necessarily tell whether there is active or inactive disease present. Clinical status and treatment is not usually determined by this test. Bacteriological study is the most accurate way of defining significant active disease. As the disease progresses, there may be a series of small extensions in one or both of the lungs, and the degenerated tissues that are broken off are eliminated through coughing. After ulceration, especially of the bronchial walls, bleeding may occur. This bleeding from the lung is called *hemoptysis*. Usually the bleeding takes the form of staining or streaking, rather than the elimination of large amounts of blood. In some acute forms, debilitation results from fever; weight loss; and a general feeling of sickness and tiredness. Acute disease may exist without significant symptoms. If the disease becomes chronic with considerable destruction of lung tissues, it may interfere with the lung's ability to take in air and to expel carbon dioxide.

Treatment

Treatment of tuberculosis is a long-term problem. In the early days, the primary treatment consisted chiefly of bed rest, and this was fairly effective. Good nutrition, fresh air, and various factors of that type were considered the most important things in the earlier days of the disease. Sanitoria were established throughout the world, which specialized in giving the fresh air and the old mountain type of environment which at that time was thought to be most beneficial to the tuberculous patient. Doctors since have discovered that environment plays very little part in the control of disease; rather it is the rest and the general improvement of health of the host which is most effective in controlling it. The disease itself is a continued battle between the host's resistance and the virulence of the invading organism.

Other forms of treatment somewhat related to this consist of local rest of portions of the lung. This is brought about by so-called collapse therapy. One of the earliest forms of collapse therapy consisted of *pneumothorax*. This is a treatment in which air is introduced into the chest cavity, allowing the lung to collapse. In comparing this with our original illustration, we would introduce air between the box and the balloon, thus lowering the negative pressure and allowing the balloon to go down. In the same manner the lung would collapse; theoretically the cavity would be closed and eventually heal and obliterate. Pneumothorax carried with it many complications, such as rupture of the cavities, adhesions, empyema, etc., and has been almost entirely abandoned in the present day.

Another form of collapse therapy consisted of *thoracoplasty.* Thoracoplasty is a means of collapsing the lung by removing some of the ribs holding the chest wall in position. This, of course, is a fairly mutilating procedure and one in which there is considerable blood loss and many complications. However, for many years this was the standard form of treatment of advanced cases of cavitary tuberculosis and the results with this operation were reasonably good. The disease was controlled in more than 85 percent of patients treated this way.

One type of operation involves the removal of ribs from above downward. Sometimes a very large portion of the chest wall must be collapsed in this manner to collapse cavities in order to promote healing. A person who has an inactive tuberculous condition may nevertheless have a serious respiratory impairment. As indicated above, the lung tissue may have been lost or changed in such a way that function is reduced. Such reduced function may result from loss of lung tissue, loss of ability to ventilate (move air) or to diffuse (pass oxygen across the alveolar membrane), or a decrease in blood flow carrying oxygen to other parts of the body.

In some cases, surgical resection or removal of a portion of a diseased lung may be performed. If an entire lung is removed, thoracoplasty is usually performed to collapse the chest wall over the space previously occupied by the lung. Surgical resection of the diseased portion of the lungs is now not reserved for far-advanced cases or cases with cavities which will not heal. It is being performed increasingly frequently on early cases in which healing does not progress properly although the disease has not caused ulceration. Thus, the fact that surgery has been performed does not mean that the tuberculosis was extensive.

With the introduction of the *chemotherapeutic agents* (antimicrobial drugs such as streptomycin), a new era in the surgery of tuberculosis was opened. It now became possible to resect portions of the lung which were heavily diseased with tuberculosis, such as cavitary lesions. Previously, this would cause a tremendous amount of spill across good lung tissue resulting in spread of the disease. Streptomycin was, however, very effective in preventing the spread of disease during surgery, and since the introduction of this drug, resection surgery has increased. Some credit also must be given to the improved methods of anesthesia and surgical techniques. At the present time, the major foci of the infection of the tuberculous disease can be removed. This diminishes the number of organisms attacking the host and frequently helps control the generalized disease.

Rehabilitation

Tuberculosis remains a serious disease in this country and throughout the world. It is still the most common infectious disease known. Though the death rate has fallen greatly, the incidence of tuberculosis is still considerable. Treatment is long-term therapy, and the problems of rehabilitation are fairly obvious. Patients who have been treated for tuberculosis are rehabilitated on the basis of the extent of their disease. Those with very extensive disease must certainly be trained in new jobs. They must be brought from a sanitorium existence back into the normal world of competition and work. They must be taught to have frequent checkups to be certain that they are not infectious and to avoid contaminating others in case they should become reinfected. Sheltered workshops, in which patients can begin working under ideal circumstances with gradual increasing activity in new lines of work, are extremely helpful in rehabilitation.

Bronchiectasis

Bronchiectasis is a disease primarily of the bronchial tubes toward the periphery of the lungs. It is usually caused by either a chronic lung infection or a severe lung infection such as pneumonia. Most often in the past it has been due to a severe episode of whooping cough in early age. It also may be caused by a foreign body in the lung or following a lung abscess. Occasionally it is seen following a tuberculous infection in the upper lobes. Usually it occurs in the lower lobes. The patient has a chronic cough which is often productive of a foul-smelling, thick, purulent sputum. In fact, the odor is such that many times a patient presents himself because of his foul breath or because of foul putrid sputum. This is embarrassing to the patient and a source of concern. The infection which has occurred has destroyed the elastic membrane of the bronchi, causing a loss of tone in that area. The branchus dilates and does not push the mucus and sputum upward in a normal manner where it can be passed on outward and coughed up normally. Instead it acts like a water bottle which fills with pus. When the patient lies down, the pus pours up to where it is felt and he coughs, raising large amounts of secretion. Complications may occur if a blood vessel is eroded by the infectious process, if metastasis through the bloodstream occurs and causes a brain abscess or abscess in other organs of the body, or if continued infection from one segment of the lung to another goes on until the patient has so much destroyed lung that he becomes extremely dyspneic.

Treatment

The treatment of bronchiectasis is primarily surgical. If the disease can be found in the stage when it is well localized, removal of a segment of the lung or even of a lobe of the lung can give complete cure. Medical treatment provides only temporary relief. This would be directed at keeping the bronchial tree as clean as possible. Such things as medications to thin out the secretions, postural drainage to get secretions out mechanically, antibiotics, and various other supportive measures will diminish the symptoms, cut down the sputum raised, and relieve the infection temporarily. However, as long as the dilated, destroyed bronchi are present, the disease will recur with its full symptomatology. If this disease has progressed for a long period of time, frequently fibrosis takes place and there is much scarring of the lung and much diminished pulmonary area for respiration.

Emphysema

Emphysema is a disease primarily of the alveoli rather than the bronchi, although occasionally it is a result of bronchitis or obstructive disease within the bronchial tree itself. Emphysema also can be a late result of asthma. In emphysema, the air sacs become overdistended. The patient can take in air but has difficulty in breathing it out. There is a loss of the elasticity of the lungs, in that they do not expel the air in a normal manner. It is obvious that as each increment of air is taken in, a small amount of oxygen is contained within it. The patient that expels the entire contents of the alveolus can take in fresh air on inspiration and would be all right. But since he cannot expel the contents of the alveolus, but can only get a little out and then add the small increment of fresh air each time, he is very much limited in his breathing capacity. These patients develop barrel chest, are unable to carry on much activity, and become extremely short of breath on exertion.

Chronic emphysema can cause a slight heart strain because the heart to push against the pressure within the thorax to get blood into the lungs. It is thought that smoking plays a very important part in the development of emphysema due to its chronic irritating effect on the bronchial tree, thus causing obstruction in the outlet of the alveoli.

Treatment

Treatment of emphysema varies depending on the involvement in this case also. If it is a diffuse emphysema, treatment is based primarily on cleaning out the lungs so that what oxygen is taken in can be absorbed through the alveoli. In addition to this, the patient is taught breathing exercises and the importance of emptying all of the air from the lungs as much as possible. Intermittent positive pressure breathing and the use of aerosolized detergents and antibiotics is also important.

Rehabilitation

The rehabilitation problem in this patient, obviously, is based on his markedly diminished functional capacity. He must find an occupation which is quite sedentary. Frequently it is important that he find a job in which he is not exposed to noxious fumes or to air which is polluted in any gross manner. He certainly must be educated against the use of cigarettes.

Asthma

Asthma is a disease primarily of the bronchial tree and is essentially one of spasm of the bronchi. Asthma may be due to allergic manifestation, it may be secondary to infection, or it may be somewhat on an emotional basis. These three factors all play a part in increase in secretions of a mucoid type of output from the glands of the bronchi and cause a spasm of the bronchi so that air can be taken in but is expelled with difficulty against pressure and with a high-pitched wheezing sound. This is due to forcing of air past the mucoid secretions and the narrowed lesser bronchi and bronchioles.

Treatment

Treatment of asthma, of course, begins with determining its etiology. That is, if it is caused by allergy, desensitization must be carried out. Infection should be cleared up as much as possible, and triggering zones such as infection, bronchiectasis, or lung abscess should be removed in order that recurrent infection does not occur. Emotional aspects must be carefully worked out with the patient under psychiatric help.

Rehabilitation

Rehabilitation depends largely on the etiologic factor involved in the asthma. If it is an allergic asthma, the patient must be taught to avoid the substance to which he is allergic. His environment must be altered so that such avoidance is possible. If it is on an emotional basis, rehabilitation may be a very difficult problem and one which should involve a careful evaluation of the underlying emotional facets and a complete readjustment of the patient's emotional outlook.

Fungus Infection

Fungus infection of the lungs is somewhat similar in nature to tuberculosis; however, it is not as highly contagious. The disease is not transmitted from human to human but valley fever (coccidioidomycosis), for instance, is picked up in dust or sand in the southwest part of this country. This disease was first described during the second world war and appeared to originate in the San Joaquin Valley of California. It has moved eastward until now the endemic area extends as far east as the western part of Texas.

Treatment

Treatment of fungus infection is somewhat similar to that of tuberculosis in that rest is necessary. Resection is indicated in localized disease, cavitary disease, or bleeding. Rehabilitation again must depend on the extent of the patient's involvement.

Pneumoconiosis

Pneumoconiosis is a term referring to all the chronic diseases caused in the lung as the result of prolonged inhaling of injurious dusts. The most common is silica. Dust containing high concentrations of fine particles of silica may produce serious disease. These fine particles penetrate to finer air passages of the air cells of the lungs which perform the function of exchanging air. They then create tissue nodules wherever they become lodged. These nodules themselves replace normal tissue or interfere with proper function of remaining normal tissue. The end result is decreased lung function.

Pneumoconiosis may be classified according to the degree of lung involvement. Where the disease has not progressed beyond the root portion of the lungs (hilar areas), those areas where the bronchi, blood vessels, nerves, etc., enter the lungs, or the nodules produced by the disease remain a small size and do not coalesce, the disease is usually classified as first-stage pneumoconiosis. Where a greater portion of the lungs is involved and the nodules are greater in size but the damaged tissue is in the form of separated and discrete nodules with normal tissue between, the disease may be classified as the second stage. Where the nodules conglomerate into larger solid nodular tissue, the condition may be classified as third stage.

In advanced cases, the diseased lung is a mass of such nodular tissue. The tissue cells that are formed as indicated above are not elastic as is normal lung tissue and do not function as breathing cells. Disability is caused by this condition to the degree that the lungs lose breathing efficiency, i.e. they do not supply adequate oxygen for absorption by the blood or they do not perform adequately their function of taking carbon dioxide out from the blood. As in many other respiratory conditions, the most common symptom is shortness of breath. The diagnosis may be made by means of a careful history and the observations of the physicians and x-ray films to determine the extent of disability.

It is now known that extensive lesions seen on x-rays may cause immeasurably small change in the person's ability to breathe. Likewise, minimal lesions seen on x-rays may occasionally cause severe handicaps to breathing. Tests of breathing should include, first, ventilatory tests, and in fewer instances, diffusion tests, as previously discussed. The reader will note that breathing tests for pneumoconiosis are similar to those for emphysema. This is so because the type of function lost is the same, namely ability to oxygenate.

A common form of pneumoconiosis is silicosis produced by stone or dust. This disease is sometimes called miner's asthma.

Histoplasmosis

Histoplasmosis is another fungus infection somewhat similar in nature to the previously mentioned diseases. It is endemic in the Mississippi River Valley and causes calcification throughout the lung, fibrosis, and some diminished pulmonary function. Here again, the contagious aspect is not a great one, and rehabilitation is primarily dependent upon the amount of respiratory impairment present.

Pneumonia

Pneumonia has become a much less common problem than it used to be a generation ago. We see lobar pneumonia less frequently due to antibiotics which are available. However, it is interesting to note that within the past few years, lobar pneumonia has apparently been on the increase, particularly in antibiotic-resistant diseases and in the staphylococcic type of pneumonia. The significance today lies not so much in the disease itself as in the residual effect. These include emphysema, bronchiectasis, and occasionally asthma.

Cancer of the Lung

Cancer of the lung is an increasing problem throughout the world today. The incidence of cancer has risen dramatically within the last decade. Recent statistical surveys have indicated that the primary etiologic agent in cancer of the lung is cigarette smoking. The exact mechanism of this is not as yet determined, though it is thought to be chronic irritation caused by various factors such as the temperature of the smoke, the excessive volatilization of tars and waste within the cigarette, and actually a radioactive substance within the cigarette paper. At any rate, it has become very obvious that education for the control of smoking is essential in order to control many of these pulmonary diseases. Lung cancer today has with it a very high mortality, and the rate of curability is somewhat less than 15 percent in some of the best clinics in the country.

The biggest problems seem to lie in early detection of cancer. Cancer of the lung, in its curable stages, carries with it very few symptoms or physical signs. It is only when it has gone on to a stage where cure is almost impossible that the symptoms become very obvious. Physicians therefore urge the patients to have frequent x-rays, at least annually, in order to find any very early evidence of lung cancer. Patients who are heavy smokers should have x-rays taken at six months' to three months' intervals. Aside from x-rays, diagnostic measures include studies of the sputum, looking for cancer cells (bronchoscopic examination).

In a very large percentage of lung cancer, the tumor can actually be visualized within the bronchial tree and biopsies can be taken. Bronchography, the instillation of a radioopaque substance into the bronchial tree, will frequently outline a suspected area.

Some of the symptoms which are considered as warning signs in lung cancer include chronic dry cough, chest pain, weight loss, blood spitting, and shortness of breath. Any of these symptoms should be carefully investigated to determine its cause and to rule out the possibility of malignancy of the lung.

Treatment

The cure for cancer of the lung lies in early and radical excisional surgery. If the cancer is found early enough, a lobe may be removed with complete cure. If the lesion is more extensive, it may be necesary to remove the entire lung. Exploration of the chest is a diagnostic procedure in many cases, and when a cancer is suspected and cannot be definitely identified, exploratory thorocotomy should certainly be carried out.

Other methods of treatment which are utilized in lung cancer which cannot be cured surgically include radiation therapy in which high-voltage x-ray or cobalt therapy is applied to the involved area. This is highly effective and in many cases brings about relief of symptomatology, if not complete cure. A third treatment is a chemotherapeutic one, in which alkylating agents and other drugs are used to affect the rapidly multiplying cells seen in malignancy. In this way, the lesion is slowed down and at times some actually may be absorbed. The outlook for cancer of the lung, however, is poor in those patients who cannot be treated surgically to start.

Rehabilitation of Cancer-of-the-Lung Patient

Rehabilitation of the cancer-of-the-lung patient depends upon the individual situation which arises. The patient who has resectional surgery and is cured very frequently can go back to a completely normal existence and can carry on almost the same activities as he did before. Other patients who have perhaps a pneumonectomy or have some disease in the opposite lung may be found to have a marked respiratory deficiency, and their rehabilitation may need to include adjustment to diminished abilities to get about and to carry on their previous activity. The patients in whom cure cannot be accomplished may need to be adjusted to a certain amount of discomfort and pain. Physicians feel that it is wise to get these patients back into some sort of activity because if they are not active, they lose hope and go downhill more rapidly.

Rehabilitation of the Respiratory Patient

There are, in general, several basic and underlying rehabilitation projects which must be considered in all pulmonary diseases. These depend to a certain extent upon the type of underlying pathology, as we have discussed, and its effects on the organism as a whole. Environmental changes and the learning of new productive activity in order to make a living are important to one's self and one's family under limitations of strength and breathing difficulty. The psychological adjustment to various types of lung diseases has been considered and certainly formed the basis for rehabilitation programs. By understanding the basic pathology involved and its effect on the human organism, one can deal more adequately with the needs of the individual to readjust to his environment and to society and its requirements.

SUGGESTED READINGS

Bates, D. V., Macklen, P. T., and Christi, R. V.: *Respiratory Function in Disease*. Philadelphia, W. B. Saunders, 1964.

Gibbon, J. H., Jr., Sebastian, D. C., and Spencer, F. C.: *Surgery of the Chest*. Philadelphia, W. B. Saunders, 1969.

Hinshaw, H. C.: *Diseases of the Chest*. Philadelphia, W. B. Saunders, 1969.

Marshal, G., and Perry, K. M. A.: *Diseases of the Chest*. St. Louis, C. V. Mosby Co., 1952.

Chapter IX

RESPIRATORY DISORDERS AND THE REHABILITATION PROCESS

John W. Knapstein

In this chapter, the rehabilitation of patients with respiratory disorders will be discussed from a psychological and/or social vantage point. This particular frame of reference all too frequently has been given low priority in texts on rehabilitation, even though a great deal is said relative to the medical care, cure, and physical rehabilitation of these patients. There is an ever-growing realization that physical illness has not only psychosomatic features but also somatopsychic features. Thus more attention is being given to nonmedical aspects of all physical illnesses.

In general, the nonmedical aspects of the rehabilitation process for respiratory patients are considered important only for more severe and chronic disorders. These aspects have been viewed and treated in a manner similar to the way they are managed for patients with any chronic, severe, or long-term illness. Though this position may be more correct than incorrect, there is a need to consider these patients, their needs, and their problems in more detail.

Until recent times, a discussion of patients with respiratory problems was equated with a discussion of patients with tuberculosis. Today tuberculosis is not as threatening a disease as it once used to be. Research and improved diagnostic acumen have expanded the spectrum of topics now sharing the spotlight with tuberculosis, e.g. lung cancer, emphysema, asthmatic conditions, air pollution, etc.

The goal of this chapter is to present a discussion of some of the more recent and current thinking and research on the problem of respiratory disorders. A frame of reference, backdrop, or foundation will be presented so the reader can gain a general knowledge and have some basic expectancies concerning respiratory patients. Then the reader can more intelligently begin to synthesize the sometimes vast, and sometimes meagre, literature in the area.

INTRODUCTION

Respiratory disorders, ranging from the common cold and pneumonia to tuberculosis, lung cancer, emphysema, etc., have a wide variety of debilitating effects. Except for instances of psychosomatic etiology, respiratory illnesses follow the same course as any physical disease, i.e. (a) organism contact with some infecting or aggravating agent, (b) virulent invading agent breaking down organism defenses, and (c) organism resistance overcoming the invading agent. The contact element of this three-point model (contact-attack-counterattack) is inevitable, particularly in crowded metropolitan areas. It is a combined miracle of modern medicine and of the internal physical/physiological strength of man that prevents people in the ghetto from being eliminated by epidemics and disease.

It appears that respiratory disorders have a greater incidence rate with lower socioeconomic groups. For example, the National Tuberculosis and Respiratory Disease Association estimates that people in these groups have four times the chance of contracting tuberculosis as the general population does. Similar data concerning other respiratory disorders are not readily available, and tuberculosis is the most notorious of the diseases of the respiratory system to be associated with lower socioeconomic living conditions. However, it is not unreasonable to assume that some of the very same factors which elevate the incidence rate for tuberculosis also elevate the rate for other respiratory disorders with this same group of people.

The rehabilitation of people suffering from respiratory disorders involves much more than merely coping with the physical components of the various diseases. Haliday (1953) was one of the pioneers in the movement that has resulted in medical people becoming more cognizant of related and important psychological factors associated with physical illnesses. He noted that the proportion of patients who reported the same or similar disorders in close relatives was significantly higher than what one would expect from the general population. He argued that heredity (genetics, nature), common socioeconomic-cultural setting (environment, nurture), and imitative learning are potential explanations for this finding. He felt that some combination of these factors was in operation and he called for research that would clarify which factors are important in the various disorders. Even today the same question is being asked.

Crisp (1970) pointed out that many factors are found to correlate with having cancer. They may not be related or even relevant to having the disease. Onset of cancer does not appear to be the simple product of an isolated encounter between some etiological agent and an individual. Crisp also called for research to clarify relevant genetic and psychological factors in cancer.

The National Tuberculosis and Respiratory Disease Association has emphasized the nonmedical components of tuberculosis for some time (*The T B Clinic*, 1967, p. 9). "The most formidable obstacle to the eradication of tuberculosis is no longer the microorganism and the pathologic process of the disease, but the complex problems of the human host in whom they are found." As far as this organization is concerned, case holding has become just as important as case finding. Its whole approach to case holding is governed by sound psychological and sociological principles.

This emphasis is not restricted to tuberculosis. Krakowski (1970) made the same point for disease or illness in general. He emphasized the psychophysical unity of the human organism and took the position that psychosomatic problems must be dealt with, whether they be primary to, concurrent with, or secondary to, some organic or physical illness. He went even further when he expounded on a two-way interaction relative to illness in man: (a) psychosomatic-psychological factors affecting physical factors, and (b) somatopsychic-physical factors affecting psychological factors. In Germany, Enke (1970) even went to the point of being critical of hospital settings which foster the dependency needs of patients to the detriment of other psychological factors. He particularly pointed out the socio-medical problem of regression early in an illness as an example. He deplored attitudes of some hospital staff which counteract progression by patients out of a state of depression, anxiety, fear, and enforced/exaggerated dependency.

Thus the emphasis today is one of treating the patient *in toto*. The physical factors cannot be overemphasized to the detriment of the psychological and social ramifications and effects of a disease. One affects the other in a very complex fashion; if one component is in an upset state, complications of some sort may be expected to arise in the other component. Therefore, hand-in-hand with physical rehabilitation, other forms of rehabilitation must be undertaken. The other areas of rehabilitation can be classified into three major categories for academic purposes: psychological (emotional), social, and vocational. (These classifications are by no means absolute. This schema only serves as a frame of reference for this chapter.)

The emotional component of the rehabilitation process involves such matters as a patient's acceptance and understanding of the disease he has, of the treatment regimen required for the disease, and of the changes the disease will effect in his life. Social rehabilitation focuses on problems associated with returning the patient to the community per se, e.g. length and frequency of hospitalizations for the disease, change of lifestyle (and financial base for a lifestyle), social stigma associated with the disease, etc.

Vocational rehabilitation focuses on the world of work as limited by the aftereffects of a patient's disease, i.e. performing in an occupation which will not aggravate any conditions resultant from the disease and which will allow the patient to perform adequately and successfully. With respiratory disorders, what a person can do for gainful work is primarily a function of his loss of respiratory capability and of his need to avoid noxious agents (foul air, fumes, etc.). Ability, interests, complicating concurrent disabilities and so forth are separate but related matters which further influence the direction a person will take in his vocational rehabilitation.

COMMON COLD

Turning from general considerations of psychological, social, and vocational problems in respiratory diseases, specific respiratory illnesses will be presented from the point of view of the rehabilitation counselor. The common cold, pneumonia, asthma, tuberculosis, lung cancer, emphysema, and the smoking habit will be discussed.

Research on the common cold is indeed rare. Almost universally this illness has not been considered severe enough to warrant discussion in texts on rehabilitation. Most certainly it does not have great implications for vocational change, but it carries some implications for performance in industry. The meagre data in the area raises questions relative to overall adjustment and also suggest several possibilities for research. The implication is clear, namely, the so-called common cold and related illnesses may not be as simple and "common" as is usually believed.

One only has to do a bit of reflection to realize that a person does not function as well psychologically when he suffers from a cold. Richter (1943) was among the first to publish an article about emotional factors as related to chronic colds. He described several postillness behaviors in children who returned to school after having recovered from colds. He interpreted his observations to reflect deep-seated conflicts concerning aggression impulses. He reportedly found more apathy and depressive behaviors, more dependence and subservient behaviors, greater meticulousness in dress and habits, and more avoidance behavior for quarrels and displays of anger.

Despert (1944) reported that he found chronic absence of children from school for colds to coincide with broken home situations and a variety of emotional problems. Ruddick (1963) reported his observations in a study of women clients who had chronic colds. He took the position that some chronic colds with his clients were associated with emotionally stressful situations of separation and loss.

PNEUMONIA

It is generally felt that adverse psychological effects related to pneumonia are minimal; respiratory problems which may grow out of pneumonia may involve more important psychological factors. Nevertheless, Wittkower and White (1959) related that the onset of bacterial and viral pneumonia frequently was found to be preceded by periods of emotional stress. They observed that a depression which had developed over a period of weeks was at maximal proportions shortly before the pneumonia set in.

The findings and models of these researchers may not be specific to colds and pneumonia. Though the conclusions drawn do not preclude other factors as being important, these studies do suggest that the common cold and pneumonia may be more involved than what meets the eye. Undoubtedly, a specific germ or virus can be found in their genesis. However, that alone does not adequately explain contraction of the respiratory disorder at a time of emotional strife, nor explain the association these respiratory illnesses seem to have with stressful life situations.

ASTHMATIC CONDITIONS

A classical example of a psychosomatic respiratory disorder is asthma. A classical fallacy would be to generalize that all asthma patients are suffering from a psychosomatic disorder. There are several psychological theories relating to the causes of asthmatic conditions. Yet asthma can be a very real and uncomfortable physical disorder. This dual nature of asthma, combined with a complex array of physical aggravants, probably makes this respiratory disorder one of the most perplexing with which to deal. Wittkower and White (1959) have pointed out that the problem is enmeshed within a whole constellation of factors: emotional/psychological genesis, constitutional susceptibility, autonomic or endocrine lability, true allergies, inherited/acquired proneness to respiratory dysfunction, and sociocultural factors. In short, the problem encompasses the entire gamut of possible etiological agents.

One need not go far to demonstrate the difficulties encountered in conducting research in this area. Arnds and Studt (1969) studied 50 asthma patients and 50 random hospital patients with the goal of trying to determine personality differences between the two groups. On the basis of test results of a combination objective and projective test battery, they concluded that asthma patients were emotionally more reactive and that had more unexpressed negative feelings concerning society. However, they also concluded that asthmatics have maladjustments common to many other psychosomatic syndromes.

Researchers generally treat asthma as one group in the general category of allergies. Rawls, Rawls, and Harrison (1971) studied 1,190 children, ages six to eleven. They drew the conclusion that children with no allergic involvement were in an overall healthier physical condition and were rated superior to the asthmatic group along several social, emotional, and academic dimensions. In essence, they confirmed what has already been found for some time in texts on abnormal psychology.

Spiegelberg, Betz, and Pietsch (1970) described the results of research with 1,001 psychiatric and neurological outpatients. The patients attending their clinic had close to an 18 percent incidence rate for allergic conditions. They found no major differences between the allergic and nonallergic patients along several psychological and sociological dimensions. They did find a significant correlation between childhood motor inhibitions and the onset of allergic conditions. They concluded that in addition to psychosomatic theories to explain certain allergies, one must bear in mind somatopsychic theories as well as theories of psychoses.

Despite the difficulties encountered, a considerable amount of research on asthma has been accomplished. Two basic theories have evolved. Wittkower and White (1959) suggested that there is basic agreement on the dynamics of psychosomatic asthma: (a) inordinate need for maternal love, (b) ambivalence about the mother figure, and (c) fear of alienating or losing the mother figure.

Alexander and Flagg (1963) expanded on this model and added the concept of separation anxiety. They suggested the sequence of attack as follows: (a) arousal of a strong emotion or impulse viewed to be dangerous, (b) inhibition (frustration) of this emotion or impulse for fear of loss of love, and (c) appearance of the first symptoms of the asthma attack due to a breakdown of better defenses.

The second theory is essentially a learning model which grew out of animal experiments. For example, Turnbull (1962), among others, successfully used various conditioning procedures to reinforce asthmalike reactions in animals. In applying the results of these experiments to the human organism, the model is something like this. If crying does not succeed in gaining needed attention for an infant, he will try to use other means to get it. If he learns that sighing, coughing, and wheezing do gain the attentive behaviors of an adult, he will use them again to try to satisfy his needs. With continued reinforcement, these behaviors become part of his *modus operandi,* and they will persist as long as they reduce anxiety. Even when more effective behaviors to gain attention are learned, the person will still regress to these behaviors.

As with the common cold and pneumonia, asthmatic conditions do not frequently involve vocational change. When they do, the counselor needs to be cognizant of the aggravating agent and of the severity of the disease the patient has. Not atypically, a counselor will need to deal with adjustment factors, particularly if the process is a psychosomatic one or if the asthma has recently reached severe proportions.

TUBERCULOUS CONDITIONS

Outside of the cold and pneumonia, tuberculosis is probably one of the oldest diagnosed respiratory disorders known to man (Knapstein, 1970). Of the disorders of the respiratory system, it has been by far the topic of more psychological research than any other similar disorder. Though it is still a serious disease, its importance has waned because of the discovery of better drugs, better therapeutic procedures, and early methods of identification. It has fallen from being the number 1 killer of man to being the number 20 killer of man.

The National Tuberculosis and Respiratory Disease Association (*The TB Clinic,* 1967) has considered that tuberculosis has been becoming a disease of lower socioeconomic groups for some time now. United States Department of Health, Education, and Welfare statistics give ample evidence for this position. This is not to say that more affluent groups are not susceptible to the disease—far from it. Tuberculosis respects no socioeconomic group. However it is felt that the more affluent can better afford to maintain their overall state of health and that they can more easily take preventive measures. There are probably a multitude of other reasons for this phenomenon. The important thing is that this is the situation which exists and with which one must deal.

One of the primary and most consistent findings in research on the personality functioning of tuberculous patients is that they have an elevated level of anxiety (Knapstein, 1970). In and of itself, this is not too surprising, considering the social stigma and drastic life changes that are involved with the disease. However, researchers have found the elevated anxiety level or the presence of stress-laden life experiences to have been in existence for some time prior to hospitalization (Holmes, Hawkins, Bowerman, Clarke, and Joffe, 1957; Moran, Fairweather, Morton, and McGaughram, 1955). The presence of feelings of inadequacy and aggression, and a lowered capacity to cope seems to be important both before and during hospitalization.

Another general finding in the research seems to be centered around a series of withdrawing behaviors (Knapstein, 1970). The use of the term "introversion" is slightly deceiving because of its variant meanings to different people. Some of its components do not always appear in studies dealing with tuberculosis patients. Threat-sensitivity and sobriety (serious, taciturn) are frequent findings; but the lack of social dominance and the reliance on one's own resources are sometimes not found (Cattell, Eber, and Tatsuoka, 1970). In general, there appears to be a tendency to be introspective and self-abasive. Also, a series of behaviors appears that might be labeled as a lessened zest for living, i.e. narrow interests, disinterest in becoming involved and active in outside interests, and a lowered level of intellectual and emotional activity (Charen, 1956; Ellis, and Brown, 1950).

Subdued *modus operandi* appears to be related to this (Knapstein, 1970). Conformity would appear to be a descriptive term that best describes tuberculous patients' reliance on others for support, their respect for the established ways of doing things, and their tendency to be mild mannered. Kahn (1955) labeled these traits with the term "reactivity." In other words, tuberculous patients tend to be reactive to their environment as opposed to being active (creative) in it. Docility, amiability, acquiescence, etc., are not uncommon research findings (Moran, Fairweather, Morton, and Fisher, 1956; Vernier, Barrell, Cummings, Dickerson, and Hooper, 1961).

Any review of the literature leads one to the definite conclusion that tuberculous patients do have adjustments to make. Sometimes their attempts at adjustment may become problematic for hospital staff (Fagerbaugh, 1970). What may appear to staff, who are not sophisticated in the area of deviant behavior, as being symptomatic of deep-seated disturbances may be nothing more than an acute situational anxiety reaction.

Considering the long-term nature of the therapy and the necessity for temporary isolation from outside contacts, as well as a whole host of related problems, adjustment counseling becomes an important part of the entire rehabilitation process. The overall rehabilitation may present few problems or it may present problems from a variety of different sources. These problems are not dissimilar to those experienced by people with most chronic or long-term illnesses, so some of them will be discussed later in this chapter.

There is one matter that seems to be important and should be pointed out here; it will be brought up again. Favorable response to medical treatment seems to be a function of appropriate psychological adjustment to having tuberculosis, to the hospital, and to the treatment regimen. Severity of the disease, slow recovery, and a poor prognosis are invariably found to be related to maladaptive hospital reactions or to unhealthy psychological functioning.

LUNG CANCER AND EMPHYSEMA

These two disease processes will be discussed together not because of the similarity of their nature but because of a common and widespread aggravating agent in modern society—smoking. Statistics on smoking relating it to lung cancer and emphysema are readily available. The merits of the statistics which are used to demonstrate the relationship will not be argued pro or con. The fact of the matter is that the great majority of patients suffering from these diseases are, or have been, heavy smokers. The habit of smoking introduces a foreign agent into the lungs on a recurring basis, and has, at the very least, been shown to be an unhealthy habit.

Very little is known about the psychodynamics of the patient with emphysema. Yet, hospital staffs are seeing more and more patients with the disease. Treatment is very frequently long-term, as with tuberculosis, and these patients are handled similarly to patients with any chronic long-term illness. The nature of the disease brings about lessened respiratory capacity. If severe enough, it can be lethal, but it is not yet considered a major killer of man.

Lung cancer, on the other hand, is considered a deadly disease. Admission to a hospital for it is emotionally tantamount to an admission of imminent death by the patient. It, too, is a disease process that is seen with more and more patients in medical and surgical hospitals.

Between 1930 and 1965 (James, 1966), the death ratio associated with lung cancer increased from 2 per 100,000 to 23 per 100,000. This change may reflect an increase in rate of incidence, better diagnostic identification, earlier identification, etc. Survival rates associated with treatment are poor if lung cancer is not treated in its early stages. Even then the five-year survival rate is only 42 percent. Holding constant the severity of the disease upon diagnosis, the five-year survival rate with treatment is about 7 percent. The most successful treatment procedure, lobectomy, has about a 30 percent rate of success (survival five years or more). If the disease is discovered in the last stage of development, the chances for survival for five years or more is less than 1 in 50.

Relatively little research has been done on the topic of lung cancer alone. Psychological researchers have included it under the general topic of cancer. The general thinking seems to be that the reactions involved with cancer will not be altered that much by involvement of one organ over another unless that organ has some particular significance for a patient. One of the more important and interesting findings in cancer research seems to center around the concept of a psychological resistance to cancer. Blumberg, West, and Ellis (1954) reported a relationship between recovery from cancer and lower anxiety, lessened defensiveness, and greater tension release via motor activities. (This is not dissimilar to the same kind of thing found for tuberculosis.) The finding was picked up at the University of Texas M. D. Anderson Hospital, but the research team broke up and to date nothing official has been published; hopefully the work is being continued.

For the most part, the rehabilitation of cancer patients is handled similarly to that of patients with a chronic illness. However, because of the high mortality rate associated with cancer, a counselor will, in all likelihood, find himself in a situation in which he will need to work with terminally ill patients (Cobb, 1962; Boscue and Krieger, 1971). This can be a very difficult task. It may involve more skill and professionalism than counseling with a physically healthy person. The counselor must also come to grips with his own feelings about dying and death. There are several plausible goals that can be established. Anxiety reduction about death and dying is probably the most immediate and obvious goal. Other goals might possibly be related to getting the patient to accept death as a natural consequence of life, to maintain purposeful activities during his remaining time, or to keep his dignity and self-respect. In many cases, interpersonal support will need to be given to help the patient overcome feelings of isolation and rejection. In short, the counselor takes on the role of someone who cares, who wants to help the patient come to grips with his last major adjustment, and who is going to resist the patient's merely surrendering and vegetating.

Smoking Behavior

For some time, both lung cancer and emphysema (Waldbatt, 1953) have been known to be related to, or aggravated by, smoking. Smoking is also known to be instrumental in coronary artery and peripheral vascular diseases. It is an interesting phenomenon, insofar as it is not considered a disease, even though it has some mildly addictive features and is considered an important etiologic agent in several diseases. The classical models of smoking behavior (Bergler, 1946) have included concepts of masochism, oral pacification, aggression release, neurotic substrates, etc. As early as 1945, Finnegan, Larson, and Hoag began describing the habit in a different manner. They emphasized (a) social pressure to conform as being important in initiating the habit, (b) nicotine itself as perpetuating the habit, and (c) emotional factors as determiners of amount and occasion of smoking. The nicotine dosage (Frankenhaeuser, Myrsten, and Post, 1970) appears to be important in causing a sort of physiological emergency reaction in the smoker, e.g. increased adrenalin output, higher blood pressure, increased heart rate, decreased skin temperature, and decreased hand steadiness. Frith (1971) found that the desire to smoke seems to be associated with low-arousal situations for men and with high-arousal situations for women. These studies would suggest that need for stimulation to maintain a high level of stimulation is important in smoking behavior.

"Kicking the habit," so to speak, is not an easy accomplishment. There are probably as many ideas on how to stop smoking as there are proponents of stopping smoking. There are several commercial pills and secrets that smokers can purchase, hopefully to help them stop smoking. Various forms of therapy from various disciplines have been tried with varying degrees of success.

Among the more recent attempts to help smokers cease smoking (using a psychological base), certain behavior modification techniques seem to be showing promise. Marrone, Merksamer, and Salzberg (1970) used short-term group treatment involving stimulus saturation techniques, i.e. chain smoking followed by total abstinence. They had one group chain smoke for twenty hours (long duration) and another for ten hours (short duration). At the end of four months, all the members of the short duration group had relapsed to prior levels of smoking behavior. The members of the long-duration group had achieved a 60 percent abstinence rate.

Another technique that has been reported for slowing down the rate of smoking involves the use of social and interpersonal reinforcements. Janis and Hoffman (1971) worked with several smokers who had a common objective of reducing smoking behavior. All the smokers were grouped into pairs and attended five sessions together over a five-week period with a consultant. There were three categories of pairs based on amount of interpersonal contact there was between partners: (a) high contact—partners phoned each other every day, (b) low contact—partners only spoke to each other at the time of the consultation, (c) no contact—different partners were paired for each of the consultations. At the end of the five weeks, the high-contact group had more positive attitudes about the entire situation. At the end of a year, the high-contact group was found to have continued to reduce smoking, while the other groups reverted to prior levels of smoking behavior.

The reduction of smoking behavior is an area in which the surface has only been scratched. A few answers relative to smoking have been found. A few inroads have been made into the unknown area of smoking behavior. Some of the dynamics of this behavior are becoming better understood. There is a great deal more that needs to be understood.

The Counselor's Challenge in Respiratory Disease

Upon entering a hospital (Cobb, 1962), patients with severe lung disorders (tuberculosis, cancer, emphysema, etc.) have basically two major adjustments to make. The first is immediate and deals with the hospitalization, i.e. treatment regimen, disrupted social and family life, isolation, hospital routine, etc. The second is more remote and centers around discharge from the hospital, e.g. return to previous social setting, potential rejection experiences, changed way of living, possible job change, etc. These patients face rather serious problems such as lengthy and costly treatment, family support, and business maintenance. It is no surprise that depression, anxiety, and fear are almost universally reported with admission of these patients to a hospital. All too frequently, admission to a hospital for such a problem is perceived as being the same as death or as having had a close call with death.

The major impediments to a good prognosis have been labeled by some as being: (a) discouragement and hopelessness and (b) pessimism and rebelliousness. To do rehabilitative work with such patients involves understanding the "whole person" (to use a much overused cliché) (*The TB Clinic*, 1967). In other words, staff members need to approach problems in the context of the patient's own particular needs, his problems, his background, his living conditions prior to hospitalization, etc. It means that they will encounter diverse social backgrounds and value systems. All too often a patient will belong to some minority group; it is important for staff members to understand the sociology of that group and to contend with any language barriers that may exist.

Staff members need to gain an understanding of what hospitalization, the hospital regimen, the disease itself, and the healing process mean to a patient, not only cognitively but also emotionally. With a problem patient, it is particularly necessary to create a model of how he operates in order to deal with stress and anxiety. One needs to ask why the patient is having a problem, on the basis of the model. Then he can work to resolve the cause of the problem.

The problem patient is trying to cope with stress; chronic stress does not appear to help the patient recover. Favorable and unfavorable prognoses appear to be positively correlated with an ability to deal with the psychological stress associated with acceptance of having a chronic or severe disease.

The initial steps (Cobb, 1962) toward a healthy adjustment are taken by the physician who informs a patient about a diagnosis. He starts a process of education about the disease, its treatment, and its curability. The theory is that understanding something strange and dangerous engenders courage to cope with it, as well as a willingness to cooperate with people who can help one cope with it. The physician remains the focal point for the patient; the relationship between these two people is extremely important.

For the most part, the counselor (whatever his profession by training) functions as an extension of the physician. He will do considerable liaison work between patient, physician, staff, family, etc. He needs to know about the disease and its progression as well as to have an updated knowledge of treatment procedures for the disease. Then he can more effectively deal with misconceptions and teach facts (not fiction) about the disease. Last, but not least, he needs to be able to handle the anxieties of the family in order to convert their misconceptions and fears into understanding, empathy, and support. These are just some of the attributes important to a counselor when working with clients with respiratory disorders.

In addition to performing adjustment counseling, the counselor needs to be able to function in an interpretive role. He needs to know the needs of the patient in the doctor-patient relationship, as well as the physician's philosophy relative to this same relationship. He needs to open and keep open effective two-way communication between the patient and the physician so that the physician will discuss various aspects of the treatment with the patient. The patient needs to feel that something is happening; he needs to be prepared for what is going to happen. If a patient does not perceive that there is movement in his treatment, he will want to know why (Cobb, 1962). Often this will involve repeated explanations of the facts about a disease process, of treatment reactions, and of side effects of medicine.

Not infrequently the counselor becomes an educator also. He needs to reeducate the patient to a healthier manner of living and often he needs to help the patient find work he can do when he leaves the hospital. Proper rest, exercise, regular eating, proper nutrition, and general hygiene, as well as assorted topics related to the world of work, are not alien to the counseling session.

Multiple Disease Processes

In the previous sections of this chapter, several respiratory disorders were discussed without consideration for complicating factors such as combination diseases, e.g. tuberculosis plus alcoholism, lung cancer plus some psychiatric condition, etc. Knapstein (1970) and Martinez (1969) investigated tuberculous alcoholic patients and found that they appeared to be operating with many of the dynamics of both tuberculous and alcoholic patients. The result was that they were different from both groups and were considered problem patients. In these same studies, two cultural groups—Spanish and Anglo—were also studied and differences were found. This gave further evidence that different cultural groups react differently to given disease processes and treatments. They also demonstrated that simultaneous disease processes can complicate the picture and result in a patient's reacting in a manner that is unexpected or in a manner that is labeled uncooperative. At present the counselor must use his own diagnostic acumen in working with these patients. Complicating matters such as cultural beliefs, cultural behavior patterns, and multiple disease processes occur. These matters have important implications for rehabilitation that need to be clarified and investigated.

REFERENCES

Adar, L. D.: An investigation of the relationship of some aspects of frustration to pulmonary tuberculosis. *Dissertation Abstracts International, 31:*4322, 1971. (Abstract)

Alexander, F. and Flagg, G. W.: The psychosomatic approach. In Wolman, B. B. (Ed.): *Handbook of Clinical Psychology.* New York, McGraw-Hill, 1963.

Arnds, H. G. and Studt, H. H.: Psychodiagnostische beiträge zur persönlichkeitsstruktur von asthmatern. *Zeitschrift für Psychosomatische Medizin und Psychoanalyse, 15:*113, 1969. (*Psychological Abstracts,* 1971, 46, No. 3472).

Bergler, E.: Psychopathology of compulsive smoking. *Psychiatric Quarterly, 20:*297, 1946.

Blumberg, E. M., West, P. M., and Ellis, F. A.: A possible relationship between psychological factors and human cancer. *Psychosomatic Medicine, 16:*277, 1954.

Boscue, L. O. and Krieger, G. W.: Considerations in counseling the terminally ill. *Journal of Applied Rehabilitation Counseling, 2:*97, 1971.

Cattell, R. B., Eber, H. W., and Tatsuoka, M. M.: *Handbook for the Sixteen Personality Factor Questionnaire.* Champaign, Ill., Institute for Personality and Ability Testing, 1970.

Charen, S.: Regressive behavior changes in the tuberculous patient. *Journal of Psychology, 41:*273, 1956.

Clark, T. J. and Cochrane, G. M.: Effect of personality on alveolar ventilation in patients with chronic airways obstruction. *British Medical Journal, 1(*5691):273, 1970.

Cobb, B.: Cancer. In Garrett, J. F. and Levine, E. S. (Eds.): *Psychological Practices with the Physically Disabled.* New York, Columbia University Press, 1962.

Crisp, A. H.: Some psychosomatic aspects of neoplasia. *British Journal of Medical Psychology, 43:*313, 1970.

Despert, J. L.: Emotional factors in some young children's colds. *Medical Clinics of North America, 29:*603, 1944.

Ellis, R. W. and Brown, G. G.: The nature of Rorschach responses from pulmonary tuberculosis patients. *Journal of Clinical Psychology, 6:*298, 1950.

Enke, H.: Regressive tendenzen des patienten im krankenhaus. *Praxis der Psychotherapie, 15:*210, 1970. (*Psychological Abstracts,* 1971, 46, No. 3648)

Fagerbaugh, S.: Mental illness and the tuberculous patient. *Nursing Outlook, 18:*38, 1970.

Finnegan, J. K., Larson, B. S., and Hoag, H. B.: The role of nicotine in the cigarette habit. *Science, 102:*94, 1945.

Frankenhaeuser, M., Myrsten, A. L., and Post, B.: Psychophysiological reactions to cigarette smoking. *Scandinavian Journal of Psychology, 11:*237, 1970.

Frith, C. D.: Smoking behavior and its relation to the smoker's immediate experience. *British Journal of Social and Clinical Psychology, 10:*73, 1971.

Haliday, J. L.: Concept of a psychosomatic affect. In Welder, A. (Ed.): *Contributions Toward Medical Psychology.* New York, Ronald Press, 1953, vol. 1.

Holmes, T. H., Hawkins, N. G., Bowerman, C. E., Clarke, E. R., and Joffe, J. R.: Psycho-social and psycho-physiologic studies of tuberculosis. *Psychosomatic Medicine, 19*:134, 1957.

James, A. G.: *Cancer Prognosis Manual.* New York, American Cancer Society, 1966.

Janis, I. L. and Hoffman, D.: Facilitating effects of daily contact between partners who make a decision to cut down on smoking. *Journal of Personality and Social Psychology, 17*:25, 1971.

Kahn, D. M.: The relationship of certain personality characteristics to recovery from tuberculosis. *Dissertation Abstracts,* 1955, 15, 1256 (Abstract).

Knapstein, J. W.: A cross-cultural study of certain personality features of tuberculous alcoholic patients. Unpublished doctoral dissertation, Texas Tech University, 1970.

Krakowski, A. J.: Psychosomatic or comprehensive? The role of the physician in the total management of the patient. *Psychosomatics, 11*:587, 1970.

Kraus, A. S., Steele, R., Ghent, W. R. and Thompson, M. G.: Predriving identification of young drivers with a high risk of accidents. *Journal of Safety Research, 2*:55, 1970.

Lechtenstein, E.: Modification of smoking behavior: Good designs—ineffective treatments. *Journal of Consulting and Clinical Psychology, 36*:163, 1971.

Marone, R. L., Merksamer, M. A., and Salzberg, P. M.: A short duration group treatment of smoking behavior by stimulus saturation. *Behavior Research and Therapy, 8*:347, 1970.

Marston, A. R., and McFall, R. M.: Comparison of behavior modification approaches to smoking reduction. *Journal of Consulting and Clinical Psychology, 36*:153, 1971.

Martinez, F. H.: A crosscultural study of the psychological aspects of alcoholic and tuberculous alcoholic patients. Unpublished doctoral dissertation, Texas Tech University, 1969.

Mausner, B.: Some comments on the failure of behavior therapy as a technique for modifying cigarette smoking. *Journal of Consulting and Clinical Psychology, 36*:167, 1971.

Mayer, L. and Isbister, C.: Report on group therapy for mothers of children with intractable asthma. *Medical Journal of Australia, 18*: 887, 1970.

Mezei, A. and Levendel, L.: Rorschachpróbával diagnosztizált testvázlatzavar prognoszlikai ertíke krónikus betegségben. *Magyar*

Pszichólogiai Szemle, 27:78, 1970. (Psychological Abstracts, 1971, 2, No. 3652)

Moran, L. J., Fairweather, G. W., Fisher, S., and Morton, R. B.: Psychological concomitants to rate of recovery from tuberculosis. *Journal of Consulting Psychology, 20*:199, 1956.

Moran, L. J., Fairweather, G. W., Morton, R. B., and McGaughram, L. S.: The use of demographic characteristics in predicting response to hospitalization for tuberculosis. *Journal of Consulting Psychology, 19*:65, 1955.

Rawls, D. J., Rawls, J. R., and Harrison, C. W.: An investigation of six-to-eleven-year-old children with allergic disorders. *Journal of Consulting and Clinical Psychology, 36*:260, 1971.

Rentsch, S.: Katamnestische untersuchung nach behandlung lungentuberkulösen mit autogen training. *Praxis der Psychotherapie, 15*: 200, 1970. (*Psychological Abstracts*, 1971, 46, No. 3656)

Richter, H. G.: Emotional disturbances following respiratory infections in children. *American Journal of Psychiatry, 100*:387, 1943.

Ruddick, B.: Colds and respiratory introjection. *International Journal of Psychoanalysis, 44*:178, 1963.

Spiegelberg, U., Betz, B., and Pietsch, B.: Zur psychosomatik allergischer krankheiten. *Nervenarzt, 41*:587, 1970. (*Psyschological Abstracts*, 1971, 46, No. 3659)

The TB Clinic. New York, National Tuberculosis and Respiratory Disease Association, 1967.

Turnbull, J. W.: Asthma conceived as a learned response. *Journal of Psychosomatic Research, 6*:59, 1962.

Vernier, C. M., Barrell, R. P., Cummings, J. W., Dickerson, J. H., and Hooper, H. E.: Psychosocial study of the patient with pulmonary tuberculosis. *Psychological Monographs*, No. 510, 1961.

Waldbatt, G. L.: Smoker's respiratory syndrome. *Annals of Internal Medicine, 39*:1026, 1953.

Wittkower, E. D. and White, K. L.: Psychophysiologic aspects of respiratory disorders. In Arieti, S. (Ed.): *American Handbook of Psychiatry.* New York, Basic Books, 1959.

Wright, L. and Jimmerson, S.: Intellectual sequelae of hemophilus influenzae meningitis. *Journal of Abnormal Psychology, 77*:181, 1971.

Chapter X

DISEASES OF THE KIDNEY

A. LEE HEWITT AND FRANK LAWLIS

MEDICAL ASPECTS

This discussion of the rehabilitation of patients with genitourinary tract pathology will follow the premise that a patient requires rehabilitation when he is afflicted with a longstanding or chronic, disabling or partially disabling problem involving any or all of the structures in this system. In order to best understand the abnormalities which can occur and appreciate the rationale for their treatment, a basic knowledge of the structures which make up the genitourinary system and their function is imperative.

Figure X-1 shows details of the upper urinary tract structures. There is one kidney on each side. The kidneys are behind all of the abdominal structures, outside the peritoneal cavity which contains the liver, the spleen, the stomach, and all of the intestines. Furthermore, the kidneys lie just inside the lowermost ribs, where they are protected from injury and are connected to the urinary bladder by means of two long muscular tubes. The muscles in these tubes propel the urine toward the bladder so that the forces of gravity are of no practical significance in this regard. These long muscular tubes, the *ureters*, pass through the bladder wall in an oblique manner so that a pseudovalve exists, which prevents regurgitation of urine back up the ureters once it has reached the bladder. The urinary bladder is simply a reservoir; the ureters and the *urethra* (which is the channel through which the urine passes from the bladder to the outside) act only as conduits so that the urine does not change character in any respect once it leaves the kidneys. In the urethra is a sphincter muscle which is under voluntary control and which is a part of a very complex system allowing the bladder to function as a reservoir and then empty in response to a voluntary stimulation in the central nervous system. This complex system allows one to urinate or not to urinate voluntarily.

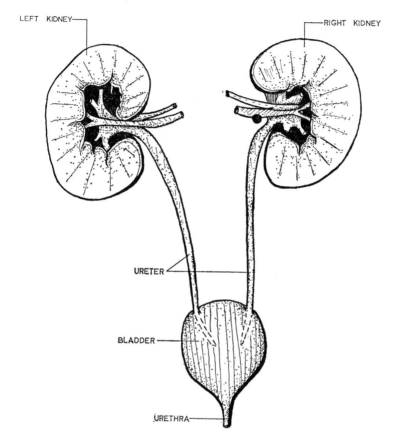

Figure X-1. Kidneys and lower urinary tract. (Illustration by Ruth Ann Rogers, Arkansas Rehabilitation Research and Training Center, University of Arkansas, Fayetteville, Arkansas.)

Figure X-2 shows the location of the sphincter in the male urethra just distal to the prostate gland. The prostate is a collar-like structure which completely surrounds the urethra at the bladder neck. It looks much like a breakfast doughnut with a hole in the middle. When the urine passes from the bladder to the outside through the urethra, it goes "through the hole in the doughnut." Contrary to popular opinion, the prostate has no vital function. Although it is under the influence of the male hormone, its secretion merely adds bulk to the seminal fluid and lubricates the lining of the urethra. Other glands do the same thing, so that except for the trouble that the prostate causes in many patients, it is of no particular significance.

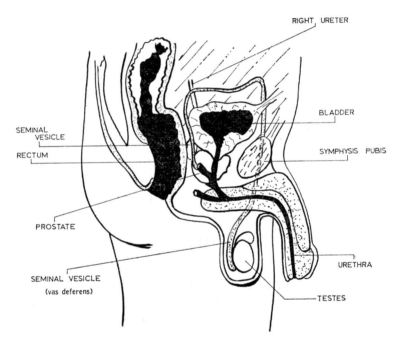

RIGHT URETER

SEMINAL VESICLE

RECTUM

BLADDER

SYMPHYSIS PUBIS

PROSTATE

SEMINAL VESICLE
(vas deferens)

URETHRA

TESTES

Figure X-2. Male pelvis. (Illustration by Ruth Ann Rogers, Arkansas Rehabilitation Research and Training Center, University of Arkansas, Fayetteville, Arkansas.)

Behind the prostate and extending up under the base of the bladder posteriorly are the two seminal vesicles which are reservoirs for the sperm that are manufactured in the testicles. The sperm mature as they pass through the long convoluted tubules of the epididymis which is located on the back side of each testicle, and then they pass up the *vas deferens* to be stored in the seminal vesicles until the time of ejaculation. At that time, the sperm are exuded into the urethra through the ejaculatory ducts which are located in the middle of the prostate.

Figure X-3 shows the relationship of the lower urinary tract structures to the genital organs in the female. The urethra is 2½ to 4½ cm in length and its outside opening is just inside the margins of the vagina. The musculature of the urethral sphincter can be found throughout the entire length of the urethra.

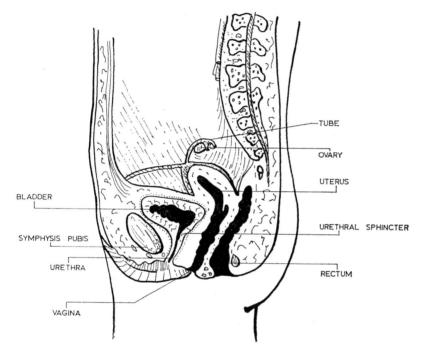

Figure X-3. Female pelvis. (Illustration by Ruth Ann Rogers, Arkansas Rehabilitation Research and Training Center, University of Arkansas, Fayetteville, Arkansas.)

Production of urine by the kidneys is a very complex mechanism involving two separate steps. The first is filtration of all components of the blood except the larger molecules, the blood cells and proteins, through *glomeruli* into a long tubular system. The second is selective reabsorption by the cells lining the tubules of certain components from this filtrate which the body needs. Any components in this filtrate which are waste products or which are in excessive amounts are not reabsorbed and make up the urine in its final form. Blood comes into the kidney (see Fig. X-4) through very large arteries, but immediately these arteries begin dividing and redividing into smaller and smaller vessels until they reach the glomeruli which are nothing more than tufts of convoluted capillaries, only one cell in thickness. The filtrate is passed through these thin-walled vessels in the glomerular tufts into the long, convoluted collecting tubules (see Fig. X-5). Together the glomerulus and the tubule make up the "nephron." In each kidney, there are over a million separate nephrons. The cells lining the tubules are "specialists," those in a certain area reabsorbing one thing (such as sugar), those in another area something else (such as sodium) from the filtrate. This reabsorbed material is then passed into small blood vessels which lie adjacent to the tubules, once again to become part of the circulating blood.

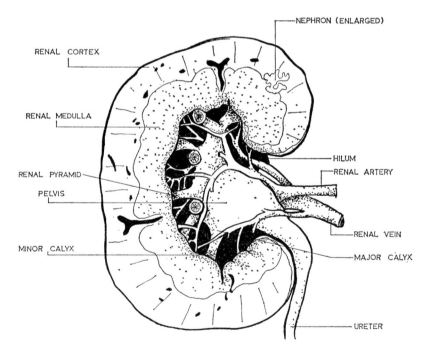

Figure X-4. Kidney in cross section. (Illustration by Ruth Ann Rogers, Arkansas Rehabilitation Research and Training Center, University of Arkansas, Fayetteville, Arkansas.)

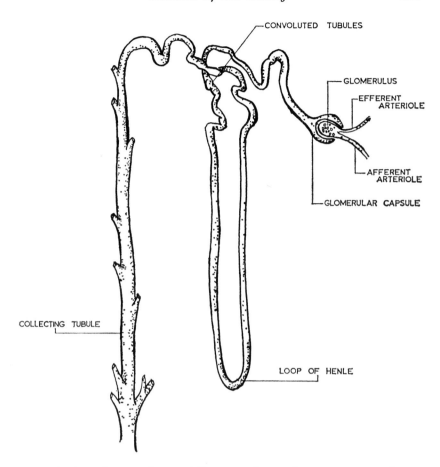

Figure X-5. Kidney nephron. (Illustration by Ruth Ann Rogers, Arkansas Rehabilitation Research and Training Center, University of Arkansas, Fayetteville, Arkansas.)

Components of the filtrate which are waste products from metabolism and certain chemicals which the body uses but which are in excessive amounts, pass on through the tubular system to emerge as the urine in its final form. We see, therefore, that the production of urine by the kidneys, its involuntary passage to the bladder where it is temporarily stored, and its voluntary expulsion to the outside represent some very complicated physiologic processes.

The mechanism of normal urination is a very complex one, and it is not clearly understood even today. Thirty years ago it was believed that bladder function represented a balance between expulsive power of the bladder muscle and blocking power of the urethral sphincter. This was based upon the fact that there are different nerves coming into these different structures—the sympathetic nerves and the parasympathetic nerves. The muscles innervated by the sympathetic nerves (the bladder) have opposite actions of those innervated by the parasympathetic nerves (the urethral sphincter). However, such a simple explanation is not the whole story. It is much more complex than this.

The sympathetic and parasympathetic nerves are automatic. In other words, the muscles which are activated by these nerves are *not* under voluntary control. The sensory and motor nerves, otherwise known as the somatic nerves, provide voluntary control to the muscles they serve. However, all of these nerves—the somatic, the sympathetic and the parasympathetic—interact in a perplexing manner to make urination partially automatic and partially voluntary. This is particularly important to know in trying to understand the problems of rehabilitation of patients who have lost voluntary bladder control.

Normally the bladder shows wavelike contractions of variable rate and amplitude but increasing in intensity and frequency as filling occurs. As the normal capacity of the bladder is reached, the strength of these contractions increases the pressure inside the bladder enough to cause the nerve endings in the bladder wall to be stimulated. This causes a message to be sent to the central nervous system where a desire to urinate registers in the conscious mind. Until the normal capacity of the urinary bladder is reached, voiding is prevented by subconscious inhibition of sensation which originates in the brain. As the bladder fills and the urge to urinate is experienced, it is possible to strengthen the inhibition voluntarily which makes it possible to refrain from urinating even though the urge is strong. With voluntary relaxation of the inhibition, the involuntary impulses are no longer overcome, and urination occurs.

It is the increase in pressure inside the bladder rather than the fluid volume in the bladder which is the chief factor in bringing about the desire to urinate. This pressure can show great variation as a result of various influences. One such influence is irritative in nature such as that which accompanies inflammation of the lining of the urinary system. In this circumstance, the nerve endings are stimulated by a much smaller amount of urine in the bladder, requiring frequent emptying. Another influence is of psychic origin, which may be demonstrated by the marked frequency of urination noted by people under a situation of stress—final exams, getting married, etc. Even peripheral reflex stimuli, as running water or exposure to the cold, can increase the pressure inside the bladder to cause the desire to urinate before the normal amount of urine is present which would ordinarily be required to create such a stimulation.

NEUROMUSCULAR UROPATHY

Patients with neuromuscular uropathy (which means interference with the normal voiding mechanism) constitute the greatest number of patients who require rehabilitation. Abnormalities such as this can be most serious frequently resulting in symptomatology, marked disability, and death. Paraplegics make up the majority of cases with abnormalities such as these. Such patients are frequently young, they have the normal enthusiasm of youth, and they can be most successfully rehabilitated with proper supervision. Of course, paraplegics have other rehabilitation problems too, but among the most serious are those in the genitourinary system.

Classifications of the neuromuscular disorders in the urinary system are by no means simple, and the authorities are not always in agreement. In general, however, it may be said that the lesions responsible for these problems are congenital, acquired, or unknown. The acquired group make up the largest number of cases, and of these, the lesions associated with physical trauma constitute the largest single group of patients with whom rehabilitation counselors will be associated. The physical trauma which is most common is partial or complete transection of the spinal cord, resulting in paralysis of all structures whose nerve supply comes off the spinal cord below the level of injury.

There is a predictable course of events which follows trauma to the spinal cord insofar as the urinary bladder is concerned. The *first* thing which occurs is a state of spinal shock. Beginning immediately, there is complete inability to empty the bladder. The bladder is without tone and fails to respond to any type of stimulation. This period of spinal shock lasts from one to several days. The only treatment is catheter drainage, without which death would result from urinary sepsis. It is important to insert the catheter using sterile technique and to maintain asepsis at all times to avoid urinary infection. The urinary tract is very susceptible to infection under these circumstances, and careful attention to the catheter with irrigations, proper drainage systems, and antibiotic therapy make up a vital part of the treatment.

The *second* phase of bladder reaction following spinal cord injury is that of the development of an autonomous bladder. This begins sometime during the first year after injury, and it begins with feeble contractions of the entire bladder muscle. There is no stable reflex or activity at this time, and without the aid of a catheter, the urine merely dribbles out constantly. The bladder remains full or almost full most of the time. Catheter drainage or drainage through a tube inserted into the bladder through an abdominal incision is necessary during this phase of recovery also.

In male patients, suprapubic drainage is preferable to a drainage through a retained urethral catheter if an artificial appliance of this nature is necessary for a long period of time. The reason for this is that the urethra does not tolerate a foreign body such as a catheter over a long period very well. Strictures, abscesses, etc. are frequently seen in cases treated with long-term urethral catheter drainage. However, long-term urethral catheter drainage is better tolerated in the female than in the male.

The *final* stage of recovery of the bladder following serious spinal cord injury is the development of an automatic bladder. This is characterized by periodic involuntary reflex urination in which the bladder musculature suddenly has a strong contraction, at which time it empties completely or almost completely. This mass reflex can be triggered frequently by a pinprick, tapping of the abdomen, sudden motion by the patient, etc. Such a mass reflex is often predictable, and the patient has time to "get ready" before the bladder actually empties.

As time goes on, the bladder gets stronger and thicker, and sometimes obstruction occurs at the bladder neck. This interferes with the efficient emptying which an automatic bladder would normally provide, and removal of the obstructing tissue using an instrument through the urethra is sometimes necessary.

In some cases, no effort at conservative treatment is successful in reestablishing any semblance of normal urination, and some type of permanent urinary diversion becomes necessary. Previously it was mentioned that catheter drainage through the urethra is essential during the early phases of recovery following injury to the spinal cord, but it was also mentioned that catheter drainage of this type is not suitable for long-term use, especially in the male patient. For permanent urinary diversion, a tube inserted into the bladder through an abdominal incision is likewise unsatisfactory, because any foreign body in the urinary bladder over a long period of time, even though it might be changed frequently, ultimately results in secondary infection, stone formation, etc. It becomes necessary, therefore, to institute a type of urinary diversion which does not involve any foreign body inside the urinary system.

The most commonly used and most successful method of permanent urinary diversion is the creation of a conduit to carry the urine from the ureters to the skin in a constant flow. Surgery is performed in which a short piece of intestine is isolated from the rest of the bowel and into which the ureters are attached. This intestinal conduit is then connected to the skin through the abdominal wall. Satisfactory devices are available which glue on to the skin to catch the urine. Such devices are completely water-tight, odor-proof, and need to be changed only about once a week. Certain patients other than those who have had spinal cord damage also require permanent urinary diversion, and this technique has worked out most satisfactorily in all types of cases. Such patients are frequently able to go swimming, ride horses, etc., without difficulty.

In addition to the measures necessary to reestablish some type of urinary control in paraplegics, it is of great importance that attention be given to the avoidance of secondary problems in the genitourinary system that are frequently caused by the primary problem of bladder dysfunction. Such secondary problems as infection, stone formation, etc., often cause increased morbidity and are frequently responsible for early death in patients who otherwise could have been rehabilitated. The overall prospect of fairly good health in these paraplegics has markedly improved in the past few years by the maintenance of good general condition, prevention of constipation, development of scientific diets using vitamins, antibiotics, etc., when necessary. Insofar as the genitourinary tract is concerned, however, the two most important considerations in paraplegics are (a) the prevention, control, or cure of infection and (b) the maintenance of free urinary drainage.

BRIGHT'S DISEASE OR GLOMERULONEPHRITIS

Whereas a good bit of time has been spent so far in discussing the problems of neuromuscular uropathy because a great percentage of patients who have genitourinary tract problems requiring rehabilitation fall in this category, there are other patients with other problems who need rehabilitation also. Such a problem is chronic glomerulonephritis. This is otherwise known as *Bright's* disease. This is a condition which begins as an acute infection in some area of the body away from the urinary system such as the throat, intestine, etc. The toxins from the bacteria causing this acute infection damage the kidney in such a way as to interfere with the normal filtration and selective reabsorption functions. The damage is originally acute and is usually characterized by generalized swelling, gross bleeding into the urine, and high blood pressure. However, the serious part of the disease is later on, after the acute phase has passed, when a gradually progressive deterioration of the kidney occurs. In such cases, a cure is frequently impossible. It is possible, however, to institute a therapeutic regimen in many of these cases so that the patient is able to carry on a fairly normal schedule without endangering his health.

In the discussion earlier, it was pointed out that part of the kidney's function is to get rid of waste products which are found in the blood and which are the result of the normal breakdown products from use of energy. The more physical activity, the more energy is expended, and the more waste products result which have to be excreted. In cases of advanced kidney diseases such as glomerulonephritis, the kidneys must be spared any excess work. It is impossible to put the kidneys in a plaster cast, such as is done with a broken bone. It is not possible to put the kidneys at rest by injecting them with air such as is done in certain chronic lung diseases. In fact the only way to put the kidneys at rest so that they can utilize this opportunity to gain strength or at least keep from getting weaker is to limit the work they have to do by limiting the amount of waste material they have to excrete. Therefore, to place the patient at relative rest in regard to physical activity is an important part of the treatment program. Certain foods such as proteins are metabolized in such a way that the breakdown products must be excreted by the kidneys. Kidneys involved in severe disease processes like this are also unable to handle other chemicals otherwise handled normally. Measures to limit the intake of foods high in these chemicals become important. Therefore dietary control is necessary.

In advanced cases in which the waste products build up in the blood because the kidneys are unable to get rid of them, some type of artificial removal of these waste products becomes necessary. Artificial kidneys have been developed which are of great value in this regard. The patient's blood is introduced into a long tubing which is then immersed in a special solution which draws the waste products out of the blood. The blood is then reintroduced into the patient's system. Such a procedure is very time consuming, expensive, and difficult for the patient to tolerate. Another means of ridding the body of waste products is by peritoneal dialysis which is performed by introducing a tubing into the abdominal cavity through a small incision. A special solution is introduced through this tube which bathes the intestines and draws waste products out of the tissues. Another tubing carries this solution with the waste products to the outside. Recent engineering has developed such apparatuses for home use which makes these procedures much more economical for the patient.

ORGAN TRANSPLANT

Intensive investigation into the feasibility of transplantation of organs from one individual to another has been of great interest recently. In the same manner and for the same reasons that skin grafts from one individual to another are unsuccessful, except in the case of identical twins, transplantation of whole organs has been far from completely successful. An adverse immunological response is the reason. Identical twins are the only patients in whom outstanding transplantation success has been experienced. In some cases, the immunological similarities of brothers and sisters, mothers and offspring, etc., are such that prolonged success is experienced following transplantation involving such closely related people. However, scarcely more than a year or two of survival can be expected in most cases. Transplantation of organs from one unrelated person to another has been even less successful. It is hoped, however, that continued intensive research will ultimately solve the various problems which exist and therefore make such transplantations of organs a therapeutic triumph in cases of advanced renal disease.

OTHER RENAL DISEASES

Advanced renal disease of other types is also a problem of rehabilitation. Such problems, however, fall into essentially the same rehabilitation category as chronic glomerulonephritis. Characteristic lesions are chronic pyelonephritis, which is an infection of the functioning tissue of the kidney; congenital polycystic disease (a hereditary disease in which the functioning tissue is replaced by nonfunctioning cysts); and nephrosclerosis (which is hardening of the arteries of the small blood vessels of the kidney associated with high blood pressure); generalized arteriosclerosis, diabetes, etc.

Another problem requiring a good deal of rehabilitation because of its chronicity is recurrent *kidney stone* formation. Whereas there are many contributing factors in problems of this sort, the overall "cause" of kidney stones remains essentially unknown. The problem of stasis is an important one. This is a condition where the urine is impeded in its passage from the kidneys to the outside by some obstruction. Such a problem might be neuromuscular dysfunction of the lower urinary tract structures seen in paraplegics as was discussed previously. And, in fact, the formation of kidney stones repeatedly is a very real problem in such patients. Other patients who have to be in bed for a long period of time such as those with severe bone fractures, severe heart disease, etc., frequently have the problem of urinary stasis due to inactivity, with ultimate kidney stone formation. Another frequent contributing factor in the formation of kidney stones is persistent infection somewhere in the urinary tract. Any type of foreign body such as purulent material, dead tissue, etc., can serve as a center around which a stone might develop. The urine is characteristically full of crystals and other components which can precipitate or "settle out" to cling around such an area. These solid urinary constituents then can grow as a stalagmite grows by having one layer after another of crystals deposited on it. Ultimately it gets large enough to be considered a stone. Here again we see the relationship to the paraplegic who frequently has persisting urinary tract infections, and we once more can see the importance of controlling infections in such patients.

There are some instances of familial tendencies to stone formation. Such families may not have a single member who escapes a kidney stone attack at some time or another during his life time. Certain races have great predilection to the formation of kidney stones. For example, the Negro race has fewer kidney stones than the Caucasian race.

Certain areas of the world are considered kidney stone belts. It is believed that the food and water which are consumed in those areas are largely responsible. Climate plays an important role in some cases. Certain chemical imbalances in metabolism are related to the formation of kidney stones. Such instances are the kidney stones associated with gout and with overactivity of the parathyroid glands. However, the great majority of patients who have kidney stones have them for reasons which are largely unknown.

Once a kidney stone has been retrieved, it is frequently possible to place a patient on some type of medical and/or dietary regimen which will be successful in preventing further stone formation. This is possible by determining the exact chemical composition of the kidney stones and by prescribing medications and diet accordingly. Large fluid intake is an important adjunct in the treatment of recurring kidney stones. The urine is much like a glass of iced tea, for it can become a supersaturated solution just as a glass of iced tea can if too much sugar is added. When one teaspoonful of sugar is added to a glass of tea, it all dissolves. A second spoonful only partially dissolves, whereas the third spoonful settles to the bottom almost *in toto*. In the case of the urine when a small urinary output is present, the kidneys are placing too many chemicals for them all to remain in solution. Consequently, some of them precipitate out into solid form. These solids can become kidney stones. If, on the other hand, there is a large fluid intake, the resulting large urine output in its dilute form is such that all of the urinary constituents can remain in solution. To keep the urine dilute enough, drinking a gallon of water a day is recommended.

CONGENITAL ANOMALIES OF THE URINARY TRACT

There are seven times more congenital anomalies in the urinary tract than in any other single system in the body. This is probably due to the complicated embryological development of this system. To be sure, most of these abnormalities are minor and cause no problems. However, there are many which are significant and which require specific treatment if the patient is to have a relatively normal existence. There are many possible abnormalities ranging from peculiar blood supplies, abnormalities in position of the kidneys, reduplication or "double" kidneys and ureters, and obstructions anywhere along the urinary canal system. There is such a thing as exstrophy of the urinary bladder in which the bladder actually opens on to the abdomen rather than through the urethra. There is such a thing as an extopic opening of an extra ureter whereby the bladder is completely bypassed, with the ureter draining into the vagina in female patients. There are other very peculiar anomalies, all of which require definitive treatment, usually surgical, in order that the patient not only be healthy but be acceptable socially.

PSYCHOLOGICAL AND REHABILITATION ASPECTS OF GENITOURINARY TRACT DISABILITY

The phrase "to be accepted socially" is of particular importance from a psychological standpoint, since patients who are continually wet with urine are unacceptable socially even though there is no serious disease process present. The problem of being "wet all of the time" as well as the odor which accompanies this condition necessitates definitive treatment if the patient is to be rehabilitated. An example is a child with congenital meningocele. This is a condition which is characterized by an abnormality of the spinal cord which results in paralysis of the lower extremities and inability to control the bowels and kidneys. Such a child is perfectly content and gets along very well until it comes time for him to attend school. Other children will tolerate a child in a wheelchair but will not tolerate his persistent uriniferous odor. He therefore might suffer irreparable psychologic damage unless something is done to correct this condition.

In such a case, the creation of a conduit taking the urine from the ureters to the skin by means of a small piece of intestine as was described previously is a logical solution. The bladder becomes atrophic and causes no trouble, the urine is collected in a receptacle which is waterproof and odorless, the child becomes socially acceptable, and further damage to the urinary system is avoided. The bowels are controlled with a single enema every day, and the child manages satisfactorily from his wheelchair.

Adrenogenital Syndrome

In congenital adrenogenital syndrome there is hyperplasia of a portion of the adrenal glands. These glands are located above the

kidneys and exert a profound influence over the entire physiological function of the body. In addition to many other functions,
the adrenals produce a certain amount of hormones, both male
and female. When the portion of the adrenals which produces
one of these hormones becomes hyperplastic, an unusual amount
of hormone is produced which sometimes conflicts with the normal
hormone-producing program of either the male or the female.
For example, should an individual with normal female structures
be subjected to an adrenal change which causes an unusual amount
of male hormone to be produced, dire results are noted. When
such things occur in growing children, the secondary sex characteristics are frequently altered from normal. It is sometimes
difficult to tell whether the child is male or female. Problems like
this are psychologically devastating if they are allowed to persist,
and rehabilitation must be begun early if such individuals are to
lead a normal life. Definitive treatment involves removal of the
hyperplastic adrenal tissue and corrective plastic surgery to the
external genitalia if necessary.

Chronic Urethritis

The psychological aspects of problems referable to the genitourinary tract are of considerable importance because the organs
involved in this system are so frequently directly related to
psychosomatic problems and even actual psychic disturbances.
In many cases there is a significant overlap of symptoms which
are actually based on pathologic changes and those which are
entirely psychic in origin. In females, for example, there is a
large percentage of patients of all ages who have a degree of
chronic urethritis. Some of these patients complain bitterly of
symptoms referable to this condition, while others have no symptoms whatever. It becomes of great importance, therefore, to delve
into the problem carefully so that a psychological problem cannot
be made worse by treating a pathological problem which is actually of no clinical significance. A physician treating patients with
problems of this sort must be a psychologist as well as a surgeon,
internist, therapist, etc.

Enuresis

A very common problem which has a psychological cause in the great majority of cases is *enuresis*, which means nocturnal incontinence. This usually occurs in children, but it sometimes persists into adulthood. Although occasionally there is some actual physical cause for this condition, it usually means that the child has not formed an emotional bond with his mother of sufficient strength to make him want to control his urination adequately. In other words, if there is an insufficient desire on the part of the child to please his mother by staying dry, he concerns himself only with his own comfort and empties his bladder at the slighest provocation. Either the child or mother or both can be at fault. The mother must have qualities of leadership in her personality if she is to guide her child into successful bladder control. She must expect the child to control his urine, show him that she expects this, and then reward him when he is successful. Adequate urinary control normally occurs around the age of two to three years. Beyond that age, the child can be considered to have a psychological problem if enuresis persists.

It is improper to advise parents that the child will "outgrow" this problem. The reason is that even though the enuresis stops, the basic problem of psychological insecurity persists and manifests itself in more serious ways as the child grows older. Also, the years of bedwetting, shame, embarrassing situations, and painful scenes often cause a worsening of the basic psychological problem.

Sexual functions are almost always impaired in the presence of severe psychological instability. In only very rare cases are any actual pathologic problems found in the sex organs. For this reason, further consideration of this subject as well as all psychological implications related to this discussion will be left to the psychologist.

Impact of Treatment

A very important aspect in the process of dialysis is considered to be the psychological emphasis. The general importance of psychological factors involved in dialysis treatment was emphasized by Gombos, Lee, and Harton (1964, p. 462).

> . . . psychological factors were clearly recognized as important considerations in the treatment program. Notwithstanding its life-prolonging promise, hemodialysis was felt to be an obviously stressful affair. Immediately apparent were potential stresses of disrupted work pattern, diminished income and generally altered life activities. It was agreed that anxiety was a more subtle but important factor surrounding treatment by dialysis. The possibility arose that an individual might not be able to tolerate the degree of dependency necessitated by the program. It is clear that information concerning potential emotional reactions of a prospective patient were of high practical interest in the selection of candidates for treatment.

This article by Gombos, Lee, and Harton (1964) starts out by referring to the possible suicide of one of the patients of dialysis who died shortly after initiation of intermittent dialysis. The authors report that the patient pulled his arteriovenous shunt apart and exsanguinated.

In a study of nine patients by Shea, Bogden, Freeman, and Schreiner (1965) reported rather severe psychological problems were found. For example, the authors state (p. 562): "As a result, the additional stress of hemodialysis seemed to precipitate schizophrenia-like episodes in two patients, a psychotic depressive reaction in one patient, and a number of severe neurotic reactions in all but one of the other patients."

Shea *et al.* (pp. 562-563) concluded that the reaction to intermittent dialysis programs has a serious psychological implication.

> Reactions have been divided into those occurring before dialysis, consisting mainly of irritability, apprehension and insomnia; those occurring during dialysis, namely anxiety while being connected to or disconnected from the dialyzer, restlessness, irritability and anxiety and often depression when technical difficulties arise; and those occurring after dialysis, especially relief that the procedure is over. The patient's attitude toward the cannula, the dialyzer, the diet, and the other patients is also important. The severe reactions that can occur and the inability to compensate have impressed us with the necessity to develop a more intensive program of psychotherapy for patients on the chronic dialysis program.

Wright, Sand, and Livingston (1966) observed that on MMPI profiles, the depression score was considerably elevated in this group of patients. The authors made reference to a need for ". . . a stable doctor-patient relationship, a meaningful goal in life for a patient, and the meaning of the symptom or disability to the patient."

Most of the studies stress the importance of evaluation of patients' psychological states in order to assess their potential for adaptation to a dialysis program. These studies indicate that psychological problems can be triggered by the dialysis program and are apparent within the context of the treatment procedures. As already indicated in the Gombos study (1964), one of the five patients observed may have committed suicide. No serious psychological complications were reported in the remaining four patients in Gombos' series. However, there were other problems expressed in the form of anxiety, depression, agitation, noncooperation, and withdrawal.

Furthermore, there are references to possible changes in body image, which are disturbing to the patients but usually denied. Nevertheless, there is some projective test evidence for the existence of body-image disturbances. The importance of the "significant other" or family members in the treatment program is stressed. It is suggested that group meetings or group therapy with the spouses of the dialysis patients be utilized to help deal with the anxieties and readjustments in relation to the possible unrealistic expectations of all involved parties. It is evident that the interpersonal relations of the patient with his outside world, especially his family, are of great importance.

In dealing with the patient with renal disease, it is very important to remember the essentials of rehabilitation. The patient is in need of help, but the cluster of personality dynamics causes the patient to react to his needs in a multitude of directions. Because of the nature of renal disease, it is often observed that the patient feels extremely guilty for his condition. It is crucial that an empathic understanding be communicated to the patient in order that rehabilitation be achieved to the fullest extent.

REFERENCES

Gombos, E., Lee, T. H., and Harton, M. R.: One year's experience on intermittent dialysis program. *Annals of Internal Medicine, 62:*462, 1964.

Shea, E. J., Bogden, D. F., Freeman, R., and Schreiner, B.: Hemodialysis for chronic renal failures IV, psychological considerations. *Annals of Internal Medicine, 62:*558, 1967.

Wright, R. G., Sand, P., and Livingston, G.: Psychological stress during hemodialysis for chronic renal failure. *Annals of Internal Medicine, 63:*611, 1966.

Chapter XI

THE GASTROINTESTINAL SYSTEM

Stanley Holgate and James R. Matthews

The vocational rehabilitation counselor is in a position which brings him in contact with the field of medicine on a daily basis. Hence, the rehabilitation counselor, in order to perform proficiently, should attain a basic understanding and knowledge of the field of medicine. The purpose of this knowledge is to allow him to communicate effectively with medical practitioners. The counselor will need to be able to understand and evaluate medical reports, understand the physical limitations of the client after debilitation, recognize the complications involved in the specified treatments, and construct a rehabilitation plan based upon the information he is given by the medical staff.

The primary purpose of this chapter is to provide the student of vocational rehabilitation with a basic knowledge of some of the disorders of the gastrointestinal system which are debilitating in nature and the vocational implications which are involved.

BASIC ANATOMY AND FUNCTIONS OF THE

DIGESTIVE SYSTEM

The structures and functions of the digestive system can best be described by following the passage of food through the system. Food taken in the mouth is reduced physically by the teeth, moistened, and subjected to its first chemical breakdown by the secretions of the salivary glands. The tongue aids in moving the food into the pharynx where it mixes with air from the nose. The food and air cross paths in the pharyngeal chiasma, and the food passes then into the esophagus which by peristaltic action moves the food on down to the stomach. Two sphincters, one at each end of the esophagus, prevent the food from reversing its path. Peristaltic action in the esophagus is accomplished by alternate contraction and relaxation of both circular and longitudinal smooth muscles.

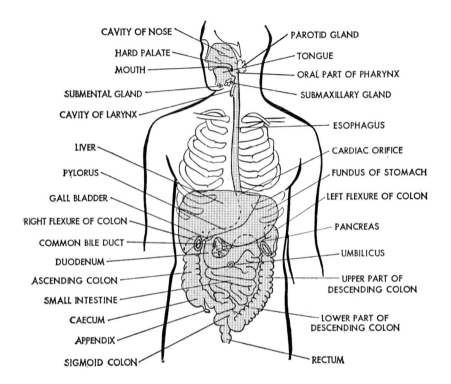

Figure XI-1. The digestive system. (Courtesy of U. S. Department of Health, Education, and Welfare. *Descriptions of Common Impairments.* Washington, D.C., U. S. Govt. Printing Office, 1959.)

Food then passes into the stomach, a J-shaped structure, lying in the upper left portion of the abdomen. The stomach is a collapsible sac consisting of the fundus, the body or corpus, the pyloric antrum, the canal of the pylorus, and the pyloric sphincter through which the food passes to the duodenum. After the food enters the stomach from the esophagus via the cardiac orifice, it is reduced to a semiliquid consistency, and the process of digestion is begun as the food is changed chemically through the action of hydrochloric acid and the enzyme pepsin. These two chemicals are secreted by special cells in the stomach wall. Muscular contractions of the stomach wall aid the chemical process by grinding and crushing the food. This process is completed in approximately four hours, and the liquefied and partially digested food is passed into the duodenum.

The duodenum comprises the first portion of the small intestine, a structure which is approximately 23 feet long. The small intestine is comprised of two portions in addition to the duodenum. Comprising the middle portion is the jejunum, and comprising the last or distal portion is the ileum. Stomach contents enter the small intestine in an acidic state and are neutralized by intestinal secretions which complete the necessary chemical process of preparing the food for absorption into the walls of the small intestine. The nutrients from the food are absorbed into the walls of the small intestine and whatever food remains is passed on to the large intestine or colon via the ileocecal valve which prevents the return of the food to the small intestine.

In the large intestine, the food wastes are converted from liquid into a semisolid state and moved on to the rectum for elimination through the anal sphincter. Passing through the ileocecal sphincter, the food enters into the cecum from which it passes up the ascending colon, across the transverse colon, down the descending colon, through the sigmoid or S-shaped colon and into the rectum. As the waste material moves along these parts of the large intestine, the liquid is absorbed by the blood vessels lining the walls of the large intestine, and what remains is called fecal matter. The fecal matter is eliminated through the anal sphincter.

In addition to the digestive system proper, as described above, there are four accessory organs whose basic anatomy and functions should be considered. The first of these organs are the salivary glands. There are three pairs of salivary glands: the parotid, sublingual, and submaxillary. Salivary glands secrete saliva which consists of 95 percent water and 5 percent mucin, a lubricant, and ptyalin, a digestive enzyme.

The second accessory organ to be discussed is the pancreas, which is located posterior to the stomach. It secretes three digestive enzymes—trypsin, amylase, and lipase—which serve to break down starch into sugar, fats into glycerine and fatty acids, and proteins into peptones and amino acids. The enzymes reach the digestive tract via the pancreatic ducts and the common bile duct. In addition to these enzymes which are secreted through a duct, the pancreas also produces insulin which is secreted directly into the bloodstream. Insulin is needed by the body to aid in the storage of glycogen, an animal starch, in the liver, muscles, and skin, to facilitate the combustion of glucose, which is the chief source of energy for the tissue cells, and to support the utilization of protein and fat. The scarcity of, or lack of, insulin in the system will lead to a condition known as diabetes mellitus, which will be discussed thoroughly in a later section.

Located in the upper right side of the abdominal cavity, just beneath the diaphragm, is the liver, the third accessory digestive organ to be discussed. It is divided into lobes and is suffused with blood. One function of the liver is the secretion of bile for the purpose of fat digested food. Bile is conveyed from the liver via the hepatic ducts and then by way of the common bile duct to the duodenum. Additional biochemical functions of the liver are the following: synthesis of protein, manufacture of fibrinogen and vitamin A, removal of toxic substances from the blood, and destruction of red blood cells for the conservation of hemoglobin.

Finally is the gallbladder, which is located beneath the right lobe of the liver. It is not a manufacturing organ but a storage organ for bile until the bile is needed for the digestive process. After bile is produced by the liver, it flows through the hepatic ducts and the cystic ducts where it is stored until needed. The bile flows from the gallbladder into the common bile duct and then into the duodenum. When bile incurs an obstruction in the common bile duct, it backs up into the bloodstream and is evidenced by the characteristic yellow color commonly found in jaundiced patients.

SYMPTOMATOLOGY

Perhaps all that is necessary for the rehabilitation counselor to know is that there exist such symptoms as pain, dysphagia (difficult swallowing), indigestion, vomiting, constipation, diarrhea, weight loss, weakness, anemia, disagreeable taste, coated and sore tongue, bad breath, hunger disturbances, pyrosis, aerophagia, headaches, vertigo, and others in disorders of the gastrointestinal tract and accessory organs. However, a limited knowledge of some of these symptoms is necessary for him to better understand the discomfort and difficulties which his client faces.

Pain

Historically pain was viewed as an emotion opposite that of pleasure, but with the technological advancements made in the field of science, it is now viewed as an experience which comprises not only the perception of noxious stimulus but also the resultant secondary physiological and psychological reactions to the stimulus and their consequences. Pain is beneficent in the fact that it provides the organism with a warning system which causes an individual to seek the aid of a physician. Pain, however, may exceed its protective value and become deleterious to the organism. A knowledge of pain localization seems to be appropriate for the rehabilitation counselor to consider. Pain located in the region of the umbilicus is indicative of functional or organic disturbances of the small bowel somewhere between the duodenojejunal junction and the ileocecal valve. Upper right quadrant abdominal pain is primarily suggestive of diseases of the liver, gallbladder, or bile passages. Another source of pain in the upper right quadrant is irritation of the peritoneum in that region. However, irritation of the peritoneum is usually accompanied by tenderness and muscle guarding, or rigidity of the overlying abdominal wall. Regarding pain in the upper left quadrant of the abdomen, the rehabilitation counselor should note that a pressure type of pain in this region is frequently reported by patients in whom there is no evidence of organic disease. Pain in this region should not be neglected, however, because it could be indicative of heart disease, a hiatus hernia, or a gas pocket in the upper loculus of the stomach.

In the lower left quadrant, pain arises from such causes as spastic colon, colonic redundancies, organic colotides, constipation, and various types of obstruction to the distal colon. Pain in the lower right quadrant of the abdomen is indicative of disease in the appendix, terminal ileum, or cecum of the colon. Back pain is often indicative of disease in any portion of the alimentary canal.

Pain localized in the midline of the body which is the result of disturbed alimentary function is generally regarded as true visceral or splanchnic pain. Alimentary disturbances which usually evidence themselves in the midline of the body are those such as peptic ulcer, obstructive appendicitis, cholecystitis, the colic pain of functional spasm, and mild inflammatory lesions of the small intestine.

To be sure, only a few of the pain symptoms have been described here. It is hoped, however, that it is sufficient coverage to bring to the attention of the rehabilitation counselor the numerous disturbances which are indicated by the presence of pain. Unfortunately some disturbances are located in what may be referred to as silent areas, and subjective discomfort does not arise until the disease is far advanced. Examples would include tumors of the body of the stomach located some distance from the pylorus or cardia; a gastric ulcer, similarly located; lesions of the wider right colon; and disease of the liver not involving the capsule of the organ.

While most pain is the result of an organic gastrointestinal disturbance, some pain is the result of a psychological disorder and is called "psychogenic pain." Psychogenic pain cannot be accounted for by peripheral stimulus as in the case of the phantom limb pain. The rehabilitation counselor, as well as the physician, must be alert to psychogenic pain, especially as it is used as an escape mechanism to release the patient from a disagreeable duty. Although pain is not specific to any psychological disorder, it is commonly demonstrated in the depressive and anxiety states, psychoneurosis, psychopathic drug addiction, toxic psychosis, and delirium. Psychogenic pain has its obvious implications in vocational rehabilitation, such as the client who has by all medical standards recovered from a gastrointestinal disturbance, such as an indirect inguinal hernia, and yet persists in not returning to his job because he "hurts" and is convinced that the hernia has not healed.

Dysphagia

Pain, although it may be the most common symptom which suggests a disturbance in the gastrointestinal tract, is not the only symptom of value in aiding the physician in making a diagnosis. Actually, pain has more value in the fact that it causes the patient to seek medical assistance. Many other symptoms aid the physician in making his diagnosis or in leading him to employ diagnostic equipment such as gastroscopy. One such symptom is dysphagia or difficult swallowing. It is not to be confused with globus hystericus, a feeling that something is lodged in the throat, or with the emotional reaction of a neurotic who says he cannot swallow. Dysphagia occurs only during attempts at swallowing and during or within seconds after the act of swallowing, in any of the three stages of swallowing: (a) moving the food from the mouth into the pharynx, (b) transportation of food through the pharynx, and (c) moving the food through the esophagus. Any lesion of the mouth or tongue may produce dysphagia. The most common cause is probably acute pharyngitis with such diseases as scarlet fever, diphtheria, mumps, peritonsillitis, carcinoma or syphilis scleroderma, and others.

Vomiting

Vomiting, or emesis, the forceful expulsion of gastrointestinal contents through the mouth, may be associated with all of the organic diseases of the alimentary tract and its appendages, as well as organic diseases of almost every organ in the body, disorders of the automonic nervous system, and functional and psychogenic disturbances. Hypersalivation, nausea, and retching (labored rhythmic activity of the respiratory musculature) usually precede the act of vomiting. Clinically, the time of onset is often significant. A toxic cause is indicated in the case of vomiting in the early morning before breakfast. Such toxic causes include uremia and pregnancy. Also, chronic gastritis resulting from an alcoholic condition or hypersensitivity may give rise to early morning empty-stomach vomiting. Usually, vomiting which occurs soon after eating is of functional origin, although the possibility of an organic stomach disease must be eliminated. Vomiting of large amounts of well-digested food suggests the presence of pyloric obstruction. Migraine is indicated by periodic vomiting preceded by hemicranial headaches. Unlike vomiting caused by an alimentary disorder and preceded by nausea, vomiting produced by a central nervous system lesion, such as a brain tumor, is not normally preceded by nausea. Functional vomiting is more commonly found in women and as a rule occurs as the result of some psychic trauma. Furthermore, the vomiting act is infrequently associated with retching or preceded by nausea, and rarely are all of the contents of the stomach evacuated.

Oral Cavity Symptoms

Among the oral cavity symptoms of a gastrointestinal disturbance would be disagreeable taste, coated tongue, sore tongue, and bad breath. In the case of disagreeable taste, a first step is to eliminate local causes such as chronic nasal conditions, pyorrhea alveolaris, chronic gingivitis, and poorly fitting dentures. Other possible causes to be eliminated are lower esophageal obstruction, chronic bronchitis, bronchiectasis, and diabetes. Bitter taste may be attributed to chronic gallbladder disease or even cholecystectomy. In functional cases, constant bitter taste is often the result of neurosis, usually of a depressive nature. A coated tongue may or may not reflect the condition of the gastric mucosa. A sore tongue in association with atrophy of the lingual papillae in conjunction with achlorhydria may be symptomatic of pernicious anemia, macrocytic tropical anemia, pellagra, and sprue. Bad breath or halitosis is most commonly associated with disturbances in the nose, throat, or lungs. However, it may also be indicative of chronic colon stasis and obstructing lesions to the esophagus, stomach, and upper small intestine (duodenum). Bad breath may also be of functional etiology in cases involving neurotics.

Hunger Disturbances

Hunger disturbances as symptomatic of gastrointestinal disorders include the following: anorexia, anorexia nervosa, hyperorexia, bulimia, acoria, and parorexia. Anorexia or the loss of desire to eat may be indicative of carcinoma of the stomach, advanced renal disease, and chronic gastritis. Anorexia nervosa is the term applied to anorexia when it is the predominant manifestation in a neurotic or psychotic personality. Sitiophobia is the fear of eating arising from painful sensations which occur after eating. Although sitiophobia more commonly results from anxiety, it may also stem from an organic disease in the upper gastrointestinal tract which causes distress after the ingestion of food. One who overconsumes may be suffering from hyperorexia—excessive appetite. Hyperorexia can be either functional or organic in origin. In the latter case, it is usually associated with parasitic infestation, diabetes, chronic pancreatic insufficiency, sprue, hyperthyroidism, gastrointestinal fistulas, and certain other hypermetabolic conditions. Bulimia is a rare symptom associated with psychoneurotics and is an abnormal return of the hunger sensations soon after eating. Acoria is the complete absence of satiety and is primarily functional in origin, although it may occur as the result of a brain tumor. Parorexia, an appetite for unusual foods, is also primarily functional but may be associated with a metabolic derangement or electrolyte imbalance.

Pyrosis

Pyrosis or heartburn is a sensation of warmth, burning or heat generally located behind the lower sternum or high in the epigastrium. Heartburn may be functional (the most common), organic, or psychogenic in origin. Functional pyrosis is many times found at the cardioesophageal junction as a result of faulty eating habits, nervous tension, fatigue, and certain foods. When pyrosis occurs as a result of an organic disturbance, the most frequent incidence is in the case of the hiatal hernia. Other organic causes would include pyloric or duodenal ulcers, esophagitis with or without the presence of a peptic ulcer, and antral spasm. Psychogenically, heartburn may constitute a monosymptomatic neurosis in which case the heartburn occurs in the absence of all physiologic activities.

Aerophagia

Syndromes resulting from aerophagia, air swallowing, are the most common to be encountered in gastroenterology. Aerophagia has several possible causes, among which are the following: bad habit, excessive swallowing of saliva and hence air, underlying nervous disturbance, habitually induced belching, and faulty habits of hygiene. The diagnosis of aerophagic syndromes (esophageal belching, magenblase syndrome resulting from a large air bubble in the stomach, splenic flexure syndrome, and intestinal flatulence) requires primary consideration of heart disease, hiatus hernia, carcinoma of the stomach or pancreas, peptic ulcer disease, pyloric obstruction, biliary tract disorders, intestinal obstruction, and the functional enterocolonopathies.

Headaches

Headaches are often considered by patients to be symptomatic of gastrointestinal disorders, but alimentary tract disease *per se* is not regarded as a common cause of headaches. Headaches which occur in conjunction with gastrointestinal disorders are probably the result of tension produced in the scalp and neck muscles. The "morning-after" headache which is commonly associated with nausea, retching, and chronic gastritis is more attributable to cerebral edema and stretching of the menigeal or vascular attachments of the brain resulting from alcoholic excesses rather than from the gastric distress. Migraine headaches are the most common ones associated with gastrointestinal disorders. However, directing the cure to the gastrointestinal disorder will not relieve the migraine.

Other Symptoms

Other symptoms such as constipation and diarrhea are more nearly disorders themselves.

Jaundice, another disease symptom, will be discussed with the diseases of the liver. Vertigo, sensations of dizziness and giddiness, have not been found to be caused by gastrointestinal disorders, although improvement occurs with the initiation of appropriate bowel regimen, regulation of the diet, correction of faulty hygiene, and frequent rest periods.

DISEASES CAUSED BY STRUCTURAL DEFECTS

Hernia

Definition and Etiology

A hernia is a structural defect in which there is a protrusion of an organ or part of an organ or other related structure through the wall of the cavity in which it is normally contained (Felton, Perkins, and Lewin, 1966). There are many types of hernias, and they are classified by location, such as the following: inguinal, femoral, umbilical, epigastric, and diaphragmatic. The most common of these hernias is the inguinal hernia which occurs nine times as often in men as in women. The inguinal hernia may be congenital (indirect) or acquired (direct) through trauma. Hernias are precipitated by extreme intraabdominal pressure which arises from lifting heavy objects, coughing, or from an intestinal obstruction.

Indirect inguinal hernias are characterized by a viscus extending along the inguinal canal, following the course of the spermatic cord, and emerging through the abdominal or external ring. Such hernias remaining in the inguinal canal are incomplete. Those descending into the scrotum are complete. Direct inguinal hernias protrude directly through the abdominal wall between the deep epigastric artery and the edge of the rectus muscle. Incarceration occurs when a portion of the herniated structure becomes "stuck" in the canal at some point. Obstruction of food passage can occur but does not always develop. If the blood supply is cut off as a result of a constricted hernial ring, gangrene can occur as a complication. A reducible hernia is one in which the hernia sac can be manually returned to the abdominal cavity. An irreducible hernia cannot be returned in this way because of a constricted hernial ring, or adhesive scars.

Diagnosis of Hernia

Pain is commonly experienced because of the displaced, unprotected viscus. In the case of a strangulated hernia, associated symptoms include severe colicky pain, nausea, and vomiting. If the pain is severe enough, temporary collapse may result. Palpation and percussion may be used to diagnose an inguinal hernia. In percussion, a tympanitic note is given by the imprisoned bowel. The presence of gut in the sac frequently can be demonstrated by a lateral x-ray film (Wangensteen, 1949). Strangulated hernias usually are associated with tenderness and lack of impulse on cough. Impulse and slight tenderness are present on cough in incarcerated hernias. A hernia may be differentiated from a hydrocele by transillumination of the mass, as hydroceles are translucent.

Treatment of Hernia

Hernias are treated exclusively by surgery. An incision is made in the abdominal surface, and the herniated organ is returned manually to the abdominal cavity. The hernia orifice is then sutured followed by suturing of the abdominal wall. In the case of a strangulated hernia, a return of the normal luster of the bowel and pulsation of the vesicles is adequate evidence for returning the loop to the abdomen (Wangensteen, 1949).

Vocational Implications

Hernias ordinarily become the subject of surgical techniques. This fact alone suggests that they will, prior to treatment, become a disabling condition rendering a man unemployable. However, except in cases involving one kind of complication or another, hernias, once treated, place no limitations on a man's employability. Employment of persons with known and untreated hernias is refused by most companies due to insurance rates and in some states due to regulations in the Workmen's Compensation Act. Seldom will the rehabilitation counselor encounter a client who has been treated for a hernia because except for physical restoration, the client can return to work. Cases do arise when emotional problems complicate the treatment during physical restoration. In such cases the counselor may be called upon to help reduce the client's anxiety about returning to work.

DISEASES OF THE GASTROINTESTINAL SYSTEM

This discussion will consider diseases of the esophagus, stomach, small and large intestines (bowels), liver, and pancreas.

Esophagus

Two diseases of the esophagus will be presented: achalasia (cardiospasm) and esophageal ulcers.

Achalasia

The primary condition is a neuromuscular disorder of the body of the esophagus resulting from idiopathic destruction of the myenteric plexus.

There is a similar condition termed "cardiospasm" which refers to spasm of the distal esophageal sphincter. This condition is less chronic than the primary condition of achalasia and usually occurs in tense and anxious persons.

Improper emptying of the esophagus into the stomach can produce several complications, including dysphagia (painful swallowing), regurgitation of esophageal contents, stagnation esophagitis, and more rarely, strictures (or scars) of the lower esophagus.

Treatment depends on the severity of the disease and includes medical management with antacids, antispasmodic medication, and appropriate use of tranquilizers. Surgical treatment is sometimes required to relieve obstruction and scarring.

Esophageal Ulcers

Esophageal ulcers are etiologically the result of regurgitation of gastric contents into the esophagus, and treatment consists largely of attempts to prevent the regurgitation. The therapeutic regimen ordinarily used is the patient's avoidance of the following: overeating and overdrinking, lying down after eating, bending from the waist down after eating, and eating just prior to bedtime. The patient should eat at least five small meals a day and remain upright for at least one hour after eating. The patient's bed should be at least six inches higher at the head than at the foot. Anticholinergics are contraindicated.

Stomach

Diseases of the stomach discussed include hiatus hernia and peptic, marginal and jejunal ulcers.

Hiatus Hernia

This is a disease that may give a picture similar to achalasia. In this disease, a portion of the stomach breaks through the diaphragm into the chest. This may cause backing up of gastric juice into the esophagus, causing inflammation and scarring. In far-advanced cases, large hiatus hernias may produce shortness of breath by imposing pressure upon the heart and lungs.

Peptic Ulcer

DEFINITION AND ETIOLOGY. Peptic ulcer is, by definition, an erosion which occurs in the portions of the gastrointestinal tract that come into contact with gastric juice. The erosions are caused by hydrochloric acid and pepsin, and approximately 80 percent of such ulcers occur in the duodenum. Etiologically, the peptic ulcer is of great significance. Although the action of the acid and pepsin is the final determining factor in the formation of the peptic ulcer, it is probably the variable stress which plays the greatest role in its formation. Stress may be physically or psychologically based. Physical bases of stress include severe burns, brain injury, lung disease, surgery, fractures, and acute temperature changes. Yet, psychological stress is the more frequent origin of factors leading to peptic ulcer as a final result.

The personality factors involved in psychological stress are of importance to the rehabilitation counselor. It should be noted that peptic ulcer is peculiar to civilized *Homo sapiens* except when experimentally produced in organisms lower than man on the phylogenetic scale. Individuals in whom a peptic ulcer is present normally can be described as being driving, active, versatile, restless, successful, responsible, determined, conscientious, and overextended (Sullivan and McKell, 1950). In addition, peptic ulcer patients do not tend to openly vent their anxiety and rage. Certainly, not every person with these personality traits develops peptic ulcers, but these personality traits are predisposing factors in peptic ulcer development. The precipitating situation associated with a peptic ulcer may be strong or weak, depending on whether the individual is low or high in peptic ulcer personality traits, respectively.

DIAGNOSIS OF PEPTIC ULCER. An individual who has developed a peptic ulcer will characteristically present a "pain" syndrome having four major aspects. These can be discussed under the following headings, according to Bockus (1963): (a) character and intensity of pain, (b) location and radiation of pain, (c) rhythm of peptic ulcer pain, and (d) periodicity and recurrence of the ulcer attack.

The "pain," or something simulating pain, is usually described by the patient as "gnawing," "exaggerated hunger," "burning," or "dull aching." Pain intensity and character is influenced by such factors as location, size, sensitivity, serosal involvement, and associated complications. Ulcers in the body of the stomach usually cause less pain than those in the cardiac stomach, pylorus, or duodenum. The intensity of the pain usually is relevant to the size of the erosion. Larger erosions tend to cause more pain. Also, the pain threshold of the patient influences the intensity of the pain; some patients are more sensitive than others. The pain is reported as being greater also in cases in which there is serosal involvement. But in cases involving subacute and acute perforation, the pain increases and becomes constant.

The patient usually feels the ulcer pain in the upper left portion of the abdomen. The radiation of pain is related to the severity of the ulcer. In more severe cases, the pain tends to radiate toward the back and spread over a greater area of the organ with the ulcer. Radiation of pain is also dependent on the pain threshold of the patient. In addition, greater penetration of the ulcer produces greater radiation of pain.

Pain in the peptic ulcer syndrome seems to follow a rhythmic pattern associated with the emptiness or fulness of the stomach.

When the stomach is relatively empty, the pain increases and then subsides after food is ingested. Because of this rhythmical relationship between ingestion of food and pain, most patients eat several times a day and when awakened from sleep will usually drink a glass of milk. However, when the ulcer is very severe, food brings less relief, and the pain often becomes constant and intense.

Periodicity is a very important diagnostic characteristic which the physician considers in the diagnosis. Uncomplicated ulcers often tend to follow a pattern in which pain occurs in a rhythmic pattern with the digestive cycle for several weeks. Then a period ensues during which the symptoms disappear with healing of the active lesion. Odd as it may seem, ulcer attacks are often seasonal in nature, with spring and autumn being the seasons of most common recurrence.

In addition to the ulcer syndrome described above, there are several symptoms of diagnostic significance which should be mentioned. The first of these is the presence of nausea, vomiting, and regurgitation. Ordinarily, repeated episodes of nausea and vomiting are not present in uncomplicated peptic ulcer. During active ulceration, however, isolated events of nausea and vomiting do occur. Vomiting occurs more often in cases of gastric ulcer than duodenal ulcer. Secondly, there is a constant presence of appetite, at times excessive. The presence of anorexia is usually indicative of pyloric obstruction. Third, occurrence of colonic dysfunction in association with an active ulcer is not uncommon. Usually the dysfunction is in the form of constipation which may be the result of the dietary regimen employed. Finally, some ulcer patients incur episodes of mental irritations, lack of concentration, and weakness, which tend to disappear following the ingestion of food.

A third portion of the diagnosis is the physical examination. Symptoms of clinical significance which may be revealed in the physical examination of the abdomen are circumscribed parietal epigastric tenderness and deep tenderness. The general physical examination is important for gaining a better understanding of the patient's personality and also for the possible detection of concomitant abnormalities.

The fourth step in the diagnostic procedure is the use of x-rays, gastroscopy, gastric analysis, cytologic examination, and blood count. Frequently, the presence or absence of an ulcer can be determined by a good medical history and a physical examination. The use of x-ray techniques is for confirmation. On the x-ray film, a gastric ulcer will usually be visible as a niche or crater. In the case of duodenal ulcer, one ordinarily must use the compression technique to demonstrate the presence of an ulcer. With the coming of x-ray techniques, gastroscopy is not used as much. In gastric analysis, particular attention is paid to the acidity and volume of the gastric secretion. The blood count is usually lower in cases involving a gastric ulcer than in those involving an uncomplicated duodenal ulcer.

TREATMENT OF THE PEPTIC ULCER. Treatment of the various forms of peptic ulcer (esophageal ulcers, gastric ulcers, duodenal ulcers, and marginal or jejunal ulcers) will be the same as that described by Conn (1966). Treatment of an uncomplicated duodenal peptic ulcer depends on whether it is acute, chronic, recurrent, or one of the Zollinger-Ellison syndrome. Acute ulcers are best treated by an hourly mild antacid, anticholinergic-to-tolerance program which is designed to decrease the acidity of the stomach contents. This program is maintained for 10 to 14 days. Then additions are made to the diet until a normal diet is approached, normally in about a month. Patients are encouraged to avoid overeating, fatigue, alcohol, caffeine, and the use of tobacco. Anticholinergics may be contraindicated for patients with glaucoma, elderly male patients with obstructive prostatic symptoms, and patients with cardiospasm.

Treatment of a chronic ulcer is the same as that of the acute ulcer except when surgery is advised. Employment of surgical treatment is dependent on the frequency of occurrence, response to treatment, and time lost from work. Recurrence is best treated by the use of anticholinergics and sedation as well as abstinence from irritants. Ulcers which fit the Zollinger-Ellison syndrome are characteristically surgically treated.

Gastric ulcers are treated in a manner similar to that of the duodenal ulcer. Ordinarily, less anticholinergic is required to reduce gastric secretion. Because gastric ulcers may be malignant, a trial period for healing is used. If the symptoms do not lessen or disappear, surgery and biopsy are used to determine the nature of the ulcer.

Marginal or Jejunal Ulcers

Marginal and jejunal ulcers are treated medically the same as duodenal ulcers, although the treatment is not usually as successful. Because of unsuccessful medical treatment, surgery is usually indicated. If an adequate subtotal resection was used in the first operation, the subsequent surgical procedure to be used is a vagotomy.

Vocational Rehabilitation

A period of rehabilitation follows diagnosis and medical treatment. It is this period of time during which the rehabilitation counselor plays a most important role in the patient's therapy. It is of primary importance to educate the client to the need for strict adherence to the dietary regimen and the avoidance of stressful situations, both physical and psychological.

The rehabilitation counselor will have the task of amelioration of differences between the client's personality and his environment, as it seems that these differences are most significant in ulcer development. As a general rule, psychotherapy and counseling are sufficient to improve the personality factors. One of the chief problems is getting the client to ventilate his tensions arising from his environmental conditions, including his vocation. In some cases, it may be easier to alter the environment than the personality.

With regard to the client's vocation, the counselor will find it necessary to locate the client in a nonstress-laden position. Also, a client should not work on a rotating shift because he must adhere to a regular medicinal and dietary regimen. The task of the rehabilitation counselor becomes complicated in postoperative cases, especially when gastrectomy is involved. The major task lies in reassuring the client in order to keep him motivated. Most statistical reports indicate that between 75 and 90 percent of gastrectomized patients return to their usual occupations when properly rehabilitated. The essential factors in rehabilitation include the client's task ability, level of training, job experience, and motivation. Programs which attend to these factors generally produce good results.

The rehabilitation counselor should have a knowledge of postoperative complications such as the dumping syndrome and remain alert to the symptoms in clients during counseling sessions. However, when careful preoperative procedures are employed, many postoperative complications can be avoided, such as anemia, edema, and others, including those of a psychological nature.

DISEASES OF THE SMALL AND LARGE INTESTINES

The diseases discussed concerning the small and large intestines will include colitis and regional enteritis.

Colitis

Definition and Etiology

Colitis refers to inflammation of the colon. Physicians have applied many meanings to the term and added many prefixes such as mucous and ulcerative. Actually, mucous and ulcerative colitis are the same disorder varying in severity. In mucous colitis, the most prominent symptom is the passage of large amounts of mucus, resulting from inflammation of the mucous membrane of the colon. Progress of the disease continues until the mucous membrane is eaten away and ulcers form, leading, logically, to the term ulcerative colitis (Montague, 1956).

Mucous colitis ("mucous colic" is preferred by Alvarez, 1954), it is frequently agreed (Cantor, 1951; Montague, 1956), has its origin in psychogenic factors which produce autonomic nervous system (ANS) dysfunctions and central nervous system (CNS) tension. Of secondary importance are effects of endocrine secretions and allergies.

The etiology of ulcerative colitis may not be quite as simple as stated above by Montague. Yet there does seem to be argument for a strong psychogenic component. Several bacterial origins for ulcerative colitis have been suggested.

Diagnosis

Mucous colitis is associated with such symptoms as constipation or diarrhea, flatulence, painful spasms, and the presence of large amount of mucus in the stools. A general examination of the patient usually reveals that he is hypersensitive, neurotic, and unstable in his basic nature. Often, hyperaction reflexes, hand tremor, excessive general and palmar perspiration, and tenderness in the colon (when palpated) are present. Negative results are obtained from stool examination (for ova and parasites), serologies, and sigmoidoscopies, except when complications are present. In short, mucous colitis is best diagnosed from the negative results of tests for organic disorders because mucous colitis has only a functional pathology.

Ulcerative colitis presents many suggestive symptoms, including extreme illness, inflamed colon mucosa, pain, weakness, and bloody, foul-smelling stools. Often the disease is associated with diseases of the joints, eyes, or skin. But, as in mucous colitis, ulcerative colitis is diagnosed largely from negative test results for organic pathology.

Treatment

Mucous colitis may best be treated by psychotherapeutic drugs or, in more severe cases, with psychotherapy in conjunction with the drugs. Frequently, education of the patient toward the emotional etiology of the disorder and the fact that it is actually not colitis but irritable colon is sufficient treatment.

Ulcerative colitis presents a little more complicated process. The treatment includes systemic, local, and psychiatric therapy. Psychiatric management, in conjunction with the control of the disease by supportive therapy, must be put in force during the earliest stages of treatment. The acute case usually requires bed rest if the individual is febrile or the frequency of bowel movements and the amount of blood lost seriously weakens the patient.

Vocational Implications

The role of the vocational rehabilitation counselor in such cases is primarily that of "counselor." His function is amelioration of the stress factors which tend to initiate the disorder and aggravate it. Also, in chronic situations, he must help the client find a calmer means of support. When rehabilitation fails to serve its function, complications may require the use of surgery (colectomy).

Regional Enteritis

Regional enteritis is a chronic, nonspecific inflammatory disease of unknown etiology which involves chiefly the small intestine— usually the terminal portion of the ileum (regional ileitis)—but may affect any region from the lower part of the esophagus to the rectum (Conn, 1966).

Acute enteritis is associated with edema and inflammation of the bowel wall, and the chronic enteritis is associated with superficial mucosal ulceration in the early stage with later cicatricial changes leading to thickening of the bowel wall and constriction of the lumen. The unfortunate fact about enteritis is that it usually becomes chronic with or without repeated attacks and remissions. The chronic stage often occurs with local complications such as fistula, abscess, obstruction, perforation, and bleeding, or such systemic disorders as anemia, arthralgias, skin changes, deficiency states, and visceral changes in the liver or kidneys.

Treatment is medicinal in nature, except when complications arise; then treatment is usually surgical. Medicinal treatment is originally set up during the acute stage and is later modified as required. The basic treatment is supportive, established for providing rest, improving nutrition, and correcting any infection or complication. Generally, treatment is carried out over an extended time, since complete recovery seldom occurs.

The vocational rehabilitation counselor is a necessary factor in the often prolonged therapy. The primary vocational implications arise from the mere prevalence of the disorder in young adults. The disease is proportionally more common in Jewish persons than Negroes. Frequently, due to a chronic condition, the client will have to be trained for a position which produces minimal physical and psychological stress. Clients entering employment following treatment for enteritis should have continuing medical supervision.

DISORDERS OF THE ACCESSORY DIGESTIVE ORGANS

There are three major accessory digestive organs: (a) liver, (b) gallbladder, (c) pancreas. Because the disorders of the liver are those most commonly encountered by the rehabilitation counselor, they shall be given the most consideration.

Disorders of the Liver

The primary disorders of the liver include jaundice, hepatitis, and cirrhosis.

Jaundice

Jaundice is a morbid condition characterized by yellowness of the skin and eyes, associated with a deep-yellow color of the urine. This condition is due to the presence of bile pigments in the blood and tissues. Actually, jaundice is more correctly considered to be a symptom of liver disease than a disease itself. In cases in which there is a history of colics, a jaundice, beginning with pain and persisting in varying intensity for several weeks, is usually indicative of stones in the bile duct. When cholangiography fails to remove the obstruction, operative exploration of the biliary tree is usually necessary. A jaundice condition preceded by itching is suggestive of liver disease. Especially in the absence of colics and in older persons, a steadily deepening jaundice suggests cancer of the pancreas or bile ducts (Alvarez, 1954). Infectious jaundice in young persons is usually painless and of short duration.

Hepatitis

Hepatitis is simply an inflammation of the liver. The two types of hepatitis commonly found in the general population are of either short incubation, Virus A, or long incubation, Virus B. Virus A is transmitted via the fecal-oral route, requiring strict hygienic habits to prevent its spreading. Patients are to be considered contagious for a period of about one month following clinical appearance of the disease. Virus B is transmitted only by parenteral routes. Most commonly it is spread by intravenous administration of blood or blood products or through the use of contaminated syringes and needles and today is most commonly found in drug abusers. Blood donors with a history of hepatitis are refused. The presence of hepatitis in the liver may be detected by the presence of abnormal screening liver function tests such as serum transaminases and bilirubin.

Despite generally high sanitary standards in the United States, approximately 12,000 cases of hepatitis were reported by the Public Health Service during the first four months of 1965 (Conn, 1966). The initially debilitating features of the disease, relatively long convalescence, time lost from work, and occasional chronic disability make hepatitis a major national and world health problem. Because of the above-named factors, one can see the obvious importance of knowledge of the disease to the vocational rehabilitation counselor.

Therapy for uncomplicated hepatitis is usually nonspecific and supportive, consisting of bed rest and diet control. Hospitalization is usually recommended for at least the initial symptomatic portion of the disease. This period of institutional care facilitates clinical and laboratory evaluation, permits patient education, and enables supervised control of activity. Progression of the disease is checked by means of serum bilirubin tests, followed by bromsulphalein (BSP) tests. Patients are fed less and at more frequent intervals. The optimal diet is a normal one. Drug therapy is nonspecific and is designed to control symptoms. Adrenal steroids are not usually prescribed for uncomplicated hepatitis. A complication which may arise consists primarily of liver failure, which is corrected by stopping protein intake and administering prescribed doses of neomycin.

Following discharge, the patient is advised to abstain from alcohol for half a year and eat a normal diet. Checkups should be done at three and six months after discharge. If the patient is asymptomatic at six months, he is considered cured and advised to return to a normal existence.

For clients who are engaged in employment requiring great physical stress, vocational rehabilitation is implied. The client should be trained for more sedentary work. The counselor should also attend to the task of reassuring the client of his ability and constantly keep before him the fact that he should not overtax himself, a probable cause of complications.

Cirrhosis

Cirrhosis of the liver is a chronic inflammatory disorder resulting in fibrosis with hardening caused by excessive formation of connective tissue followed by contraction. The etiologic factors in cirrhosis are mostly speculative in nature. Therefore, the first steps in therapy involve the elimination of the following suspected etiologic agents: (a) alcohol, (b) biliary obstruction, (c) hepatoxic drugs, and (d) hepatic poisons. A thorough evaluation of all systems, particularly the cardiovascular system, is warranted (Conn, 1966). In some instances, chronic heart failure and constrictive pericarditis may be implicated in the etiology of cirrhosis.

Therapy is generally nonspecific and supportive in nature. Characteristically, the patient is emaciated from malnutrition. The protein intake is normally increased, and vitamins and minerals are added to the diet to overcome the malnutrition. The caloric consumption is increased somewhat. In general, palatability is the most important dietary factor as long as the protein requirements are met. The diet has to be modified for many of the possible complications of the disease which include the following: (a) ascite abdomen, (b) hemorrhage, (c) anemia, (d) jaundice, and (e) renal failure.

The long-term prognosis is not favorable. Rehabilitation includes bed rest, at least for the period during which the disease is most active. As the disease becomes more chronic, the patient will have to be his own judge of the amount of physical activity he can endure without fatigue. The patient with cirrhosis can continue to work until such time as disabling symptoms appear. A possible important function of the rehabilitation counselor is that of keeping the emotions of the cirrhotic client as stable as possible and helping the client face his disability realistically.

Diseases of the Gallbladder

Cholecystitis and cholelithiasis are two disorders to which the gallbladder is subject. In the acute forms, these disorders leave no disabling conditions after treatment, which is usually surgical. In the case of unequivocal diagnosis of chronic cholecystitis, especially when cholelithiasis is demonstrated and there is a history of repeated biliary colic, the treatment of choice is surgical. However, medical management is reserved for the aged and debilitated, for patients with associated conditions contraindicating operation, for patients who refuse operation, and for those cases in which the diagnosis is equivocal and it is uncertain whether stones are present or whether a chronically diseased gallbladder is truly responsible for symptoms (Conn, 1966). In such cases, the rehabilitation counselor will probably be called into service.

The patient may be ambulatory and permitted to indulge in mild exercise. However, he should avoid activity that involves jarring or abdominal twisting or bending. His diet should be low in fat and high in protein and carbohydrates. Weight reduction is usually advised.

Disorders of the Pancreas

The only disease of the pancreas to be studied in this discussion of the gastrointestinal system is diabetes mellitus.

Diabetes Mellitus: Definition and Etiology

Diabetes mellitus may be defined as a metabolic disorder originating in insufficient insular activity of the pancreas and characterized by a disturbance in the utilization and storage of the dextrose molecule by the body. As a result of the diminished insular activity, several metabolic disturbances occur. These include the effect on water and salt metabolism, protein metabolism, and fat metabolism.

Many experimental investigations have been made into the etiology of diabetes mellitus with many different explanations resulting. However, the mainstream of etiological evidence points to the failure of the pancreas to produce sufficient insulin to meet the body's needs. The insulin failure may be caused by the hyperfunctioning of some other gland—possibly the anterior pituitary, adrenal cortex, or thyroid. The validity of the latter statement is held questionable in light of three established facts: (a) diabetes is completely corrected by proper insulin dosage, (b) diabetes can be induced in normal organisms by complete destruction of the pancreas, and (c) the normal pancreas possesses a large safety factor.

Other possible etiological factors may be placed in two categories. The first includes diseases which may depress the production of insulin, and the second includes the metabolic disturbances which require greater amounts of insulin to be produced, thereby placing a strain on the pancreas. Diseases which depress pancreatic function include acute and chronic pancreatitis, pancreatic stone, pancreatic cyst, and hyalinization of fibrosis of the pancreas. Examples of the second category include obesity, hyperfunctional disorders of the central nervous system, and finally, climate. Precipitation factors involved include occupation, economic status, and extent of civilization.

Diabetes mellitus has familial implications of etiological significance with which the rehabilitation counselor should carefully attend. Diabetes, although it does not have a direct gene linkage, is inherited as a predisposition for occurrence. In marriages in which both of the spouses have diabetic conditions, 44 of 100 children will also develop diabetes (Felton, Perkins, and Lewin,

1966). In 70 percent of identical twins, both twins will develop diabetes if one develops it (Wilder, 1940).

Diagnosis of Diabetes Mellitus

Correct diagnosis of diabetes mellitus is critical. Its presence must be established beyond a doubt and also its chemical and pathological severity must be determined both qualitatively and quantitatively. The symptomatology of diabetes may be grouped under two categories: (a) symptoms related to biochemical factors which derive from carbohydrate metabolism disorders and (b) symptoms produced by complications of diabetes.

Included in the first category are polyuria, polydipsia, polyphagia, weight loss, weakness, nocturnal cramps, paresthesias of the tongue, and blurring of vision. Polyuria refers to the increased volume of urine excreted and is one of the most outstanding of the symptoms noticed by the patient. Polydipsia is the excessive thirst which is created as a result of the polyuria. Polyphagia or excessive appetite frequently occurs as the result of the depletion of dextrose from the body. A new diabetic usually incurs a weight loss which results primarily from water loss and secondarily from dextrose loss. Weakness normally develops in unchecked diabetes because of the marked reduction of the glycogen content in the liver and skeletal muscle. Frequently, nocturnal cramps occur in the calf of the leg. These cramps can probably be best explained by the depletion of glycogen in the skeletal muscles. Paresthesias of the tongue, which includes taste disorders and burning, prickly, and leathery sensations, can be explained by the presence of glycosuria and possibly a deficiency of riboflavin and other vitamin B factors. Finally, the occurrence of visual blurring, which results from the water content of the vitreous and lens being affected due to dehydration, is fairly common in diabetics.

The second category of symptoms will not be discussed in this paper. Instead, the complications which manifest these symptoms will be listed as follows: acidosis, hypoglycemia, arteriosclerosis, eye diseases, vitamin deficiencies, and infections.

However, diabetes may be asymptomatic, and in such a case

its presence is usually "accidentally" detected through a urinalysis. Even when symptoms are present, the physician employs laboratory procedures for confirmation of the diagnosis. The primary function of the laboratory tests is to verify the presence of high amounts of sugar in the blood and urine.

The presence of sugar in the urine, or melituria, is the simplest of the laboratory procedures. Testing for the presence of sugar in the urine is not only used in the hospital laboratory but is also utilized daily by the diabetic in the self-management regimen. The laboratory urinalysis includes tests for the presence of acetone and ketone bodies in the urine. One method of testing the urine for sugar involves the following steps: (a) five drops of urine are placed in a test tube, (b) a reagent tablet is added, (c) heat is generated in the tube, and (d) the resulting color is matched against a color chart.

Excessive sugar is present in the blood before it is present in the urine in the case of diabetes. The rehabilitation counselor will frequently be presented with blood sugar charts among the clinical records. He should be familiar with the interpretation of these charts. The standard unit of measure found on blood sugar charts is milligrams percent (mg %). The normal blood sugar range is 70 to 110 mg %. The diabetic's chart will commonly read between 160 and 220 mg %. Sugar normally appears in the urine when the count is above 180 mg %.

The standard test of blood sugar level employed is the glucose tolerance test. The procedure is outlined below:

1. The patient maintains a normal diet for about three days prior to the test with no restriction on normal carbohydrate consumption.
2. The patient undergoes a 12-hour fast preceding the test and just prior to and during the test is not allowed to smoke.
3. A blood sample is taken prior to the test to determine the fasting blood sugar level.
4. The patient then drinks 300 ml of water containing 100 gm of sugar.

5. Blood samples are taken at four half-hour intervals, and usually additional hourly samples are taken to a total time of three to five hours.
6. The results of the test are graphed and an interpretation is made.

Normally the blood sugar level reaches a peak a short time after the initiation of the test and returns to normal by the end of the two-hour test period. Also, a normal reading should not exceed 160 mg %, and there should be no sugar present in the urine. The chart of a diabetic normally reaches a peak but does not decline very rapidly. The "diabetic curve" normally remains above 160 mg %. Other diseases may also present a "diabetic curve," including the following: hyperthyroidism, Cushing's syndrome, acromegaly, adrenal cortical tumors, asphysia, acidosis, and brain tumors.

Treatment of Diabetes Mellitus

The treatment of diabetes mellitus as prescribed in Conn (1966) is divided into adult and juvenile treatment. Discussion here will be limited to adult diabetes. First to be discussed is adult therapy of the "middle-of-the-road" type as opposed to the "purist" and the "free-diet" types. The purist approach is often complicated by hypoglycemic shocks, emotional frustration, and compulsive perfectionism. On the other extreme is the free-diet approach in which gross disregard of diet produces a greater incidence of degenerative sequelae in long-standing diabetes.

The therapeutic regimen of diabetics has to be planned on an individual basis, preferable under controlled conditions present only in a hospital. Quite clearly, it is important that a proper balance be maintained among the diet, insulin dosage, and the amount of exercise permitted in the daily life of the diabetic.

The diet is the most important factor in the treatment of diabetes. Weighted diets are not now considered practicable, and the Food Exchange System as developed by the American Diabetes Association, the American Dietetic Association, and the Public Health Service is recognized to be the most workable diet yet devised for the average diabetic.

The construction of the diet is made with consideration for caloric count and distribution of carbohydrates, proteins, and fats. One simple method of estimating the caloric requirements is outlined as follows:

1. "Maintenance diet": patient's weight in kilograms multiplied by 30.
2. "Reducing diet": patient's weight in kilograms multiplied by 20.
3. "Gaining diet": patient's weight in kilograms multiplied by 40.

Appropriate adjustments, however, should be made for occupational energy requirements. For uncomplicated diabetes, the distribution of carbohydrates, proteins, and fats should be 50, 25, and 25 percent, respectively. Modifications are made in the distribution to account for complications such as renal or hepatic disease.

The diabetic patient should follow at least four basic dietary rules:

1. Carefully measure all foods.
2. Diversify the "exchanges."
3. Never omit meals or prescribed snacks.
4. Record body weight at least three times weekly.

In addition, the distribution of meals should be made to fit the needs of the patient. Ordinarily, the more severe the diabetes is, the more numerous is the required number of meals. An arbitrary statement should now be made to the effect that about one third of the known diabetics can be controlled on diet alone, one third on diet plus oral antidiabetic agents, and one third on diet plus a prescribed insulin dosage. It can be stated that no child under 15 years of age can have his diabetes controlled without insulin except during remissions.

Diabetic patients may, if they fulfill three basic criteria, be placed on oral diabetic agents. Rigid criteria to be met by the *ideal* candidate might be the following:

1. Diabetic condition of 10 years' duration or less.

2. Good diabetic control with less than 40 units of insulin daily.

3. Over 40 years of age.

The following are currently used oral antidiabetic agents: tolbutamide, acetohexamide, chlorapropamide, phenformin, and phenformin sustained release. The oral diabetic agents should be, of course, prescribed by a physician. It should be noted that insulin therapy is two to four times less expensive than oral therapy.

A patient who fails to meet the criteria for oral antidiabetic agents has to resort to the use of insulin to control the diabetes. Physicians have a choice of eight different insulins to choose from. The insulin type and approximate dosage is prescribed by the physician as is indicated by blood sugar tests and urinalysis. The best dosage requirements are determined by simple trial and error.

Some patients demonstrate high resistance to insulin. Such resistance may be due to any one of several factors. This resistance requires the administration of high doses of insulin or of specially prepared insulins. Insulin overdosage can lead to insulin shock, which is usually reversed by the prompt administration of glucose. To protect the ambulatory diabetic from hyperinsulinism, he is advised to maintain in his possession a cube of sugar, a candy bar, or a small box of raisins, which are to be eaten at the first sign of insulin shock. The occurrence of local allergy in diabetics is common, and it can be controlled through the use of "special beef" insulin. Insulin injections should be made in different areas to prevent insulin lipodystrophy, which is either hypertrophic or atropic in action. Special problems occasionally arise in the treatment of diabetics. Among these problems are impaired vision, foot infections, and coronary artery disease. Surgery and other stressful events pose special problems of medical management of the diabetic condition.

Self-Management of Diabetes Mellitus

The education of the diabetic patient is of the utmost importance if he is to be able to function as near to normal as possible. Instructions for self-administration of insulin should be given by the physician or a qualified nurse. The patient will also be charged with the responsibility of controlling his own diet. Various other means also can be employed in adding to the education of the patient. The American Diabetic Association sponsors health education programs which allow diabetics and their families to meet regularly to hear lectures and view films related to self-care.

The diabetic can further his education regarding diabetes by reading such instruction manuals as the *Diabetic Manual*, prepared by Joslin, or the *Primer*, prepared by Wilder. There are many other comparable manuals that the diabetic may choose from.

Other important instructions which should be given to the patient include how to care for his equipment, how and when to make urine tests, what action to take in case of hyperinsulinism, and hygiene of the feet.

The equipment used by the diabetic includes the following: (a) the type of insulin prescribed by the physician, (b) a syringe for the administration of the insulin (special syringes are available for the blind), (c) sterile case for the syringe and needle, (d) alcohol and sterile cotton to help prevent infection, (e) epinephrine and sugar as safeguards against insulin shock, and (f) some form of identification of the nature of his illness.

Vocational Implications and the Role of the Rehabilitation Counselor

An uncomplicated diabetic who has the disease under control is placed under very few vocational restrictions. However, he should be employed in a position which is not stress laden. Because of the diabetic's need for regularity in his activities, he should not work on a rotational shift. A third factor in employment of the controlled, uncomplicated diabetic concerns the possibility of complicating infections. He should not be placed in a job which involves physical hazards which could produce infections.

There are several reasons why industry hesitates to employ the diabetic. The first of these is absenteeism. Although industry remains reluctant to employ a diabetic until reassured by the physician in charge, there have been few problems reported concerning absenteeism and the diabetic. Secondly, the juvenile diabetic poses a question of longevity. Most companies will not include the juvenile diabetic in costly training programs and long-range advancement programs. A third concern of industry is that of hyperinsulinism. As a result, many companies do not employ diabetics in positions requiring the operation of an automobile. To protect the diabetic population from the prejudices of industry and to protect industry from the employment of diabetic "risks," the Committee of Employment of the American Diabetes Association has been established to aid employers in hiring diabetics.

Employment of diabetics is increasing, and concurrently, the attitude toward employing them is becoming more liberal. Though formerly excluded from employment in the Federal Government, since 1941 the United States Civil Service Commission has changed its policy and now recommends the employment of controlled diabetics. As the leaders in industry become better educated with respect to diabetes and diabetics, the vocational plight of at least the controlled diabetic will continue to improve.

The rehabilitation counselor ordinarily will not encounter the controlled diabetic in his work. Most of the counselor's clients will be those who have complications of a physical or psychological nature, or both. Such complications include clients with visual impairments, amputation of a limb, neurologic or vascular involvement, or some psychological disturbance. The rehabilitation counselor usually must attend first to the emotional problems of these clients. He must attempt to establish a stress-free environment for the uncontrolled diabetic with whom he works most often. Another problem which the counselor must attempt to improve is that of poor self-care on the part of the client. Finally, there remains the problem of locating employment for the client, a task which presents many obstacles.

CONCLUDING REMARKS

It is difficult to conclude a subject which has obviously only been introduced. Many gastrointestinal disorders have only very minor vocational implications. The disorders discussed in the preceding pages, however, do not exhaust the field of those disorders which do have vocational implications. Many times a disorder will present only organic implications, in which case treatment of the physiological symptoms is sufficient to allow the patient to return to his customary occupation. Others involve implications of both a physiological and a psychological nature. Stress arising from both physical and emotional situations probably has more etiological significance for gastrointestinal disorders than any other single factor. The rehabilitation counselor who is able to remove this stress factor from either the client or the client's environment many times is able to remove the client's major source of debilitation. In most situations, either the client or the environment will have to be altered to remove the stress. Frequently, the easiest route would be to alter the environment; however, it would seem that until some change is made in the client, the true source of debilitation, especially in functional gastrointestinal disorders, has not been effected. Therefore, the rehabilitation counselor has a dual role to play. First, he provides supportive psychological therapy for the client's emotional stress. Secondly, he provides the client with vocational counseling and guidance.

REFERENCES

Alvarez, W. C.: *Nervous Indigestion and Pain.* New York, Harper and Brothers, 1954.

Bockus, H. L.: *Gastroenterology.* Philadelphia, W. B. Saunders, 1964, Vols. I and II.

Cantor, A. J.: *Psychosomatic Medicine.* New York, The Julian Press, Inc., 1951.

Collens, W. S. and Boas, L. C.: *The Modern Treatment of Diabetes Mellitus.* Springfield, Thomas, 1946.

Conn, H. F.: *Current Therapy.* Philadelphia, W. B. Saunders, 1966.

Felton, J. S., Perkins, D. C., and Lewin, M.: *A Survey of Medicine and Medical Practice for the Rehabilitation Counselor.* Washington, D. C., Department of Health, Education and Welfare, 1966.

Garma, A.: *Peptic Ulcer and Psychoanalysis.* Baltimore, The Williams & Wilkins Co., 1958.

Manner, H. W.: *Elements of Anatomy and Physiology.* Philadelphia, W. B. Saunders, 1962.

Montague, J. F.: *How to Overcome Colitis.* New York, The Citadel Press, 1956.

Sullivan, A. J. and McKell, T. E.: *Personality in Peptic Ulcer.* Springfield, Thomas, 1950.

Wangensteen, O. H.: *Intestinal Obstructions.* Springfield, Thomas, 1942.

Wilder, R. M.: *Clinical Diabetes Mellitus and Hyperinsulinism.* Philadelphia, W. B. Saunders, 1940.

Chapter XII

MEDICAL AND PSYCHOLOGICAL FACTORS PERTINENT TO THE REHABILITATION OF THE EPILEPTIC

LEWIS BARNES AND ALAN KRASNOFF

E pilepsy has been known for thousands of years. The first lines written about epileptics appeared in the Code of Hammurabi, King of Babylon, about forty centuries ago. For the next fifteen hundred years, epilepsy was attributed to supernatural causes. Around 450 B.C., Hippocrates wrote that epilepsy is a condition of the brain due to natural, not supernatural causes. It was not until about eighty years ago that Dr. Hughlings Jackson, the father of clinical neurology, conceived the idea that epileptic attacks are due to an abnormal discharge of energy in the brain. This idea was proved relatively recently by the electroencephalogram.

The epidemiology of epilepsy in the United States yields a rate of 0.5 percent, estimated from statistics of the Selective Service (Merritt, 1959). Kurland (1959) estimated the prevalence of epilepsy as ranging between 552,000 and 757,000. According to a pamphlet of the Epilepsy Foundation, two million people, or approximately 1 percent of the population, are said to have epilepsy. Udel (1960) estimated that there are approximately 400,-000 epileptics of working age.

The overall incidence of epilepsy is estimated to be higher in males than females, apparently stemming from the higher frequency of head injuries in men. Merritt (1959), citing data from a study by Lennox, indicated that only 59 females per 100 males had an initial epileptic seizure after 20 years of age. Hyllested and Pakkenberg (1963) offered this explanation to account for their finding of an almost two to one ratio of men to women in a study of epilepsy appearing initially at age 45 or later.

Three complex areas must be considered as the rehabilitation counselor works toward rehabilitation of the epileptic patient.

First, he must be aware of pertinent medical aspects of the disease. Second, psychological factors must be considered. Finally, the social problems related to attitudes of employers and other important people in the life of the working epileptic must be known to him.

MEDICAL ASPECTS OF EPILEPSY

Epilepsy is a word derived from the Greek term *epilepsia*, meaning a seizure. It may be defined as a chronic, episodic disturbance in function of the central nervous system which is characterized by one or more of the following usually transitory features: disruption of consciousness, convulsions, and alterations in sensory, motor, autonomic, cognitive and affective status. Livingston (1963) refers to epilepsy as a diagnosis referrable to a variety of causes affecting the brain and/or spinal cord. As such, it is a symptom reflecting a number of possible disease states (Hill, 1963). According to Penfield and Jasper (1954), a seizure is produced as a result of "an abnormal excessive neuronal discharge."

Gibbs, in *A Definition of Epilepsy* (1962, pp. 58-59), states:

> No matter what its manifestation, epilepsy results from brain disorder, not from something that floats around free; it is not an emotional disturbance, a psychological disturbance nor a social disturbance. It is evident that a brain has been harmed. . . . If we forget that epilepsy is a brain illness, we cannot understand epilepsy and we cannot give effective help to epileptics. For some strange reason we have a tendency to leave the brain out of our thinking. We try to cope with epilepsy while deeply ignorant about the way in which the brain functions and without knowledge of how some of its major disturbances are remedied. We must get the brain back into the central position if total rehabilitation of epilepsy is to succeed.

Classification

Although epilepsy may be classified in several ways, two commonly used schemes will be presented for the purposes of this summary: (a) idiopathic or essential epilepsy, for which no specific cause can be found and (b) symptomatic or secondary epilepsy, which is produced by a variety of conditions. Approximately 77 percent of the cases of epilepsy are of the idiopathic type. In the remainder, convulsive seizures are symptomatic of underlying conditions. Eight broad categories of symptomatic epilepsy are as follows:

1. *Congenital.* Includes cerebral aplasia, birth injuries, congenital syphilis, congenital idiocy, and other congenital nervous system abnormalities.
2. *Degenerative.* Includes Pick's disease, Alzheimer's disease, and multiple sclerosis.
3. *Inflammations.* Includes various types of encephalitis, meningitis, brain abscess.
4. *Vascular.* Includes arteriosclerosis, cerebrovascular accidents (strokes), cerebral vascular spasms, sinus thrombosis, cerebral aneurysm, and others.
5. *Traumatic.* Includes cerebral contusion and laceration, cerebral scarring, subarachnoid hemorrhage, subdural hematoma, middle meningeal hemorrhage, and electroshock treatment.
6. *Tumor.* Includes gliomas, meningioma, metastatic carcinoma, and others.
7. *General somatic disease.* Includes acute fevers in children, heat stroke, hyperventilation (alkalosis), hypertension, uremia, hypoglycemia, and others.
8. *Intoxications.* Includes cases of botulism, tetanus toxemia of pregnancy, water and alcohol intoxications, and various drug intoxications.

It is important to remember that epileptic seizures or a convulsive disorder may be associated with a wide variety of pathological conditions.

Epilepsy is also frequently classified according to the *type of attack* demonstrated by the patient. This classification schema is essentially a descriptive one. Four major categories may serve conveniently to encompass the variety of seizure manifestations, as follows: grand mal, petit mal, psychomotor, and miscellaneous focal seizures.

Grand Mal

Grand mal is the most dramatic form of attack. Approximately 90 percent of persons with epilepsy have seizures of the grand mal type. It is often preceded by a warning or aura typically consisting of vertigo or some other sensory experience. A shrill cry may herald the onset of the general convulsion which involves loss of consciousness and tonic and clonic movements of the entire body. This aura lasts for several seconds before the loss of consciousness and is usually specific for the individual person. It may consist of sensations of numbness or nausea, an odor, a feeling of distress in the epigastrium, or hallucinations such as flashes or hearing certain noises. The aura is usually an unpleasant feeling. The aura can be motor in nature, consisting of such things as twitching or stiffness in a certain group of muscles. Following the aura there is a stiffening and complete loss of consciousness and the patient falls. As he falls, the entire voluntary musculature goes into a continuous contraction and remains in this tonic phase from ten to twenty seconds. The peculiar sound known as the epileptic cry, which is so characteristic in grand mal seizures, is caused by the contraction of the muscles of the chest, forcing air through the larynx. At first the face is pale, but as the muscles contract, the superficial veins become enlarged. Because the patient is not breathing, aeration of the blood cannot take place, causing a blueness or cyanosis of the face. During the tonic phase and for awhile afterward, the pupils are dilated and do not react to light, and the corneal reflex is absent. Deep tendon reflexes are decreased or absent, and the Babinski reflex is present. It is during the tonic phase when the voluntary muscles are in contraction that there is often urinary and fecal incontinence. The tonic stage is followed by intermittent or clonic muscular contractions, at first rapid but gradually slowing down. It is during this stage that tongue biting occurs. As the clonic movements begin to be less frequent, respiration returns and the saliva, which could not be swallowed during the seizure, may become mixed with air and thus appear in a foam, perhaps tinged with blood if there has been injury to the tongue. In addition to biting injuries to the tongue, fractures of bones may rarely occur.

The postconvulsive coma, a variable period of sleep and stupor, lasts usually from one to four hours. During this phase, there is a relaxation of the muscles, so that if an arm or leg is lifted and then released, it drops heavily as it would in a state of flaccid paralysis. After awakening, the patient may complain of headache, fatigue, painful tongue, or of general soreness of the muscles. Following the seizure, the patient has no recollection of what occurred in the seizure. Sometimes as the patient is emerging from the coma, he is confused and may perform semiautomatic acts, fumble at his clothing or attempt to remove it. He may exhibit chewing movements or move aimlessly about.

There may be considerable variation in the pattern of grand mal seizure. They may occur at any time of the day or night. Some people have seizures only at night and may not know they have had one unless they wake up on the floor, bite their tongue, or void in bed. Attacks may occur many many times in one day or may occur only once in several years. Sometimes the convulsive phase is so brief that the seizure appears as simple fainting.

If you are present when someone has a grand mal seizure, there are several ways to help. If there is a warning, you may be able to break or guide the person's fall. A rolled handkerchief or something soft to place between the teeth may prevent tongue biting, but hard objects may injure the teeth. Keep your fingers out of the patient's mouth. Do not try to restrain the individual, but allow the convulsion to proceed naturally. Do not get excited and alarm bystanders or create a scene which will not help anything and only embarrass the person having the attack. Afterwards, try to get the patient to a quiet place where he can rest and recover away from people.

Petit Mal

Petit mal seizures are characteristic of epilepsy in childhood and rarely, if ever, begin after age 20. Petit mal customarily involves an incomplete loss of consciousness with a momentary or brief disruption of environmental contact. Oftentimes, this condition is perceived as inattention by an observer. The patient may drop objects held at the time as a result of muscular weakness and may demonstrate flickering of the eyelids or simply a fixed gaze. The duration of the attack is typically only a few seconds—at the most, a minute or two. The attacks begin and end abruptly and are without warning or sequel. The patient does not fall, although he may droop, stagger, or lose urinary control, and there may be a few jerks of an arm or of an eye muscle. Very often, these seizures are hard for an observer to recognize and may be manifested only by a momentary staring and fixed posture. Unlike grand mal, petit mal attacks occur with great frequency. In some, there may be only a few attacks daily, but in others, there may be 20 to 30 attacks in an hour. They tend to be more frequent early in the morning or while the victim is sitting quietly and are less frequent during active exercise.

The onset of petit mal is usually between four and eight years of age. It tends to disappear after age eighteen or to be replaced by other types of seizures. Grand mal and petit mal may co-exist. Two thirds of the children with petit mal subsequently develop grand mal.

Usually included in the petit mal form are myoclonic jerks in which contractions of muscles occur without alteration of consciousness. Myoclonic jerks tend to occur more frequently upon going to sleep or upon awakening. Normal individuals may have rare myoclonic jerks in drowsiness or light sleep.

Akinetic attacks are also included under petit mal and are seizures of sudden brief loss of postural tone during which the person slumps a little before catching himself or recovers just after the knees of the body touch the ground. There is a sudden hypotonia of the muscles. Following the attack, the patient resumes previous activity and may remain unaware that a seizure has occurred.

Psychomotor Seizures

Psychomotor seizures result from focal lesions of the temporal lobe(s) of the brain. Consciousness is affected in such a way that automatic behavior may occur without memory of it afterward. Reports of antisocial (Baldwin, 1960) and psychotic states (Guerrant *et al.*, 1962) have been mentioned in connection with this type of epilepsy, but the significance of the frequency of such disturbances is still a matter of controversy (Lennox, 1949). Disturbances in memory, speech, and mood, the latter involving increased irritability, have been noted (Guerrant *et al.,* 1962), but objective confirmation of these clinical impressions is still unresolved (Klove and Doehring, 1962).

Noyes and Kolb (1958, p. 102) give the following characterization of psychomotor epilepsy:

> Psychomotor epilepsy is characterized clinically by trance-like attacks and confusional episodes and is much more common in adults than in children. The patient is not unconscious, but has no memory of the episode. Some patients describe brief affective states of fear, vague alarm, terror, rage and occasionally feelings of well-being or pleasure. The patient's behavior is appropriate to his mood. Other episodic but sustained moods may be in the form of extreme irritability, depression, ill humor, or bad temper.

Sometimes these psychomotor seizures take the form of a clouded state characterized by confusion, bewilderment, excitement with hallucinations, outbursts of violence, or occasionally ecstatic moods with religious exaltation. Clinically, the clouded state suggests a delirium with liberation of aggressive and occasionally self-destructive impulses. Acts of violence may be committed in these automatisms and may be of a strikingly brutal nature; the patient may pursue his crime to a most revolting extreme. These furors are characterized by their suddenness, absence of premeditation and of precaution, and by amnesia for the victim. The extraordinary degree of discrimination and judgment displayed in the psychomotor attack often gives the patient's acts a misleading appearance of deliberation. It may be difficult to accept the fact that the author of the crime was not responsible for his acts. Usually these psychomotor seizures continue for only a few minutes, but they may go on for hours or even days. Sometimes the seizure may assume the form of a fugue. Occasionally the patient may report feelings of loneliness or strangeness to typical *déjà vu* phenomena as if he had undergone the same experience in the past. Psychomotor seizures may occur in pure form, but in many cases, grand mal seizures may also be present. Their frequency increases with age.

Among the many types of miscellaneous focal seizures, perhaps the most distinctive is Jacksonian epilepsy which results from a lesion in the motor cortex of the brain and is characterized by an organized "march" of muscular activity starting at a single point of the body and progressing systematically on the side affected, sometimes ending in a generalized convulsion.

In Jacksonian or focal seizures, contractions begin on one side of the body and consciousness is not lost until they move to the other side. This type of seizure is most commonly associated with organic brain lesions such as tumors or scars and is due to focal irritation of a portion of the motor cortex.

Despite the apparent discreteness of the above classification, the type of attack is subject to change. A Jacksonian seizure may result in a grand mal convulsion, this effect being due to the spread of neural excitation to both cerebral hemispheres. As another example, petit mal, beginning in childhood or adolescence, not uncommonly develops into grand mal later in life. Of the four categories, the most common, by far, is grand mal, which accounts for approximately 90 percent of all cases of epilepsy (Merritt, 1959).

DIAGNOSIS

The diagnosis of grand mal epilepsy, if observed by a physician or trained observer, is relatively easy, but in the case of petit mal or in atypical and incompletely developed seizures, the diagnosis may be difficult. It is important to remember the word "recurrent," because an isolated single seizure in a person does not mean the person has epilepsy. One must be very careful before labeling a person as an epileptic and be sure his diagnosis is correct because of the social and occupational stigmata associated with epilepsy.

In making the diagnosis, physical and neurological examination must always be carried out. Skull x-rays, examination of the cerebrospinal fluid for cell and protein content, spinal fluid manometrics, cerebral angiography, and air studies may be helpful and are often made. Electroencephalography is now a most objective and useful tool in the diagnosis of epilepsy. It may help in determining the type of seizure and to some extent may help in determining the prognosis. A normal brain wave does not exclude the diagnosis of epilepsy nor do minor abnormalities confirm the diagnosis. The occurrence of seizure discharges is fairly positive evidence of epilepsy. The type of brain wave varies with the type of seizure. In grand mal, rapid high-voltage spikes occur. In petit mal, there is a typical spike and dome pattern and in psychomotor seizures, slow high-voltage square-topped waves occur. When epilepsy is suspected, it is important to record the electroencephalogram while the patient is in a light sleep or at least drowsy. Sleep records often reveal abnormalities that are not present in the waking state. Hyperventilation and photic stimulation also may bring out abnormalities which otherwise may not be present.

TREATMENT

The first necessity in treatment is to get the intelligent cooperation of the patient. Sometimes it is difficult to get the patient to emotionally and realistically accept the fact that he has epilepsy. He may pretend he does not have the condition, may show a disinterest in learning a few basic facts about epilepsy, may not care what medicine he is taking, or may act as if it is a disgrace to be epileptic. The patient should be encouraged to become a member of groups interested in the welfare of epileptics such as the American Epilepsy Society, The United Epilepsy Association, and the National Epilepsy League.

The object of drug therapy is to render the patient seizure free, although this is not possible in many cases. On drug therapy, about 50 percent of epileptics can be well controlled, another 20 or 25 percent can be controlled to some extent, and the remaining 15 or 20 percent can be only poorly controlled. It is the latter group which make up the epileptic population in state hospitals. Most patients must continue to take anticonvulsive medication throughout life. However, if seizures are entirely controlled for three to five years, the dosage may be slowly reduced over a period of one to two years and finally withdrawn to ascertain if seizures will recur.

The type of anticonvulsant used depends upon the type of seizure present. Phenobarbital is one of the most likely used drugs and is usually effective in alleviating grand mal seizures. It is of little value in petit mal or psychomotor seizures. Dilantin® is used in grand mal attacks and it is also the most efficacious of the anti-epileptic drugs in psychomotor. Dilantin® and phenobarbital are often used in combination. Tridione® is often effective in the treatment of petit mal, but may aggravate other types. Other anti-epileptic drugs in use include Mesantoin®, Phenurone®, Diamox®, Mebaral®, and Peganone®. Bromides are not used much anymore. The ideal drug dosage is that amount which controls the seizures without producing side effects.

Drowsiness produced by the medication will usually wear off after continued use. Once the proper dosage of anticonvulsant is established, this should be taken regularly without fail, since omitting medication is likely to lead to seizure recurrence.

Unfortunately, all the drugs which work in epilepsy are potentially toxic, even though not seriously so in most instances. The dosage must be increased gradually with a constant watch for possible side effects or decreased gradually to avoid seizure tendency from withdrawal. Blood counts must be checked at varying intervals to make sure there is no depression of the blood-forming tissues. If one drug does not work, it is gradually decreased while the new medicine is being substituted. The common side reactions to anticonvulsant drugs are drowsiness, fatigue, nausea, dizziness, diarrhea, awkwardness, double vision, fever, or skin rash. It is not always necessary to discontinue a drug because of side reactions. Sometimes by adjusting the dose, the side effect will disappear.

In addition to being properly medicated, it is important for the patient to avoid excessive fatigue and to have a simple regular daily routine, eating meals on time, taking exercises, and getting adequate sleep. Drinking of alcoholic beverages is contraindicated in the epileptic, as this often causes an increase in seizures. Emotional turmoil and conflict also aggravate seizure tendencies. Many epileptics are helped with psychotherapy (in addition to medication). In some instances, a better psychological adjustment has practically eliminated the attacks.

Every epileptic should be acquainted with the nature of his seizures and know exactly the names and doses of his medications. Those with grand mal attacks should carry a card with the diagnosis and medication to avoid any unnecessary treatment in emergency rooms.

Cause of Epilepsy

The role of genetics in relation to epilepsy is still a matter of debate. Lennox (1960) estimated that there is about one chance in forty that an offspring of an epileptic parent would develop epilepsy. Alstrom (1950) estimated the odds as being no greater than one in twenty-five if the parent has essential epilepsy. On the other hand, Livingston (1963) viewed the genetic factor in terms of a predisposition which lowers the threshold making the individual more vulnerable to seizures, given other necessary conditions. Lilienfield and Pasamanick (1954) placed greater emphasis on prenatal and perinatal circumstances and questioned the importance of hereditary factors in epilepsy.

In studies on *identical* twins, it was found that idiopathic epilepsy occurs eight times more frequently in both individuals than it does in both of fraternal twins. It is estimated that epilepsy occurs about five times more frequently among near relatives of idiopathic epileptics than it does in the general population. The existence of a predisposition to the disease in the child of an epileptic is often demonstrable in the form of cerebral dysrhythmia on an electroencephalogram record. There is also a striking likeness of brain wave abnormalities in epileptics with the same heredity.

Onset

Livingston (1963) indicated that the onset of seizures occurs from birth through adolescence in a preponderant number of instances, 90 percent before the age of twenty. In senescence, an increase in the number of cases is found after a stable and significantly lower rate through the active adult years.

Course of Epilepsy

The course of epilepsy is a variable matter, and prognosis depends on such considerations as the frequency of seizures per unit time, the presence or absence of gross brain damage, the overall length of time that the patient has suffered from seizures, and whether or not seizures began during or after childhood. The prognosis is said to be more favorable when the number of seizures has been small, when gross brain damage is absent, when the total time that epilepsy has been present is limited, and when the onset occurred after childhood. The prognosis for epilepsy with onset during the first year of life is said to be particularly serious, apparently because of the vulnerability of the brain during this phase of development (1961). Despite such complicating factors, if one considers the prognosis on an overall statistical basis, the outlook is generally favorable. Krohn (1961) stated that approximately 80 percent of epileptics have little difficulty due to seizures. Yahr and Merritt (1956) reported 75 percent of their series of patients controlled on drugs. Evans (1962) indicated that although only 13 of 31 patients with posttraumatic epilepsy were taking anticonvulsant medication, all were free of seizures. Hyllested and Pakkenberg (1963), in a 4- to 14-year follow-up of 59 patients with a late onset, noted that 35 or 40 survivors never or only rarely had seizures, despite the fact that the majority were not taking drugs to prevent them. In a follow-up of 32 patients with "pure" petit mal, twelve were free of seizures (1959). Penfield and Jasper (1954), in a study of 257 adult epileptics described as having more severe seizure problems than the average, reported that 30 percent were found to have had no attacks for at least one year, while an additional 35 percent had had no more than six major convulsions per year. Thus, the above review indicates that the vast majority of epileptics show good to complete control with medical care.

PSYCHOLOGICAL ASPECTS OF EPILEPSY

From ancient times to the present, the epileptic has been described as having various psychological aberrations. This section will include a summary and evaluation of some of the recent literature on intellectual functioning and personality disturbances of epileptics.

Intellectual Functioning

Turning to intellectual functioning first, Lennox (1960) reported that retardation is found in only a small proportion of cases. In comparing thirteen pairs of monozygotic twins, only one of each pair with chronic seizures, he reported a net difference in mean IQ of only 2.5 points. The mean IQ of the chronic seizure group was 100.7 and the mean IQ of those without chronic epilepsy was 103.2. From these suggestive findings, one might reasonably conclude that epilepsy, per se, has little effect on intelligence when the genetic basis of intellectual functioning is controlled.

Collins (1951), who evaluated four hundred patients from Lennox's office practice with the Wechsler-Bellevue Intelligence Scale, found that their IQ scores compared favorably overall with the test norms. Admittedly, these patients were drawn from a generally higher socioeconomic status than the Wechsler norms, considering that the patients were seen on a private basis. Nevertheless, these findings argue against the claims of cognitive deterioration which have been ascribed to epileptics. Folsom's review of the literature (1953) indicated that mental deficiency is not typical in epilepsy, adding further support to this view.

Lennox (1960) presents rather convincing data which suggest that intellectual functioning tends to vary with the frequency of seizures, with the number of different kinds of seizure patterns that patients experience, and with the EEG patterns that they demonstrate. Only 9 percent of patients were classified as mentally retarded of the group experiencing less than 10 grand mal convulsions, whereas 54 percent who had 1,000 or more such attacks were so designated. In relating intellectual functioning to types of seizure pattern, 12 patients, having a combination of grand mal, petit mal, and psychomotor seizures, had a mean IQ of 97.5, whereas 71 patients with only petit mal attacks had a mean IQ of 110.5. Concerning the relationship between intellectual functioning and brain wave patterns, 55 patients with "very slow" waves had a mean of 95.5, whereas 61 patients with a normal EEG record had a mean IQ of 112 and 162 patients with a "fast spike wave" pattern had a mean IQ of 109. Kooi and Hovey (1957) simultaneously recorded EEG's and administered intelligence tests to a group of patients with paroxysmal cerebral activity. They found that "higher integrative processes" were impaired at times when there were signs of paroxysmal activity on the EEG. Livingston (1963) reported that mental retardation "is exceedingly high" in patients with minor motor epilepsy. Fortunately, this kind of seizure pattern is relatively uncommon.

As might be expected, intellectual functioning is more likely to be impaired in instances of acquired, as compared with idiopathic, epilepsy. This difference is attributed directly to the presence of brain damage implicit in the former designation. Lennox (1960) reported that almost 25 percent of his office patients with organic epilepsy had IQ scores below 80, whereas only 4.2 percent of his patients with metabolic epilepsy functioned at this level. At the upper extreme of intelligence, the reverse is true. Thus, approximately one third of the patients with metabolic epilepsy had an IQ score of 120 or above, whereas only 10 percent of organic cases reached this level. Since the more severe cases of organic epilepsy are not likely to survive due to the extent of brain damage, these differences may be considered to be conservative.

The question of the influence of anticonvulsant medication on intellectual functioning has received little systematic attention. Lennox (1960) pointed out that the use of bromides for the control of seizures in the nineteenth century undoubtedly produced a reduction in mental alertness. Loveland *et al.* (1957) in a three-month longitudinal study of drug effects on epileptic patients, found no significant alteration in intellectual functioning among epileptics in comparison with a group of normal controls. Since alterations in the state of consciousness are common to practically all known anticonvulsant drugs, their influence on intellectual functioning can be assumed where overdosage occurs.

For this and other reasons, careful medical supervision is required.

Although a reversible lowering of IQ as a function of emotional disturbance among epileptics has been suggested by Livingston (1963), objective support for such an effect has not been demonstrated conclusively in our opinion. Klebanoff *et al.* (1954) reviewed a study by Goldman in which three groups consisting of idiopathic epileptics, patients with hysterical seizures, and patients with brain damage but without seizures were compared. The Wechsler-Bellevue patterns of the epileptics were said to be similar to those of the neurotics while the brain-damaged group differed from both.* However, based on clinical experience, many psychologists have come to believe that emotional disturbance produces a functional impairment in cognition. Since emotional disturbances have been ascribed to epileptics, consideration of personality aberrations in the following paragraphs would have a bearing on this issue.

Personality Disturbances

Five theories of the personality of epileptics have been discussed by Tizard (1962). Briefly stated in slightly revised form and order, they are as follows:

1. The personalities of epileptics are not discriminable from those of the normal population.
2. Neuroses (or character disorders)** are more common in epileptics than in the general population.
3. Epileptics tend to be similar to patients with brain damage.
4. Although there is no personality constellation which is common to all epileptics, there are specific personality types which are related to different types of epilepsy.
5. There is a personality constellation which characterizes epileptics in general regardless of the specific type.

---

*The validity of pattern analysis of the Wechsler subtests has been a matter of controversy for some time.

**The addition of character disorders is made by the present writers. See Guerrant *et al.* (1962).

One should note that the first and fifth points of view are diametrically opposed; thus evidence favoring one of these positions would necessarily tend to refute the other.

Lennox (1960) supported the first position indicated above. He attributed emotional disturbances in epileptics, when they occur, primarily to brain damage *per se*. Klove and Doehring (1962), in a study with the Minnesota Multiphasic Personality Inventory (MMPI), compared five groups of twenty patients each, consisting of idiopathic epileptics, symptomatic epileptics, brain-damaged patients without epilepsy, patients with primary affective disorders and a hospitalized control group. They found no significant differences in mean scale levels, no noteworthy differences in profile patterns in mean scale levels, and no noteworthy differences in profile patterns among the groups. They interpreted their findings as a failure to support the claim for a characteristic epileptic personality.

Livingston (1963) emphatically denied the existence of an epileptic personality, although he attributed the basis of personality deviations, when present, to organic causes, anxiety associated with the anticipation of having seizures, reactions to social stigmatization, inappropriate management in home or community, and drug effects. Merritt (1959) reported that the personality characteristics of egocentricity, pedantry, and emotional impoverishment have not been demonstrated to be an intrinsic aspect of epilepsy, as others have claimed. According to Merritt, psychological difficulties are associated with the degree to which seizures remain uncontrolled. Anderson *et al.* (1962) compared a group of patients with psychomotor epilepsy, a group with grand mal, and a control group with normal EEG records. They disclaimed support for an epileptic personality and attributed personality aberrations, which were frequent, to chronicity of disease.

The negative findings and viewpoints reported above in regard to the claim for the existence of an epileptic personality would also serve to argue against the position that epileptics tend to be more subject to neuroses or character disorders than nonepileptics. Klove and Doehring's (1962) failure to find distinguishing features in the MMPI for either idiopathic or symptomatic epileptics in comparison with controls is one form of negative evidence. Another problem is the issue of the base rate of neurotic and characterological disturbances in the general population. Since there is some indication that the rates of these disturbances are high among nonepileptics (e.g. the findings of Srole *et al.,* 1962), one would be hard put to show a significantly higher rate among epileptics. Although Anderson *et al.* (1962) found a high proportion of personality aberrations in their epileptic samples, they disclaimed a direct connection between convulsive disorders and personality disturbances and instead emphasized the role of chronic illness in accounting for their results.

The idea that patients with brain damage and patients with epilepsy share common personality attributes, one should note, is somewhat confounding, since by definition, patients with symptomatic epilepsy are brain damaged. A frequently cited study conducted by Piotrowski (1947) is subject to question on this ground. Piotrowski evaluated 25 epileptic patients and 25 neurotics with either conversion or anxiety reactions. The epileptics were described as not psychotic, not hospitalized, and not "conspicuously deteriorated." Whether or not symptomatic cases comprised a part of the epileptic groups is not clear. Piotrowski derived 14 Rorschach signs from this study, 6 of which had previously been identified as indicators of brain damage. Since he found that 20 of the epileptic patients showed at least 7 of the 14 signs, while none of the neurotic patients showed more than 4, he concluded that epileptics share a number of psychological traits in common. In addition to the probable confounding of brain damage and epilepsy in this study, one should also note that the results, taken at face value, argue against the theory that neuroses typify the epileptic patient. This conclusion is justified, since Piotrowski claimed that there was a marked difference between the neurotics and epileptics.

A study by Delay *et al.* (1958) involving a Rorschach analysis of 50 epileptic patients of various types is subject to criticism because no control group is included. These authors claimed to have cross-validated Piotrowski's signs of epilepsy and noted that the organic indicators were superior to the epileptic ones. Since almost half of their patients sampled were categorized explicitly as having symptomatic epilepsy, these findings are not surprising, assuming that Piotrowski's organic signs are valid. The above studies fail to support the theory that epileptics and patients with brain damage have similar personalities, unless one interprets this theoretical position as a tautology. Thus, only if one is willing to concede that the personality characteristics of patients with brain lesions without epilepsy and those epileptics with organic damage share personality characteristics in common, can one claim support for this viewpoint.

The fourth theory, that there are specific personality types which are related to different types of epilepsy, has been most strenuously pursued in studies of psychomotor epilepsy. Ever since the now-classical findings of Kluver and Bucy (1939) that destruction of both temporal lobes in monkeys produces increased tractability and activity, investigators have made efforts to extend these findings to humans. Clinical studies and case reports have produced a number of personality characteristics said to typify patients with epilepsy who have a focus in the one or both temporal lobes. Such patients have been described as being subject to unstable affect, irritability, unusual aggression, and violence which may even reach homicidal proportions.

Walker (1961) and Banay (1961) reported a number of case studies in which automatism, violence, and homicide were associated with temporal lobe seizures. Glaser (1964) evaluated a series of 37 patients with psychomotor seizures, all of whom had had interictal psychotic episodes. All patients were administered a psychological test battery consisting of Wechsler Intelligence Scales, Bender-Gestalt, Rorschach Ink Blots, Thematic Apperception Test (TAT), and an object-sorting task. There was no control group. Glaser noted considerable similarity among patients in their approach to the tasks which was not reflected in the quantitative analysis. The patients were described as having fluid thought processes with signs of confusion. There were also said to be fluctuations in alertness of these patients.

Mirsky *et al.* (1960) failed to differentiate epileptic patients with focal lesions of the temporal lobes from those with nonfocal seizures using the TAT and Rorschach. Guerrant *et al.* (1962) compared a group of patients with psychomotor epilepsy, a group with idiopathic grand mal epilepsy and a control group with chronic illness not involving the brain. Patients were carefully evaluated neurologically, psychiatrically, and by a battery of psychological tests. The hypothesis that patients in the psychomotor group would be found to have a higher incidence of functional and emotional disturbances was rejected. Both psychiatric and psychological evaluations indicated that approximately 90 percent of patients in all three groups were emotionally disturbed. Psychiatric ratings attributing a higher frequency of brain damage to the psychomotor group were not supported by the psychological evaluations. While the patients with grand mal epilepsy were judged to have a high rate of personality disorders, those with psychomotor epilepsy showed a high frequency of psychosis, and the medical controls were most often considered to have neurotic disturbances. The finding that psychosis is more frequent in the temporal lobe group than in the other two groups is supported by two other independent studies.

Roger and Dongier (1950) reported that 84 percent of epileptics admitted to psychiatric hospitals had focal damage of the temporal lobe. Baldwin (1960) found that 60 percent of a series of 235 patients with temporal lobe epilepsy had required psychiatric treatment prior to their admission to the National Institute of Neurological Diseases and Blindness. If one assumes that patients with more severe psychological disturbances are likely to be referred to a psychiatrist or to be hospitalized, then these findings stand in agreement with Guerrant *et al.* that psychosis is more common in temporal lobe epilepsy. That the psychological difficulties of patients with psychomotor epilepsy are probably not as widespread as these studies would suggest is indicated by Coleman's (1964) report that only 1.2 percent of first admissions to mental hospitals involve patients with both psychosis and epilepsy. One would gather, however, that a considerable proportion of such patients would have psychomotor seizures.

The selected review of personality theories in epilepsy presented above suggests the following tentative conclusions. There is little likelihood that epileptics, regardless of type, severity, and degree of control, share a common personality. Although neurotic and character disturbances may be commonly found among epileptics, these difficulties do not appear to be associated in any singular manner with convulsive disorders *per se*. Patients with symptomatic epilepsy may share some personality characteristics with brain-damaged patients without epilepsy due to the fact that both groups have cerebral lesions. There are some indications that patients with temporal lobe epilepsy have a greater incidence of severe personality disturbances, including psychosis, than patients with other types of seizures. From the above review, it seems clear that many contradictions remain to be resolved, and further interdisciplinary studies are needed to clarify the nature of the relationships between personality variables and epileptic conditions.

SOCIAL ASPECTS OF EPILEPSY

In addition to previously noted concerns about the medical and psychological aspects of epilepsy, further difficulties undoubtedly have been created for these patients as the result of the responses of other members of society toward them. White (1964) has pointed out that personality problems of the epileptic are not only due to the condition of his brain but also to the consequences of social disability imposed upon him by society. In this section, the social problems of the epileptic will be considered.

Legislative Limitations

The social difficulties of the epileptic are perhaps most readily documented in the legislation applied to him at both the federal and state levels in the United States. Lennox and Markham (1953) reported that federal *immigration laws* have prohibited the issuance of even a visitor's visa to those epileptics whose seizures are not due to brain damage. Legislation in a number of the states has restricted the issuance of marriage licenses to epileptics. Peer (1959) noted that seventeen states prohibited the issuance of such licenses to epileptics. Angers (1960) found that 62.7 percent of the 1,521 adult epileptics in rehabilitation programs in his study were never married, although 89.4 percent were employed. A 1965 survey of state laws undertaken by the Epilepsy Foundation (1965) noted that fourteen states permitted sterilization of epileptics under certain conditions. All of these measures apparently have been instituted as an outgrowth of public concern based on the claims of the profound significance of genetic factors in epilepsy, a matter previously noted in this chapter to be a subject of debate among experts in the field.

Another legal sphere which is restrictive toward epileptics is *licensing* to drive a motor vehicle. These restrictions are invoked typically at the discretion of the motor vehicle administrator rather than being an explicit law. According to a survey by the Epilepsy Foundation (1965), only five states have prescribed specific standards for licensing epileptics seeking a driver's permit. Elliott (1963) expressed his opposition to licensing epileptics because of the presumed hazards involved. On the other hand, Steinwall (1961) reported a study by Herner in Sweden which found an accident rate of only 2 per 1,000 attributable to epilepsy. Lennox (1960) noted a 13 percent accident rate associated with the ingestion of alcohol in Massachusetts over a three-year period, whereas none was attributed to epilepsy during this time. Barrow and Fabing (1956) analyzed driving status in the United States and noted a recent trend toward liberalizing earlier, more restrictive interpretations of various laws. Livingston (1963) presented relatively new procedures used in Maryland for licensing drivers who are epileptic. These procedures have been recommended as somewhat of a model that might be followed elsewhere.

Yet another legal sphere which has profound implications for the social well-being of the epileptic is *workmen's compensation.* Lennox (1960) has recommended that workmen's compensation laws be revised so that employers will not have to bear the burden of costs of awards for injuries deriving from epileptic attacks occurring while on the job. Perhaps the problem here is one of the employers' attitudes toward epilepsy more than anything else. This impression is supported by the following statement taken from a summary of findings concerning workmen's compensation insurance involving epileptics (Epilepsy Foundation, 1965).

> Great concern is shown on the part of the insurance companies and bureaus over the fact that some employers use a professed fear of higher workmen's compensation premiums as an excuse for not hiring persons with epilepsy. There is some sentiment that a number of employers know this fear is unfounded, but they find it to be a more convenient explanation than disclosing the real reasons for not hiring such persons.

Public Attitude

Aside from the legal strictures noted above, public attitudes toward epilepsy have been investigated directly in three national polls in the United States from 1949 to 1959. The first national sample reflected considerable aversion to epilepsy. Caveness (1949) reported that although 57 percent of the sample indicated that they know an epileptic and 56 percent stated that they had witnessed a seizure, only 57 percent stated they would *not* object to having an epileptic attend school with their children, while 24 percent would object. Fifty-nine percent of the sample indicated that epilepsy was not a form of insanity, but 35 percent thought it was. Forty-five percent thought that epileptics should be employed in the same manner as anyone else, but 35 percent disagreed. Lennox (1960) reported a second survey of public attitudes toward epilepsy by Caveness, Mangold, and Gallup with the following results. Sixty-eight percent of the sample expressed their willingness to have epileptics attend school with their children. The same percentage indicated that epilepsy was not a form of insanity. Sixty percent indicated that epileptics should be employed in a normal manner. A third poll, summarized by Lennox (1960) and conducted by Caveness (1960) found that 74 percent of the sample believed that epilepsy was not a form of insanity. Seventy-five percent thought that epileptics should be employed on the same basis as others. The gains in positive attitudes toward epilepsy were attributed by Lennox to efforts directed toward public education. Despite these gains, the surveys indicate that a significant residue of prejudice and ignorance about epilepsy remains in the general population.

Response to Prejudice

How the epileptic responds to such prejudice is suggested in a study by Hayes (Forrest, 1962). She indicated that the salient difficulty she found in carrying out a study of employment problems of epileptics was the identification of these people, "since the epileptic made every effort to keep his condition a secret" (p. 32). This impression is supported in a study of the vocational effectiveness of epileptics by Udell (1960) who found that 33 of 110 epileptics were not known to their employers as having this condition. He asserted that the majority of epileptics in an employment setting will deny having had seizures because of the fear that they would not be hired.

Probably one of the most emotionally laden social problems for the epileptic is the question, "Should a person with epilepsy marry and have children?" This must be decided on an individual basis. How seriously disabling is the disease? Aside from possible economic problems, heredity is something of a factor in all cases. A person with epilepsy who marries a nonepileptic may expect only one child in fifty resulting from the union to suffer from convulsions. As you recall, the instance in the general population is one in two hundred. Putnam (1943, p. 164) mentions three sets of circumstances, any of which may be considered definite grounds for advising a given person not to have children.

> The first is the existence of a high degree of disability resulting from the disorder. Second is a history of convulsions occurring in two or more successive generations of his (or her) ancestors. The third is evidence that there is some tendency to seizures in the family of the other prospective partner. Under any of these circumstances, the likelihood that the children will be subject to seizures has been shown to be extremely serious.

Lennox points to the following factors as tending to minimize the chances of the disease in the child of an epileptic: a family history devoid of epilepsy or migraine for the spouse as well as the patient, a minimal abnormality of their encephalograms, some acquired condition that is at least partially responsible for seizures, late onset of the illness, and a normal mentality.

The above sampling of the available literature relevant to social aspects of epilepsy indicates clearly that such patients need only be concerned with their medical and personal problems. Indeed the discrimination that the epileptic is likely to encounter on the part of the general public might well be considered analogous to a pariah's role in society. Fortunately, the previously cited material contains encouraging signs of increasing enlightenment on the part of the public. Nevertheless, not the least of the epileptic's problems is winning greater acceptance for himself in education and employment, aspects of life which account for a large portion of normal waking activity.

REHABILITATION ASPECTS OF EPILEPSY

The rehabilitation of epileptics is a multifaceted process. Since epilepsy first occurs preponderantly before the age of 20, the rehabilitation specialist is not likely to come into professional contact with many such people until after their condition has become a long-standing problem. In some instances, the epileptic will have limited experience in a vocation and may not have entered a stable occupation. Thus, habilitation to a career may be required rather than rehabilitation.

Despite the large number of epileptics estimated to be in the employable age range, a lesser number are likely to require rehabilitation services. Many undoubtedly will have resolved these problems with more or less success by themselves. On the other hand, others may have disabilities that are too severe to permit them to benefit from rehabilitation services at the time they seek such assistance.

Scope of Problem

A recent survey conducted by Dishart (1964) and sponsored by the National Rehabilitation Association indicated that of 1,240 epileptics processed by 36 state vocational rehabilitation agencies, 15 applicants were not accepted because they had insufficient disabilities; 9 had no vocational handicap; 41 were presently employed. Of 585 epileptics who were not accepted for vocational rehabilitation by these agencies, 11 percent were found to be not in need of these services for the above reasons. A total of 133, or almost 23 percent, however, were designated as having handicaps too severe at the time they were seen to make such services useful.

John W. Forrest of the Office of Vocational Rehabilitation, Atlanta, Georgia, made a powerful plea for cooperative and comprehensive rehabilitation coverage for epileptics at a national institute on rehabilitation of the epileptic in Chicago in 1960.

Vocational rehabilitation workers, social workers, physicians, psychologists and placement representatives all have a definite role to play in the vocational rehabilitation of persons with seizures. Epilepsy is as common as diabetes and perhaps twice as prevalent as tuberculosis. The many people it affects should be vocationally rehabilitated because society cannot in the normal scheme of things maintain so large a group as this in idleness and inactivity. We must start thinking of medical control as a beginning and not as an end in itself, then go one step further and help the person from seizure control into employment so that he will be able to sustain himself.

Social and emotional growth is important to people with seizures in order to keep their futures from being grim and unrewarding. But unless this social and emotional growth can find expression in remunerative employment, then this growth, like seizure control, only adds to the feelings of futility and frustration that the person with seizures must face.

Seizures constitute a difficult medical problem and a tremendous social problem which all too often has a direct effect on emotional and vocational adjustment. This letter from an epileptic typifies the situation:

> Vacant positions in and around my town are very few for the normal persons, and with the disability I have the odds are very much against me. It was or is my intention to secure employment for a few days before I begin school. However, the employers of the vicinity cannot seem to overlook the fact that once my attacks were severe but now are under control.
>
> Therefore, there are many places I could have secured employment, feeling confident I was capable of holding the position. But

so many times I have had the epilepsy thrown in my face with the answer of no and the bitter taste of defeat along with it.

These things, to a great extent, make you feel segregated socially, and to face the facts, I am. From family statements from time to time, I am sure their viewpoint is the same as employers. This is a very difficult situation to cope with.

Seizure control made this boy available for employment, but it did not do anything to resolve his family problems, or improve his concept, or alter the opinion of employers about hiring people who have a history of seizures.

This boy—we will call him Carl—has had a lifelong seizure problem. It began as a result of brain damage when he was born, along with additional physical limitations imposed by a left-sided hemiplegia.

He is the son of a prosperous farmer, but because of his spells and other physical disabilities, he was never able to contribute much to the management of the highly mechanized family farm. But he was bright and had perseverance. He finished high school and he wanted to go further but could not because of his multiple problems. His referral to vocational rehabilitation was made by a merchant in a nearby town to whom he had applied for work.

The family had some grave reservations and misgivings about vocational rehabilitation for Carl. The community attitude toward epilepsy, like the family, was rather negative. Both felt that people with seizures should be kept out of sight.

The family never discussed Carl's seizures with him. They were good to him; they loved him; but they felt just a little ashamed of him, too, and did not even like the idea of his going to the nearest town for fear that he might have a seizure and embarrass them. They also had a fear that something dreadful might happen to him and so wanted to keep him constantly under their supervision "just in case." As a result, they were rather resistant to any program that might take this boy out of the home and away from their supervision and protection, and yet they realized that he could not make a living for himself unless he got away from home.

The situation is a common one. How is the vocational rehabilitation counselor to work with this young man toward any vocational rehabilitation program unless the family can be made a part of it?

This family is going to have to gain some insight into their own feelings and what these feelings have had to do with their son and the way he feels about himself. They are going to have to accept him as a person and not as just another epileptic.

Carl had some misgivings about himself, too. He had the feeling that he was not a person that should be held in high esteem. In school: "boys and girls wouldn't play with me for having spells. They never did like me. It had made me lose confidence in myself." With girls: "My girl friend's father disapproved of me because of my seizures. My emotions have a ninety percent influence on when I have seizures, so I load up on Dilantin when I go to see her so I won't have a seizure."

He had all the same feelings that his family and community had about seizures. He had seen some other people have seizures and felt they were grim, gruesome, frightening experiences.

Because of all these things, Carl tended to withdraw. As he withdrew, he limited some of the stimulating social contact he might have had and so learned very little about how he might fit himself into his world in a meaningful, productive way.

Most people with seizures have tremendous psychological problems as well as all the other problems that the so-called normal person might have. As a group, they are more sensitive, more hostile and aggressive, more anxious, and more insecure.

Perhaps as one of the results of this insecurity, many of them indulge themselves in a considerable amount of fantasy, and Carl did this, too. He would see himself as a very able person whose contribution in his chosen field of endeavor could be so great that people would forget his epilepsy and admire him as an individual. All of us indulge ourselves in some fantasies of this nature at one time or another, but with Carl this fantasy became an all-prevailing ambition that had to be realized. Unfortunately, he did not have the intellectual endowment or the personal resources to reach this goal, and he was caught with a burning need to be more than he could be. Carl had been so defensive about these deeper feelings that no one even suspected their presence until he began working with his counselor and planning for vocational rehabilitation.

Here is an area in which the psychologist can contribute to vocational rehabilitation. He must apprise the vocational rehabilitation counselor of the dynamics of this person's personality—his level of intellectual confidence, strength, weakness, evidences of deterioration, whether he sees himself in a positive way, how he sees his environment, how he feels about other people, whether he seems motivated for work and self-sufficiency or derives some secondary gain from seizures, whether he can accept help. These are all factors essential to good vocational rehabilitation planning. They are basically psychological problems, but they are often a major obstacle to vocational success.

When Carl went into training, he had been seizure-free on medication for about eight months. However, after about six weeks in training, he began to have seizures again. The dean and the registrar of the school where he was taking a special course wanted him withdrawn immediately.

Carl was brought in for an interview and it was discovered that he still had grave doubts about himself. He had not done well on one of the tests that he had taken, and he began to feel that he was not really capable of performing acceptably in class. What resulted was a sort of subconscious defense mechanism. He began to have a block about taking his medicine, could not remember whether he had had his doses, and began to miss drug medication regularly. The result was the seizures came back. He preferred return of seizures and forced withdrawal from school to the possible admission that he did not have enough intellectual ability for the course of study he was taking. Although this happened to Carl during training, it might just as easily have happened during his period of vocational placement.

Quite often it is found that emotional tensions created by the demands of new and frustrating situations will cause return of seizures and a longing to return to a secure, protected, dependent status, even though it is grossly unsatisfying. This episode points up the need for continued follow-up. The need for vocational and emotional follow-up is as important as medical follow-up to good vocational rehabilitation.

Most of the people referred to vocational rehabilitation are not equipped to be self-sustaining, self-assured, and competent just because they have had their seizures controlled and have been placed on a job. These cases are followed with supportive counseling, reassurance, and other help that seems necessary.

Carl continued to have difficulties periodically. He had a difficult time getting a job and his first job did not last long. He refused to tell his employer that he had epileptic seizures because he felt that he would not get the job. But he developed considerable tension, had a spell, and was fired.

All clients should be encouraged to tell the employer they have epilepsy. Members of an experimental group that were not encouraged to tell the employer and members of another group that were encouraged to tell the employer were compared. Those who told the employer had a harder time getting the job initially, but once they got it, they usually stayed longer. Those who did not tell the employer sometimes developed a considerable amount of tension and had "spells" as a result.

Carl's case is a typical one. It points up the vocational needs of a person with seizures and the fact that you cannot separate vocational from social, psychological, and medical considerations.

Actually, successful vocational rehabilitation is a composite of all of these. It requires good medical supervision, good vocational counseling, adequate social adjustment, and sufficient integration of personality for the person with seizures to perform at his fullest potential.

One would surmise that symptomatic epileptics are likely to have more severe rehabilitation problems than those with cryptogenic epilepsy. In addition to the problem of controlling seizures in both groups, those with symptomatic epilepsy may have other difficulties associated with brain damage. As previously noted, for example, a greater proportion of individuals with symptomatic epilepsy are likely to have intellectual deficiencies in comparison with the cryptogenic group.

Despite some evidence to the contrary (Hill, 1963; Livingston, 1963), personality problems would be expected to be a significant complication among individuals with temporal lobe epilepsy. These people may constitute a group with especially severe personality problems (Angers, 1960; Folsom, 1953).

Regardless of type, all epileptics appear to be confronted with the problem of making an adequate social adjustment in the face of considerable rejection from other members of society. Although individual differences in this problem area might reasonably be expected, one would speculate that this sphere may be particularly troublesome to those epileptics who seek rehabilitation services. Efforts to induce modification in the attitudes of significant others as well as epileptics may be an important and necessary aspect of the rehabilitation process.

Despite these medical, psychological, and social problems, the value of rehabilitation efforts with epileptics is considerable, as shown in a study by Angers (1960). He reported on the efficacy of rehabilitation efforts with 1,521 epileptics who received services in fiscal year 1957. These services were provided under the combined auspices of federal and state vocational rehabilitation agencies. As a result of these efforts, 89.4 percent of the sample were able to achieve some form of employment. The value of these services is attested to eloquently in terms of the cash earnings of these people before and after rehabilitation. The total income of the group prior to rehabilitation amounted to 279,300 dollars, whereas following rehabilitation, earnings rose to 3,128,100 dollars. From this finding, one need not justify rehabilitation efforts on humanitarian grounds alone. A strong case can be made for the value of such services in contributing to the gross national product!

PRIMARY CONSIDERATIONS IN REHABILITATION

The successful rehabilitation of those epileptics who need it is dependent on several considerations. Such factors as accurate appraisal, rehabilitation goals, cooperation of professional specialists working with the client, the epileptics' attitudes, educational level, intellectual functioning, interest patterns all enter in, as well as the demands of the specific jobs in which they are placed. Each of these factors will be summarized briefly.

Appraisal of the Epileptic on an Individual Basis

Of primary importance is the appraisal of the epileptic on an individual basis. Generalizations derived from research studies are useful in alerting the professional in the field to be aware of certain possibilities, but individual appraisal of the epileptic's unique constellation of problems and characteristics is essential if rehabilitation is to be maximally effective.

Goals of Rehabilitation

The goals of rehabilitation programs for epileptics must be flexible. In some instances, satisfactory placement in a sheltered workshop may be all that is feasible. In other instances, goals may be more ambitious. The setting of goals and their modification should be determined on a mutual basis between the rehabilitation specialist and the epileptic.

Cooperation Among a Number of Professional Specialists

Cooperation among a number of professional specialists is mandatory if optimal results are to be obtained. The services of physicians, social workers, rehabilitation counselors, and clinical and counseling psychologists may all contribute toward the desired goal of the individual epileptic.

The physician is responsible for the assessment of the epileptic's physical status and management. Appraisal of seizure type(s), frequency, severity, degree of control, and side effects rests with the physician. The times of day when attacks occur, whether or not they are preceded by an aura and significant stimulus conditions associated with the precipitation of seizures, are important considerations to be taken into account in rehabilitation planning. Intercurrent illnesses or other disabilities need to be appraised. If seizures are frequent and severe, then the current goals of rehabilitation will have to be relatively modest until more adequate control is achieved. If seizures are invariably preceded by a reliable aura which permits the epileptic to take precautions to insure safety of himself and others, then this factor may be counted as an asset. A small proportion of epileptics experience seizures only at night during sleep, an obviously favorable circumstance from the standpoint of rehabilitation.

The Epileptic's Attitude Toward His Illness

The epileptic's attitude toward his illness should be assessed. His understanding and the degree to which he realistically accepts his condition need to be evaluated. To what extent his views are amenable to change, if such is indicated, should also be considered.

The quality of the epileptic's psychosocial adjustment is of considerable importance in the rehabilitation program. Several approaches to assessment are available in this sphere. Significant information may be obtained through careful inquiry into difficulties encountered in various life situations, including home, school, job, medical setting, and the rehabilitation facility. An informant's history of the epileptic's interpersonal relationships from a friend or relative might be helpful not only in ascertaining the epileptic's effectiveness in social situations but also the extent of conflict and ambivalence directed toward him by significant others in his life situation. To what extent personality problems are attributable to the epileptic condition and associated organic defects, if any, or are a product of psychosocial conflict may be difficult to assess. Formal psychological appraisal as well as other previously mentioned procedures may be useful in evaluating this issue.

History of the Epileptic's Educational Attainment

The history of the epileptic's educational attainment and the skills which he has acquired are important facets of information to be obtained. Furthermore, when such education and skills were attained in relation to the onset and course of his seizures should be ascertained. To what extent his functional capacity to use these attainments has been impaired, should also be appraised.

Level of Intellectual Functioning

His level of intellectual functioning, his capacity, and indications of change in this sphere should be considered. In this regard, a decision involving the need for formal testing will have to be made. In some instances, such assessment may be of the utmost value, whereas in other circumstances it may be unnecessary.

Interest Patterns

The interest patterns of the epileptic, their distinctness, and their stability should be considered. Furthermore, the bearing of these interest patterns on his vocational potential is of considerable relevance.

Demands of Specific Job

The rehabilitation specialist must not only consider the assets and liabilities of his epileptic client but also the demands of various forms of employment positions if placement is to prove satisfactory. The heterogeneity of occupational choices of epileptics with empirical documentation of persons employed in these positions has been examined by Norris (1960) for a selective sample of veterans of World War II and the Korean conflict; this information was published by the Department of Veterans Benefits. This document is a valuable reference for vocational specialists.

The processes of placement and follow-up are an essential part of rehabilitation. These activities, in addition to providing feedback on the appropriateness of the placement, also afford opportunities to serve a public relations function. The need for the latter is underscored by previously noted findings that epileptics are reluctant to inform employers of their condition and by the evidence of prejudice directed toward epileptics by some employers and segments of the general public. Angers (1960) found that epileptics compare quite well with the general population in terms of intellect, education, vocational training, and experience. He emphasized the need for equal opportunity for the epileptic in relation to his current functioning and potential.

Lennox (1949) has indicated three occupational categories

which he deemed as generally unsuitable for epileptics, namely, those positions which would constitute a threat to the lives of others, those which would endanger the epileptic's life, and those where public prejudice would create an excessive problem. Lofquist (1957) has called attention to vocational hazards of operating motor vehicles and power machinery, working in high places, and handling dangerous materials such as acids.

Our view is that one must be exceedingly cautious in making generalizations. With continued progress in the diagnosis and treatment of epilepsy, coupled with wider understanding on the part of the public, suitable occupational choices for the epileptic should become increasingly broad. At the present time, the rehabilitation of epileptics requires an individualized approach.

REFERENCES

Alpers, B. J.: *Clinical Neurology.* Philadelphia, F. A. Davis Company, 1950.

Alstrom, C. H.: *A Study of Epilepsy in its Clinical, Social, and Genetic Aspects.* Copenhagen, Munksgaard, 1950.

Anderson, W. W., Guerrant, J., Weinstein, M., and Fisher, A.: The epileptic personality—does it exist? *Neurology, 12:*301, 1962.

Angers, W. P.: Job counseling of the epileptic. *Journal of Psychology, 49:*123, 1960.

Angers, W. P.: Patterns of abilities and capacities in the epileptic. *Journal of Genetic Psychology, 103:*59, 1963.

Baldwin, M.: The problem of temporal lobe epilepsy in occupational medicine. *Archives of Environmental Health, AMA, 1:*253, 1960.

Banay, R. S.: Criminal genesis and the degrees of responsibility in epileptics. *American Journal of Psychiatry, 117:*873, 1961.

Barrow, R. L. and Fabing, H. D.: *Epilepsy and the Law.* New York, Hoeber-Harper, 1956.

Caveness, W.: A survey of public attitudes toward epilepsy. *Epilepsia, 4:*19, 1949.

Caveness, W. F.: Trend in public attitudes toward epilepsy over the past decade. *Epilepsia, 1:*385, 1960.

Chusid, J. G. and McDonald, J. J.: *Correlative Neuroanatomy and Functional Neurology.* Los Altos, California, Lange Medical Publications, 1962.

Coleman, J. C.: *Abnormal Psychology and Modern Life.* Chicago, Scott, Foresman and Co., 1964.

Collins, A. L.: Epileptic intelligence. *Journal of Consulting Psychology, 15*:392, 1951.

Currier, R. D., Kooi, K. A., and Saidman, L. J.: Prognosis of "pure" petit mal: A follow-up study. *Neurology, 13*:959, 1963.

Delay, J., Pichot, P., Lemperiere, T., and Perse, J.: *The Rorschach and the Epileptic.* Translated by Rita and Arthur L. Benton. New York, Logos Press, 1958.

Dishart, M.: *A national study of 84,699 applicants for services from state vocational rehabilitation agencies in the United States.* Washington, D. C., National Rehabilitation Association, 1964.

Elliot, A.: Motor driving and epilepsy. *Practitioner, 190*:371, 1963.

Evans, J. H.: Post-traumatic epilepsy. *Neurology, 12*:665, 1962.

Folsom, A.: Psychological testing in epilepsy. I. Cognitive Function. *Epilepsia, 2*:15, 1953.

Forrest, J. W.: Vocational rehabilitation. In: National Institute on Rehabilitation of the Epileptic: *Total Rehabilitation of Epileptics.* Washington, D. C., U. S. Government Printing Office, 1962.

Glaser, G. H.: The problem of psychosis in psychomotor temporal lobe epileptics. *Epilepsia, 5*:271, 1964.

Gibbs, F. A.: A definition of epilepsy. In: National Institute on Rehabilitation of the Epileptic: *Total Rehabilitation of Epileptics.* Washington, D. C., U. S. Government Printing Office, 1962.

Guerrant, J., Anderson, W. W., Fisher, A., Weinstein, M. R., Jarcos, R. M., and Deskins, A.: *Personality and Epilepsy.* Springfield, Thomas, 1962.

Hayes, M.: An exploration of employment problems of persons with epilepsy. Unpublished thesis, University of Tennessee, 1957.

Hill, D:. Epilepsy: Clinical aspects. In Hill, D., and Parr, G. (Eds.): *Electroencephalography.* New York, Macmillan, 1963.

Hyllested, K. and Pakkenberg, H.: Prognosis in epilepsy of late onset. *Neurology, 13*:641, 1963.

Kiorboe, E.: The prognosis of epilepsy. *Acta Psychiatrica Neurologica Scandinavica, 36*:166, 1961.

Klebanoff, S. G., Singer, J. L., and Wilensky, H.: Psychological consequences of brain lesions and ablations. *Psychology Bulletin, 51*:1, 1954.

Klove, H. and Doehring, D. G.: MMPI in epileptic groups differential etiology. *Journal of Clinical Psychology, 18*:149, 1962.

Kluver, J. and Bucy, P. C.: Preliminary analysis of functions of the temporal lobe in monkeys. *Archives of Neurology and Psychiatry,* 42:979, 1939.

Kooi, K. A. and Hovey, W. B.: Alterations in mental function and paroxysmal cerebral activity. *Archives of Neurology and Psychiatry,* 78:264, 1957.

Krohn, W.: A study of epilepsy in northern Norway, its frequency and character. *Acta Psychiatrica Neurologica Scandinavica,* 36:215, 1961.

Kurland, L. T.: The incidence and prevalence of convulsive disorders in a small urban community. *Epilepsia, 1:*143, 1959.

Lennox, W. G.: The epileptic made socially useful. In Soden, W. H. (Ed.): *Rehabilitation of the Handicapped.* New York, Ronald Press, 1949.

Lennox, W. G.: *Epilepsy and Related Disorders.* Boston, Little, Brown, and Co., 1960, Vol. II.

Lennox, W. G. and Markham, C. H.: The sociopsychological treatment of epilepsy. *Journal of the American Medical Association, 152:*1690, 1953.

Lilienfield, A. M. and Pasamanick, B.: Associations of maternal and fetal factors with the development of epilepsy. *Journal of the American Medical Association, 155:*719, 1954.

Livingston, S.: *Living with Epileptic Seizures.* Springfield, Thomas, 1963.

Lofquist, L. H.: *Vocational Counseling with the Physically Handicapped.* New York, Appleton-Century-Crofts, Inc., 1957.

Loveland, N., Smith, B., and Forster, F. M.: Mental and emotional changes in epileptic patients on continuous anticonvulsant medication: A preliminary report. *Neurology, 7:*856, 1957.

Merritt, H. H.: *A Textbook of Neurology,* 2nd ed. Philadelphia, Lea and Febiger, 1959.

Mirsky, A. F., Primac, D. W., Maksan, C. A., Rosvold, H. E., and Stevens, J. R.: A comparison of the psychological test performance of patients with focal and nonfocal epilepsy. *Experimental Neurology, 2:*75, 1960.

National Institute on Rehabilitation of the Epileptic, *Total Rehabilitation of Epileptics.* Washington, D. C., U. S. Government Printing Office, 1962.

Norris, R. W.: *Occupations of Epileptic Veterans of World War II and Korean Conflict.* Washington, D. C., Department of Veteran Benefits, 1960.

Noyes, A. P. and Klob, L. C.: *Modern Clinical Psychiatry.* Philadelphia, W. B. Saunders Company, 1958.

Penfield, W. and Jasper, H.: *Epilepsy and the Functional Anatomy of the Human Brain.* Boston, Little, Brown, and Company, 1954.

Peer, I. N.: Epilepsy and the law. *Journal of Nervous and Mental Disease, 128:*262, 1959.

Piotrowski, A. Z.: The personality of the epileptic. In Hoch, P. H. and Knight, R. P. (Eds.): *Epilepsy.* New York, Grune and Stratton, 1947.

Putnam, T. J.: *Convulsive Seizures.* Philadelphia, Lippincott, 1943.

Roger, A. and Dongier, M.: Correlations electrocliniques chez 50 epileptiques internes. *Review of Neurology, 83:*593, 1950.

Srole, L., Langner, T. S., Michael, S. T., Opler, M. K., and Rennie, T. A. C.: *Mental Health in the Metropolis: The Midtown Manhattan Study.* Blakiston Division, McGraw-Hill, 1962.

Steinwall, O.: Epilepsy and the driver's license. *Acta Psychiatrica Neurologica Scandinavica, 36:*179, 1961.

The Epilepsy Foundation: *Epilepsy: A Survey of State Laws,* 1965 (pamphlet).

The Epilepsy Foundation: *Workmen's Compensation and Epilepsy,* 1965 (pamphlet).

Tizard, B.: The personality of epileptics: A discussion of the evidence. *Psychology Bulletin, 59:*196, 1962.

Udell, M. M.: The work performance of epileptics in industries. *Archives of Environmental Health, 1:*257, 1960.

Walker, A. E.: Murder or epilepsy? *Journal of Nervous and Mental Disease, 133:*430, 1961.

White, R. W.: *The Abnormal Personality,* 3rd ed. New York, Ronald Press, 1964.

Yahr, M. D. and Merritt, H. H.: Current status of the drug therapy of epileptic seizures. *Journal of the American Medical Association, 161:*333, 1956.

Chapter XIII

REHABILITATION MEDICAL ASPECTS OF HEARING DISORDERS

LLOYD A. STORRS

To try and understand the many conditions that impair hearing, we must first know something about the structure of the ear, how it functions, and the diseases that attack it.

The ear is divided into three separate anatomical parts. These are the external ear, the middle ear, and the inner ear.

1. The *external ear* is composed of the auricle, the external ear canal, and the eardrum.
2. The *middle ear* is composed of the inner surface of the eardrum, the middle ear cavity, the ossicular chain (malleus, incus, and stapes), and the tympanic end of the eustachian tube.
3. The *internal ear* is composed of the organ of hearing (cochlea) and the organ of balance (vestibular apparatus), their various communicating channels, and the origin of their central nervous connections.

PHYSIOLOGY

The human ear is a receiving mechanism for sound of exquisite fidelity, being able to perceive from 20 to 20,000 hertz. It is tuned, however, primarily to receive the human speech frequencies which are 500, 1000 and 2000 Hz. Just exactly how this appreciation and awareness of sound takes place is not completely understood.

The sound that is produced by the human voice speaking in a normal conversational level must be amplified by the ear or it would not be audible; therefore there must be some mechanism within the ear which amplifies this sound. This has been found to be the eardrum and the ossicular chain. This mechanism amplifies the airborne sounds by approximately 30 dB. Following amplification, the sound is carried into the organ of hearing

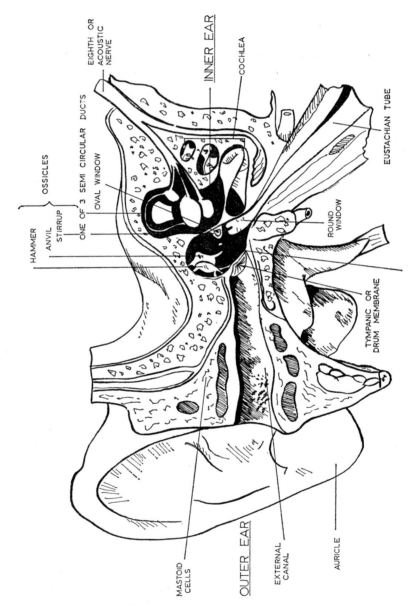

Figure XIII-1. Sectional diagram of the human ear. (Illustration by Stanley Y. Louie, Texas Tech University, Lubbock, Texas.)

which is called the cochlea. The cochlea is filled with fluid, and the hair cells, which are the nerve endings, are located within this fluid. These are the sound receivers which, once stimulated, fire messages to the central brain connections. The final authority over any auditory stimulus is the brain itself. The area of the brain which appreciates sound is in the temporal lobe called Broca's convolution. As a note of interest, it is curious that the balance mechanism is also located in the ears. Why this arrangement is interconnected remains a mystery.

PATHOLOGY

Now that we have briefly discussed the anatomy and have a working knowledge of the physiology, let us proceed to the understanding of the diseases that affect the ear and its ability to function. This is called pathology. The pathological states that affect the ear are divided into injuries, infections, anomalies, tumors, and degenerations.

INJURY. We are all familiar with injuries that can occur in automobile accidents and almost any traumatic experience that one can imagine. Other injuries can result from high sound intensities such as are found in the working environments of sheet metal workers, jet engine mechanics, military personnel, and miners.

INFECTIONS. The most common diseases affecting the ears are due to bacterial or virus disorders. Everyone is familiar with the child or adult that suddenly becomes ill with a feverish condition, generally a sore throat, and an ensuing earache.

ANOMALIES. The most outstanding examples of anomalies that involve the ear are the ones in which a part does not develop. This may involve only the external ear, the external ear canal, or only the internal ear; or there may be combinations of all involvements. An example of this is the deaf mute.

TUMORS. Each division of the ear—external, middle and internal—has its own specific tumor and each of these tumors have definite signs and symptoms. The external ear may be affected by skin cancer, and the middle ear by blood vessel tumors called glomus jugularies, and the internal ear by the acoustic neuroma.

DEGENERATIONS. The degenerative conditions which affect the hearing are those that affect the body in general. These are advancing age, hardening of the arteries (arteriosclerosis), diabetes, syphilis, metabolic disturbances, congenital disorders, otosclerosis, and many others.

Pathology of Hearing

We have discussed the pathological conditions which can cause hearing losses. Regardless of the nature of the disease which caused the difficulty, hearing losses are divided into three distinct types: (a) conductive, (b) perceptive (sensorineural), and (c) mixed. The hearing loss is generally greater than 30dB.

CONDUCTIVE HEARING LOSSES. Conductive hearing losses are due to disorders that involve the conducting mechanism of the ear, that is, the external ear, the external ear canal, and the eardrum or ossicular chain.

PERCEPTIVE (SENSORINEURAL) HEARING LOSSES. Hearing losses that are perceptive are due to diseases that affect the internal ear (cochlea and vestibular apparatuses). These hearing losses generally cause a loss of the nerve endings (hair cells) which results in profound hearing loss.

MIXED HEARING LOSSES. Mixed hearing losses are a combination of any of the other causes of hearing losses. That is, the disorder is due to both a conductive and a perceptive involvement.

Treatment

Treatment of the above-described conditions is the primary concern of the ear specialist (otologist). He is supported in his efforts by the rehabilitation and occupational therapists and other paramedical specialists.

Conductive Deafness

How does the otologist diagnose conductive deafness? A careful history is obtained from the patient regarding his past medical and surgical problems which could account for a loss of hearing. In general, the history is the first and most important clue to the diagnosis of the patient's problem.

A thorough and searching physical examination is then done. The patient's general condition is observed, as well as his ability to follow conversation, his state of awareness, and his general body development and preservation. The ear is inspected externally and with the use of the otoscope. The eardrum can be examined externally for evidence of perforation or other signs which are clues to the patient's difficulty, and finally the hearing is examined by means of tuning forks and the audiometer. Audiometric studies in conductive hearing losses reveal that the airborne sounds are not heard as well as the sounds which are borne through the skull or bone-conducted sounds. This results in an air-bone gap which is typical of conductive hearing losses. The hearing loss is usually 30 dB and the gap 20 to 30 dB. The diseases which most commonly cause conductive hearing losses are infections such as chronic otitis media and mastoiditis with eardrum perforations and otosclerosis which is a hereditary form of deafness due to an overgrowth of bone around the stapes footplate. This causes the stapes to become fused in the oval window and does not allow it to transmit sound from the eardrum to the organ of hearing.

The treatment of chronic otitis media and mastoiditis is surgical, by an operation referred to as a tympanoplasty with myringoplasty. This means that the diseased tissues in the mastoid and middle ear are removed and that the eardrum, and at times the ossicular chain, are repaired by plastic surgical methods. The treatment for otosclerosis is by an operation called a stapedectomy. The stapes bone is removed and replaced by a prosthesis made of stainless steel wire and a small piece of connective tissue.

Conductive hearing losses comprise about half of the patients with deafness and are the ones that lend themselves to treatment and in which the test results are obtained. In general, the hearing can be restored in about 50 percent of the cases of chronic otitis media and mastoiditis and around 90 percent of the cases with otosclerosis.

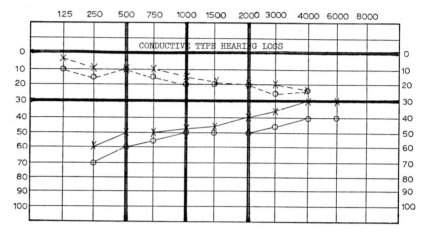

Figure XIII-2. Conductive-type hearing loss.

Perceptive Hearing Loss

A diagnosis of a perceptive hearing loss is made in the same way as that of a conductive hearing loss, that is, in an orderly pattern of a thorough and searching history and physical examination followed by a laboratory examination and audiometric studies. The audiogram in this condition shows that the airborne sounds and the bone-borne sounds are both depressed, and the higher frequencies from 1000 to 2000 Hz and above show the greatest loss. The hearing loss is generally more than 30 dB. In this condition, one does not see the air-bone gap which was seen in conductive deafness. As previously discussed, perceptive hearing losses are generally due to a loss of nerve endings (that is the hair cells in the organ of hearing). In a perceptive hearing loss, the patient's ability to understand conversation is usually severely affected. This is referred to as poor speech discrimination. Usually the speech discrimination score in this condition is below 75 percent, in contrast to the speech discrimination in conductive hearing losses, which is generally above 90 percent. Because of this difficulty of speech discrimination due to loss of nerve endings, the methods of treatment are considerably compromised. At this state of the art, the method that is used is sound amplification by the use of the hearing aid. At times, the hearing aid cannot be effectively worn, and rehabilitation methods by means of speech reading (lip reading) by trained rehabilition counselors and paramedical personnel are utilized.

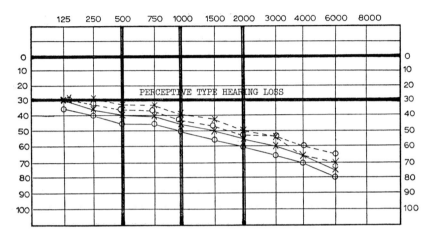

Figure XIII-3. Perceptive-type hearing loss.

Mixed-Type Hearing Losses

The diagnosis in mixed-type hearing losses is here again established by the otologist in the same orderly manner which was outlined for the two above conditions. The audiogram in this type of deafness reveals that there is a conductive as well as a perceptive element present and will show on the audiogram as an air-bone gap, with its gap being considerably less than that seen in conductive hearing losses. The hearing loss usually averages more than 30 dB. The speech discrimination score is generally below 75 percent. Because of this, a person with a mixed-type hearing loss is plagued by being unable to understanding ordinary conversation. A patient with a mixed-type hearing loss can many times be treated by removing the conductive element. That is, if the patient has a chronic otitis media and mastoiditis, this can be treated surgically and many times the conductive element eliminated so that the patient's perceptive hearing loss is now the main problem. This can then be treated by the use of a hearing aid. Depending upon the severity of the mixed loss, methods other than amplified sound may be required and those would be the rehabilitation efforts of the speech therapists and paramedical personnel.

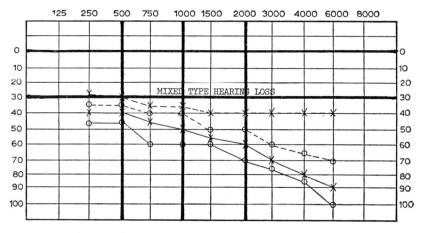

Figure XIII-4. Mixed-type hearing loss.

Chapter XIV

EDUCATIONAL AND SOCIAL FACTORS IN THE REHABILITATION OF HEARING DISABILITIES

PATRICE M. COSTELLO

For more than 150 years in the United States, physicians, educators, and others have wrestled with the problems imposed by severe to profound hearing loss. Most recently, audiologists have joined the ranks. There can be no doubt that early identification, the use of the early preschool years for special instruction, and the use of amplified sound have improved the lot of the deaf. Yet, as a group, they may be losing ground if our goal is to provide a broad general education that will enable them to solve life problems and develop skills with which they may make a living and contribute to society.

The rehabilitation counselor working with the deaf and hard-of-hearing client has a specific challenge to understand and to communicate with this client. In order to do so, he must master unique skills of communication and pertinent information related to each particular client and his specific diagnosis, type of hearing loss, speech development history, career goals, etc. It is the purpose of this chapter to summarize these essentials, including a general background of information on diagnosis, patterns of hearing loss, speech development sequence, and the influence of native ability and educational level on the prognosis for successful rehabilitation of the client. The role of training for communication through speech reading, auditory training, and the language of signs in the potential for success will be explored. Problems in psychosocial development of the deaf will be suggested, and finally, the unique questions encountered in the rehabilitation process of that client will be presented.

DIAGNOSIS AND PATTERNS OF HEARING LOSS

A physician, or otologist will be able to diagnose the underlying causes of hearing loss, determine how losses may be prevented in the first place, prevent hearing loss from increasing, or treat it so that some or most hearing returns. Before and after treatment, he may turn to the audiologist who will, with an array of electronic equipment, answer certain questions. With an understanding of problems that may affect his results he will produce an audiogram. This audiogram and the patient's case history enable the audiologist to assist the otologist in diagnosis and/or prognosis. The audiologist is also the proper professional to fit a person with a hearing aid.

Hearing loss can take a variety of patterns. There may be a far greater loss in one frequency area than another. There may be islands of hearing. Very often the child labeled "deaf" will have a moderate loss in the lower frequencies but a severe to profound loss in the critical speech range. Above this range there may be no response. This produces the typical "ski-slide" audiogram, several of which may be seen posted characteristic of a classroom for deaf children. Further, hearing can be quite different in the right and left ears. Yet we talk about "mild" to "profound" losses almost as if the normal pattern of hearing were maintained through various degrees of loss.

Alice Streng (1960, pp. 274-275) and others have written rule-of-thumb guides stating the symptoms that usually accompany various degrees of hearing loss. She also suggests services needed to help the individual.

ORAL COMMUNICATION PERFORMANCE LEVELS AND
NEEDS IN RELATION TO A LOSS OF HEARING
ACQUIRED BEFORE LANGUAGE

Level	Symptoms	Treatment
	Effect of a loss of hearing on language development, interpretation of speech, and speech development.	Special facilities, adjustments, and services needed.
Mild, 20-30 dB	Will be unable to hear faint or distant speech clearly; will probably adjust satisfactorily to school situations; will have no defective speech resulting from loss of hearing.	Speech reading; individual hearing aid for selected primary children with hearing levels approaching 30 dB; help in vocabulary development; preferential seating.

Marginal, 30-40 dB	Will be able to understand conversational speech at a distance of three to five feet without much difficulty; will probably miss as much as 50 percent of class discussions if voices are faint or if face is not visible; may have defective speech if loss is of high-frequency type; may have limited vocabulary.	Speech reading; individual hearing aid if prescribed; training of hearing; speech training if necessary; help in vocabulary development; preferential seating or, for selected children, special class placements.
Moderate, 40-60 dB	Conversational speech must be loud to be understood; will have considerable difficulty in following classroom discussions; may exhibit deviations in articulation and quality of voice; may misunderstand directions at times; may have limited language, with vocabulary and usage affected.	Speech reading; individual hearing aid, if prescribed; auditory training; use of group hearing aid for those with hearing levels approaching 60 dB; speech training; special help in language arts; preferential seating and/or special class placement for elementary pupils with hearing levels approaching 60 dB.
Severe, 60-80 dB	May hear loud voice at one foot from ear and moderate voice several inches from ear; will be able to hear loud noises, such as sirens and airplanes; speech and language are not learned normally without early amplification; may be able to distinguish vowels but not all consonants even at close range.	Speech reading; individual hearing aid, if prescribed, and training on group aid; integration of language and speech program by special teachers; special class placement at elementary level except for few pupils selected for placement in regular classes; regular classes for those high school students achieving exceptionally well in communication skills; vocational guidance, and vocational education for most.
Profound, 80+ dB	May be able to hear a loud shout about one inch from ear, or may be unable to hear anything; not aware of loud noises; speech and language do not develop.	Speech reading; training on group aid, any remnant of hearing; use of individual aid elective; special class or school for elementary children; regular class for those high school students achieving exceptionally well in communication skills; vocational guidance and education.

SPEECH DEVELOPMENT IN THE DEAF AND HARD OF HEARING

Note that under "Symptoms" the first thing mentioned is "Effect of a loss of hearing on language development." Only after that is speech and speech development mentioned. Speech is an end product, an expression and a facet of the total we know as language. To oversimplify: in the hearing child, the input is heard language augmented by a life situation that, after much repetition, allows the child to attach meaning to word, phrase, and sentence. He then begins to think in those symbols we call words. In this case, he is using his auditory memory as well as other types of memory. Probably he begins to experiment with word order. Next or simultaneously, he responds to words by action. For example, turning to his name, holding out his arms when someone says "up," etc. All this and much more occurs before he begins to speak. His family, however, may feel *sure* that when he was babbling "dadadada" he said "dada" or "Daddy." Indeed, he *might* have shortened his babbling to "dada" but he certainly did not mean to speak of or address his father.

The hard-of-hearing person having a marginal or moderate loss with a well-fitted hearing aid may yet have difficulty with speech. Since the input is defective, he will have a faulty output. His own speech will resemble, to his ears, that of others. He will need help to improve or correct his speech. He will need help to learn to discriminate among sounds, especially speech sounds. He should have instruction in speech reading.

The person who becomes moderately hard of hearing after the acquisition of language and speech may lose some sharpness of speech and may have some difficulties understanding others, but his language will be intact. The person who suffers a severe to profound loss of hearing will lose preciseness of speech sounds, especially the sibilants. Certain vowels may tend toward the neutral, or "schwa" sound (similar to short "u"). Depending on his ability to discriminate among the speech sounds he can still hear with a hearing aid and the speech reading ability he can develop, he can still communicate more or less well. His language will be intact. The deafened, then, are handicapped but can read anything with understanding that they could read before the hearing loss. They can speak and write their native language and others are able to understand them.

The time at which a hearing loss occurs is of primary importance. If a child loses hearing before he begins to talk—before basic language development was complete—he is deaf or "prelingually" deaf and will have great difficulty learning language and speech. If a child loses hearing any time after the establishment of language, he should be able to retain basic language and build on it in a near-normal fashion. This may mean keeping a three- or four-year-old talking, lipreading, and learning, a formidable task, indeed, but one that makes the difference between a deaf and a deafened person.

PROBLEMS OF EVALUATION OF NATIVE ABILITY IN THE DEAF

Pintner (1915, 1918, 1920a, 1920b, 1937) was the first psychologist of note to become interested in the deaf. He observed that the Binet scale would not properly reflect the intelligence of the deaf because of their language deficiency. He and others since have used various performance scales to better estimate intellectual capacities. Hiskey's *Nebraska Test of Learning Aptitude* has been standardized on both deaf and hearing children. Still we search for a better means of measurement because results using most present tests place the median intelligence of the deaf child perhaps 10 percent below that of the hearing child. Meyerson (1955) and Wooden (1963) speak of several studies, some of which show an even greater disparity between the intelligence of deaf and hearing groups. It is certainly possible that an insult to the human organism grave enough to cause deafness, might easily adversely affect the intelligence as well. It is just as possible that psychologists need much more effective means of communication with the deaf to conscientiously consider their test results valid.

In 1955, Lee Meyerson found that the deaf student was three to five years retarded educationally. Kirk, in 1962, said two to five years. Giangreco's doctoral dissertation shows older deaf children progressing at a decreasing rate. However, the improved scholastic abilities of applicants for admission to Gallaudet over applicants of former years reflects better research, teacher education, clinical facilities, teaching media and materials, and auditory training. It also shows the effects of the spread of preschool education of the deaf.

TRAINING FOR COMMUNICATION SKILLS

Three types of training for development of ease in communication are offered to the deaf. Speech reading is suggested for all phases of hearing loss. Auditory training has gained in importance recently, and the language of signs is still preferred by most deaf adults as the most effective mode of communication for and with the deaf. Each type of training will be briefly described.

Speech Reading

Speech-reading instruction is suggested for all ages and all degrees and types of hearing loss. Yet as a subject for instruction it has almost gone out of existence. At one time there were lipreading teachers, who used a variety of methods, texts, and workbooks. Few of these have been reprinted since the 1940's (Thompson, 1950; Stewart, 1953; Nitchie, 1913; Mayer, 1954; Phillips, 1958). New texts seem to be histories of old methods plus some suggestions which can be used to prepare materials for lip-reading practice.

As personal hearing aids came within buying range of the average person, instruction in speech reading declined almost to nonexistence. Yet every teacher of the deaf who wishes to establish oral communication knows the importance of lipreading. She constantly focuses the attention of her pupils on her lips. Well-informed parents and friends do the same. Does this mean everyone can learn to do speech reading well? Not at all. This ability is found in everyone, but in varying degrees, not reflecting intelligence. Further, the understanding of speech by a deafened person versus a deaf person must be different. A deafened person is striving to understand the speaking of a language he has known and used nearly all his life. A deaf person, however, is trying to learn and understand a language by the motions of the speech organs, only part of which can be seen (17 to 30 percent,

depending on who is making the judgment). Even more confusing, when a sound can be perfectly seen as in "p," "b" and "m,"
the sound factor which makes them quite different probably can
not be perceived by the deaf person.

Speech reading deserves a revival. Students who will instruct
the deaf and hard of hearing must learn to prepare much of the
speech-reading material they will use.

Language of Signs

It is the firm belief of most adults deaf from birth or before
language was established that the deaf could be educated more
easily and to a much higher level if only the language of signs
was used in the schools. Most people deafened before finishing
school would agree. Many teachers, some psychologists, and others support the early and continued use of the language of signs.
This is an unresolved question which has never been put to the
test of long years of careful study by trained research personnel.
In Stephen P. Quigley's (1960, p. 53) words,

> There appears to be some agreement that the language of signs
> contains all the elements of a formal language but differs from
> English in symbolic and syntactical structure at least (Stokoe,
> 1960). This raises the question as to whether it should be used in
> educating deaf children who must function in a culture where
> English is the dominant language. Such a question is worthy of
> investigation. . . .

Whether or not the language of signs will be investigated as an
educational tool in carefully controlled research, one thing is sure:
the results of such a study will not be accepted as final by large
numbers of parents and educators of the deaf. In Dr. George
Pratt's* words, "*All* methods of teaching the deaf should be researched." This is indeed true, and no one study is going to
change many attitudes.

It can be observed that the language of signs is the language
used by the deaf among themselves. One excellent reason for
this is that the speech of the deaf is so imprecise that it is difficult

---

*President of Clark School for the Deaf.

to read. It is the preferred means of communication of a great many of the deafened who lost hearing before completing their education. This does not mean that both groups may not rely on lipreading and speech in their dealings with the hearing, but it is much easier for them to communicate in signs. An evening shared by a hearing person and a deaf person who speaks and lipreads very well is an exhausting experience for both. Neither is quite sure of the other's meaning much too often and is too polite to ask for frequent repeating or rephrasing. Both will avoid a repetition of such a social evening. If the deaf person avoids a social evening with one other hearing person, how much more a social event with a large group? Imagine not being able to know who is speaking—and to whom—except by endless visual scanning. Imagine a dozen sets of lips to read. Imagine trying to follow a change in subject matter with no special clues except what can be lipread. Imagine the distractions of a moustache, the difficulty of following rapid speech, the fear that one's own speech is poorly articulated, too loud, too soft, etc. No wonder the deaf need the deaf for a comfortable, enjoyable social life. This is one reason there exists a deaf community or a deaf sub-culture.

The language of signs is the means of communication preferred not only by the deaf but (a) by those who need to communicate with them easily, directly and comfortably, i.e. the psychologist, psychiatrist, vocational counselor; or (b) by those wishing to make points easily, strongly and precisely as possible, i.e. the minister when giving the sermon, the visiting lecturer, and the news analyst. The first group, to serve the deaf best, must become fluent in signs. Most others can use interpreters.*

Auditory Training

Auditory training has gained in importance since the personal hearing aid became widely available and the group aid became

---

*Quite recently an Austin, Texas, television station has begun giving the morning news in the language of signs by interpreter while the regular newscaster speaks.

commonplace in classrooms for the deaf. Obviously type and degree of hearing loss indicate the probable value of auditory training. Here again, we discover a lack of absolutes. There may be two persons quite well matched as to age, intelligence, education, *and audiogram;* one will operate as a hard-of-hearing person, the other as a deaf person. The difference lies in one person's ability to discriminate among sounds, particularly speech sounds, and the other person's lesser ability. This is easily demonstrated. It is perhaps easiest to understand when we spend a few minutes with a typical young hearing couple.

He: What's that noise?

She: It's the faucet dripping in the kitchen. You didn't turn the water all the way off when you got a drink.

He: Oh! Now what's *that?*

She: The baby sitter just stepped on that loose front step on the porch.

(A little later. The couple is in the family car on the way to a party.)

He: Listen to that squeaky rattle. I *told* the repairman . . .

She: What squeaky rattle? I don't hear anything unusual.

Auditory training is of great importance. It deserves concentrated study with an eye to the commercial production of a great many records and tapes. The Language Master, a teaching machine, should be produced, complete with variable amplification.

As indicated above, the input or auditory signal (heard language) accompanied by a life situation eventually results in understanding and use of language by the normally hearing person. He responds by appropriate action and thinks to himself in his native language before he can speak. It is an effortless acquisition of a basic educational tool. However, the input to a deaf child, even when begun early, is largely visual. It can be any, or some selection of the following:

1. Heard speech (Watson, 1961; Whitehurst, 1966; Costello, 1958; Lowell, 1960) (a tiny remnant of that heard by the normally hearing person).
2. Lipread speech (Bennett, 1944) (only a fraction of speech is visible).

3. Facial expression.
4. Gestures, body language (Fast, 1970).
5. Fingerspelled language (Quigley, 1960; Scounten, 1960) (use of manual alphabet).
6. The language of signs (Fant, 1964; Riekchof, 1963) (use of a system of positions and motions of hands and arms for words and ideas developed in France and expanded in this country largely by teachers of the deaf. Often a word or name may be spelled in the manual alphabet to provide a word where no sign exists).
7. Cued speech (Lykos, 1960; Heneger, 1971) (a system using a manual cue for English sounds. Lipreading must be used because a given cue stands for more than one sound).
8. Reading written language (Hart, 1963) (this is indeed an input, but it is based on language acquired by understanding other inputs).
9. Vibration (Furth, 1966; Alcorn, 1938) (use of touch).
10. Other limited inputs such as smell and taste enrich language understanding.
11. Other.

These various inputs indicate the main avenues we try to substitute for normal hearing: residual hearing, sight, and to a lesser extent, other senses to overcome the lack of normal hearing. We do not completely succeed. No matter what input or combination of inputs we use, language building remains a slow, painful process for pupil and teacher alike. The deaf pupil's use of language for thinking and his output as speech (Hudgins, 1949) and written language do not approximate the language of a hearing child of like intelligence. His understanding of content subject matter such as science and social studies are limited to his understanding of the language used to teach the content. An upgrading of teaching materials, electronic devices to improve the teachers' illustrations, corrections, and drills can and have improved the input. But the basic language problem remains (Groht, 1955). The inputs we can devise fall far short of the input afforded by the normal ear. The other channels are less efficient and do not lend themselves to the easy, constant repetition we believe to be necessary.

All the above explains why the deaf child seldom equals his hearing brother in academic achievement. This achievement must be based on language, a system of symbols by which we learn, convey, and even create knowledge; a system through which we easily communicate our thoughts, feelings, needs, and discoveries.

The real handicap of deafness, faulty language, has been delineated. Lesser academic achievement can be documented. Yet a century and a half of heroic effort has not ended in gloom. Many deaf youths do achieve and go on to high school and perhaps college. Most of those who are college bound find it hard going unless (and sometimes even if) they attend Gallaudet College, a liberal arts college founded just over 100 years ago for the deaf. It remains today as the only four-year college for the deaf in the world and admits pupils from all over the world. The superintendent of a fine state residential school for the deaf once said to a group of vocational rehabilitation counselors, "The best rehabilitation for a deaf youth may well be more academic training [Mangan, 1969]." He said this after 13 or 14 years of academic study by a deaf student! Surely he had the goal of Gallaudet College in mind.

PSYCHOLOGICAL AND SOCIAL PROBLEMS OF THE DEAF

Because of the severe language problem imposed directly on the deaf by prelingual deafness, the deaf seldom speak out for themselves regarding their social and psychological needs. Hearing people can learn a great deal from the deafened (Switzer, 1967) and those hearing persons who work closely with them in their written expressions. They can learn from writings produced by a few of those who may be prelingually deaf or deafened— we do not always know which—in professional magazines such as *Volta Review* and *American Annals of the Deaf*. These are journals for professionals. Better sources of expressed ideas and needs of the deaf may be found in periodicals of and for the deaf such as *The Deaf American*, "I.A.D. (Illinois Association of the Deaf)

"D.C." (Washington, D.C.) "Eyes," etc. An examination of the latter publications would show the usual marriages, births, deaths, announcements of future meetings of various local and state groups of deaf persons, and sports events among the deaf. The papers also report progress or lack of it, in the establishment or improvement of, for example, a home for the aged deaf, sponsored at least in part by the group publishing the periodical. From time to time there are articles on the spiritual side of life and on such problems as trends in employment, purchasing, repairing, or maintaining a home.

From the organizations of the deaf has come much that is good and useful to the deaf besides a framework for socialization. These organizations resemble other community organizations in that they strive to improve the lot of their fellow man, but as with other language groups such as the Italian-American Society, it happens to be the deaf fellow man who is to benefit. Until most of the inequities a hearing world imposes upon them are removed, they will have little energy and fewer resources to help those outside their own circle.

If we think of the deaf as having made unique compensations for the stresses imposed by the complications arising from, and the handicaps resulting from, deafness, we are wrong. The adaptations made by the deaf to stress are those of other human beings under other or similar circumstances. The adaptations and the compensations are not unique, and each can be found in the hearing. In that sense, there is no "psychology of deafness" or blindness or mental retardation or any other human condition. Yet there can be seen a profile of characteristics indicating that one human reacts to the pervasive effects of deafness similarly to that of another human. A text called *Psychology of Deafness* (Levine, 1960) helps us see this profile. Furth (1966), Meyerson (1955), and Mykelbust (1962) speak of the effect of the deprivation of the constant flow of auditory language. They find that the language and communication skills of the deaf vary far below the hearing of similar age, intelligence, cultural background, and interests. Meyerson's adjustment patterns are most interesting (Meyerson, 1955, pp. 151-174). But they, and his discussion of them, show nothing unique in adjustment or treatment. He places the blame for most maladjustment squarely where it belongs: on the nonunderstanding hearing person who consciously or unconsciously discriminates against the deaf.

There is some evidence that where there are other deaf members in the family, the deaf child's life adjustment is better (Pintner and Brunschwig, 1936). However, Brill (1960) did not find this is to be the case.

Social and emotional problems start early (Gesell, 1956; Knight, 1942; Charles, 1937), change somewhat and stay late (Heider and Heider, 1943a; Heider and Heider, 1943b; Neyhus, 1964; Neyhus, 1962). Outward, obvious behavior is easy to copy. In certain recurring life situations, therefore, the deaf usually behave appropriately. Unless there is careful tutoring, and often in spite of it, the deaf lack tact. They do not understand much of humor, since so often it is based on a play on words. A favorite comedian might well be Red Skelton in his "silent spot." Flip Wilson who relies on visible innuendo would be preferred to Bill Cosby with his marvelous vocal effects. Listen to Flip Wilson without watching. He will still be enjoyable but much of his appeal is gone. Turn off the audio on your television set and watch Bill Cosby in a skit. You no longer enjoy this gifted man.

A study by Levine (1949) of 31 "normal deaf" girls at the Lexington School for the Deaf showed they (a) were retarded in conceptual forms of mental activity and (b) possessed a lag in meaningful insight into the dynamics of the world, among other findings. Levine (1960) is much concerned with lagging social maturity of the deaf. At one time she felt that the Vineland Scale of Social Maturity better reflected the *intelligence* of the deaf than any other single test. She is concerned with the effect of disturbed parents on the deaf child. The parent of any disabled child finds that child's handicap difficult to accept. The natural parent's emotional shock relates less to the fact of the handicap than to the threat to the parent's own psychic structure. A parent who adopts a handicapped child probably before the disability emerges has no more difficulty being objective about that child than any well-informed adult.

Neyhus (1962) found that the emotional and social behavior of the deaf persisted into adult life. The deaf he studied were rigid and concrete. They were also socially and emotionally immature.

Recent publications such as "Family and Mental Health Problems in a Deaf Population" and "Comprehensive Mental Health Services for the Deaf" both by Rainer and Altshuler and "Behavior Modification of the Emotionally Retarded Deaf" by Hurvitz and Di Francesca show increasing interest, study, and knowledge of the disturbed deaf. This group must pose some grave problems. Surely the frustrations imposed by deafness would tend to trigger any tendency toward emotional instability. Should a mental health problem arise which would result in admission to a mental hospital, consider the fact that deafness is an isolating condition due to the dual handicap: a deaf person's inability to understand others or to make himself understood to them. It has been said that he is wrapped in a double silence. When the deaf person becomes disturbed, he is removed from his family with whom he has some communication. He is placed—probably apart from any other deaf person—in a different world. It is no wonder that those who care about the deaf are particularly concerned when he is placed in a mental hospital. If deafness is isolating, if mental illness is isolating, if treatment is aimed at reducing isolation and establishing communication and understanding, is not the placement away from family and other deaf persons further isolation rather than part of the treatment?

Most cases, as in the general population, are not so severe. Yet parents, teachers, houseparents, and others need help to serve the deaf child with emotional and behavioral problems. Twenty-five years ago, psychologists serving the deaf in all programs in the United States could be counted on one hand. Now most of the larger state schools and many smaller schools and programs have the services of psychologists particularly interested in the needs of the deaf. We are learning to cope with more of these disturbed children, and with more difficult problems in the deaf population (Carr, 1961; Mykelbust, 1962; Neyhus, 1964; Menninger, 1923; Quick, 1960; Shontz, 1965; Thompson, 1964).

REHABILITATION OF THE DEAF AND
HARD OF HEARING

The deaf and hard of hearing pose complicated problems for the rehabilitation counselor. A realistic resume of the background of vocational training and placement of the deaf will be described. Specific needs of the normal-deaf individual and the multiple-handicapped deaf individual will be summarized. Problems of the hard-of-hearing group will be explored.

Background of Vocational Rehabilitation in Deafness

One must be realistic and focus on the deaf youth who is not academically successful to the point that higher education is possible—the deaf youth with a third- or fourth-grade reading level or less. He may have completed seventh- or eighth-grade content material, or better. How was this possible? His teachers translated content into the simpler language of which he was capable. He learned many facts through simple language. This, too, was a comparatively slow process.

This youth is not in a minority group of the deaf. He represents 90 to 95 percent of those who graduate from or leave our programs for the deaf in the United States. His teachers and their administrators knew long before he reached junior high school age that he would need vocational skills if he were to succeed as family head, breadwinner, and community member.

If the pupil is female, vocational skills will be needed, as women today spend only a few years in full time childbearing and child-rearing. Deaf women, like hearing women, increasingly leave the home to work when the children reach school age—perhaps sooner. Both boys and girls should be taught homemaking skills. Her skills for some time to come should include cooking, sewing, shopping, and cleaning. His should include simple repairing of furniture, appliances, etc. They should share childrearing. Both will be consumers and should know how to best use their income.

Granted the need for homemaking and home repairing skills, what vocational skills should be taught? One looks backward to the beginnings of special education for the deaf. The first institution established by almost every state in the union was either a prison or a school for the deaf (Mangan, 1969)! As rapidly as these state residential schools were established beginning in the early 1800's and continuing even after 1900, just as rapidly was vocational training established. Often this filled a real economic need of the school. Many of today's deaf adults will tell of the labor performed by them as children and youth, such as farming, baking, carpentry, or even ditch digging, etc. This certainly required sets of skills but also provided unpaid labor to the school. Some would call this exploitation, and by today's standards it was. Today's administrator guards against it.

Until the 1930's, it was relatively simple to determine how the deaf might make a living after leaving school. Girls were taught homemaking skills and perhaps such trades as power sewing machine operating. Most married and worked little outside the home. Boys were taught farming and returned to the family farm. Others learned such trades as baking, carpentry, shoe repair, upholstering, barbering, tailoring, and most importantly, printing. Fairly recently, floriculture, cleaning and pressing, graphic arts, and other trades have been added. Office and business machine operations are recent additions. The foregoing is not a complete list by any means, but it points up what is easily observed: residential state schools do not and never have offered a really broad spectrum of vocational choices. What they offered in the past fitted the deaf youth for yesterday's world.

More than twenty years ago, such men as Edmund P. Boatner then superintendent of the American School for the Deaf, West Hartford, Connecticut; John Nace, then superintendent of the Pennsylvania School for the Deaf, Mt. Airey, Pennsylvania; Charles M. Jochem, superintendent of the New Jersey School for the Deaf (now the Marie H. Katzenbach School for the Deaf); and Roy Parks, superintendent of the Arkansas School for the Deaf became alarmed. They tried singly to improve their own vocational programs. They succeeded admirably. As a group, they tried to find a way to establish four or five regional vocational schools for American deaf youths because they knew that isolated programs of vocational training in schools for the deaf were not keeping up with the times. Regional vocational schools have not been established, but they seemed to be a possible answer to these four men because they asked themselves these questions: How could individual schools get money for the new machines and equipment they felt were necessary? Where would they find the teachers and how would they pay them?

Basically, the problem was that a wide choice of vocations should be offered a very small group of young people. Why a small group? Fortunately, deafness afflicts few in the population. But this means that at that time, the largest school housed no more than about 500 children age 5 through 18 to 20. (Today the largest school has only a little over 600 deaf children.) Of that 500, perhaps 350 had been or were being instructed in home-making or general industrial arts. Of that 350, not more than 100 were old enough to be engaged in learning a vocation which they were expected to use all the rest of their lives.

That was the problem of the largest school. What about a school with a total of 300? 150? 75? How can a variety of vocations be offered to a small number? How do you make sure the students have been trained for a lifetime? We know now we cannot train for a lifetime. We strive to find ways to offer a reasonable variety of vocational choices, but problems at school level grow.

Public school programs for the deaf started early in our history in the larger cities. Their vocational programs were nil. Some few are now in the process of coping with the problem and it is grave. In Lubbock, Texas, there are 25 to 30 children under instruction and a few are junior high school age. How will the school system provide special vocational training to the handful who should receive it very soon?

Many public school programs solve the problem by sending 13- to 16-year-olds to the state residential schools. What happens at the state school for the deaf? It may have a good, fair, or poor vocational program. Very, very seldom is it excellent. Here is an example of what might happen. One man, Dr. John Nace, had this experience. As Vocational Principal of the Pennsylvania School for the Deaf, and extraordinary teacher of the deaf, he was in demand as a speaker for parent groups and others. In the late 1940's, a parent movement was afoot in Pennsylvania and elsewhere to establish preschool programs for deaf children near their own homes. He knew the worth of the preschool years and gave a great deal of time and encouragement to parents across the state. He watched as little schools sprang up and were subsidized by state and local funds. Then something unexpected happened. Parents decided to keep school-age deaf children in these little scattered programs rather than send them perhaps far away to one of the state schools. One can picture what happened. It is still happening. A few deaf children were pulled together to make a class. Their ages and achievements differed greatly. "Ungraded" classes were far more common than well-graded classes. Eventually the children reached 14, 15, and 16 years of age and parents knew most would not be able to go on to high school and college. They decided at that time to enter the children in the state residential school for the deaf. So the state school had an influx of children from private or public programs who had had no basic vocational skills training. They were educated side by side with children who had been at the school since the age of 5 or 6, who had learned the use of simple tools, and had learned eye-hand coordination skills beginning as early as 9 years of age. Those individuals who arrived at the residential school at about age 15 never caught up with the others in basic vocational skills.

While all the above are serious problems, it should be made very clear that the deaf are a highly visually oriented group. An occupation or vocation which requires a set of manual skills is readily learned by them (Nace, 1965; Adler, 1969; Bluett, 1937; Garrett, 1964; Rosenstein, 1962). What happened to the graduates of the state school for the deaf who were successful shoe repairmen until the 1940's and early 1950's when women found it cheaper to buy new shoes than have the old ones repaired? What happened to the deaf typesetter when his newspaper changed to offset printing? What happened to the deaf person working in a laundry or cleaning and pressing establishment when permanent press washable clothing became available? They all did the same as their hearing brothers and sisters—they turned to other ways of making a living when their jobs disappeared. A man or woman can no longer be sure of staying in the same occupation or even a profession for life. The deaf have great problems in making the transition. They will come in ever greater numbers for vocational retraining and placement.

Deafness, as a single handicap, presents greater educational problems than any other single handicap. In combination with other handicaps, it is usually the greatest obstacle to learning. However, severe language and learning disability and severe to profound mental retardation, when present along with deafness, can and do present graver problems than the deafness. Almost all the deaf, save the tiny minority who have severe visual defects, are visually oriented and alert to all motion, particularly body, or body parts, movement from point to point, change in attitude or position of body parts, etc. Since many marketable skills are based on rather precise movements, eye-hand coordination, and the use of simple tools and machines, is it any wonder that the deaf readily learn skills and find employment? Most multihandicapped deaf can learn useful skills. John Nace (1965) once did a study of the employment of male graduates of the Pennsylvania School for the Deaf during the great Depression. (This school has long accepted a high percentage of multihandicapped deaf.) Some very few were at home because their parents wanted them to be there. All the others who could be traced had jobs. They might have been underemployed, as many deaf people are today, but they were employed. With periodic updating and upgrading of the skills of the deaf as necessary, their lot should be increasingly better than during the worst economic period within the memory of men living today.

Rehabilitation Problems of the Normal Deaf and the Multiple-Handicapped Deaf

The deaf client seeking vocational rehabilitation services will be (a) the normal deaf person in need of training and placement because his skills are outmoded and (b) the multiple-handicapped deaf person who was unable to acquire a marketable set of skills in the vocational program of the school he attended. The former client presents mainly a problem of communication. He may or may not lipread and speak fairly well, but he may be puzzled without the added help of the Language of Signs. The counselor must learn it. The rehabilitation counselor needs to make a study of vocational openings where lack of hearing, in the case of the deafened, would not be a problem; where poor communication skills, faulty language, as well as lack of hearing, in the case of the deaf born or prelingually deaf, would not be a problem. There must be a constant search for openings that the deaf person could be trained to fill. Only after such study can the counselor turn to a particular deaf client with particular abilities and prepare to arrange for training in new skills.

The multihandicapped client needs special consideration and understanding. Suppose he is a deaf-blind person. He is not a deaf person who happens to be blind or a blind person who happens to have a hearing loss. He has a unique set of problems, having been deprived in more than the obvious two ways. The degree and type of vision and sight are important and, of course, age of onset. Not long ago, advice to a counselor or parent was, "Read all you can about blindness, then read all you can about deafness." Now there are publications on timeless and current problems of the deaf-blind population (Bergman, 1965; Alcorn, 1932; Montague, 1952). New publications may be obtained from the centers for the deaf-blind. The Center for the Deaf-Blind, Callier Speech and Hearing Center, Dallas, Texas, serves Texas, Oklahoma, Louisiana, and Arkansas.

The deaf-blind, including a much larger group who have a less than profound hearing loss and a visual defect, are a low-incidence group. Were it not for the rubella epidemic of 1963-65, we would have even fewer. The epidemic focused national attention on the deaf-blind and caused Mary Switzer, then Director of Vocational Rehabilitation Administration in Washington, D.C., to write a bill, later to become a law, creating centers and services for the deaf-blind.

The deaf-physically handicapped (Shere, 1960; Costello, 1960), the deaf-retarded (Wier, 1963), and the deaf with mental health problems have always existed in greater numbers, yet no law exists creating centers and services for their special needs. Between world wars we discovered the existence of the deaf person with language and learning disabilities not directly related to his deafness. We have called him by a number of names: the atypical deaf, the aphasic, the perceptually handicapped, the minimally brain injured, to name a few. Whatever the name, no law provides especially for this deaf group, either.

The needs of the multiple-handicapped deaf are just beginning to be considered by professional people who serve the deaf (Anderson, 1965; Leshin and Stahlecker, 1962; Monghan, 1964). C. Yale (1917), among a few others, made a plea near the turn of the century that we give thought to the needs of the "feeble-minded deaf." However it is only in the last decade, and indeed the last few years, that we find journal articles, books, and workshops on the deaf retarded and other multihandicapped deaf.

Rehabilitation of the Hard-of-Hearing Group

We have considered the deaf person, deaf from birth or prelingually deaf. The hard-of-hearing and deafened person has lesser problems, but may also need help in preparing for an occupation, vocation, or profession. He can communicate with hearing people, but his greatest problems may arise here. Hardy, in Davis and Silverman's (1960) *Guide for the Layman,* has these suggestions for ease of communication:

AIDS TO COMMUNICATION

1. Remember that hearing is the natural and normal way to understand speech. Therefore, be fitted with, and get instruction in the use of, the best possible hearing aid for your loss.
2. Be determined to master speech reading *now.* Don't forget that it can help you in every conversation.
3. Do not strain either to hear or to see speech. A combination of hearing and seeing enables you to understand most speakers readily. Actually, how you get it doesn't matter, just as long as you understand.
4. Avoid tension. Make every effort to relax.
5. Do not expect to get every word. Follow along with the speaker, and, as you become familiar with the rhythm of his speech, key words will emerge to enable you to put two and two together.

6. Try to stage-manage the situation to your advantage. Since lighting is important, avoid facing a bright light, and try not to allow the speaker's face to be shadowed. Keep about six feet between you and the speaker, so that you can more readily observe the entire situation.
7. Try to determine the topic under discussion. Friends can be coached to give unobtrusively a lead, such as "We are discussing the housing problem." This is particularly helpful in large conversational groups.
8. Maintain an active interest in people and events. Being abreast of national and world affairs, as well as those of your community and intimate social circle, enables you to follow any discussions more readily.
9. Remember that conversation is a two-way affair. Do not monopolize it in an attempt to direct and control it.
10. Pay particular attention to your speech. A long-term hearing loss, or even a sudden profound loss, may cause a marked deterioration of voice and articulation. This condition must be corrected, for a pleasant, well-modulated voice is a great asset.
11. Cultivate those subtle traits of personality that do so much to win friends and influence people. A sincere, ready smile, an even disposition, and a genuine sympathetic interest in other people can do much to smooth your path.
12. Remember that the education of *your* public is your responsibility. Many people are embarrassed because they have no idea of how to talk with the wearer of a hearing aid or with a speech reader. Put them at ease, and assure them that quiet, natural speech is their greatest favor to you.

She points out that speech reading can best be improved by constant practice in everyday living rather than repeated classroom sessions. It is easier to improve native speech reading skills in the early stages of hearing loss than later. The problem should not be postponed.

REFERENCES

Adler, E. P.: Deafness. *Journal of Rehabilitation of the Deaf, Monograph No. 1,* March, 1969.

Alcorn, K.: Speech developed through vibration. *Volta Review, 40:,* 1938, p. 633.

Alcorn, S.: The Tadoma method. *Volta Review, 34:*1932, p. 195.

Anderson, R. M.: Hearing impairment and mental retardation: A selected bibliography. *Volta Review, 67:*, 1965, p. 17.

Bennett, J.: Lip reading for the deaf child. *Volta Review, 46:*, 1944, p. 489.

Bergman, M. *et al.: Auditory rehabilitation for hearing impaired blind persons.* ASHA Monographs, No. 12, March, 1965.

Bluett, C. S.: Selecting vocations for the deaf. *Volta Review, 39:*, 1937, p. 677.

Brill, R. G.: A study in adjustment of three groups of deaf children. *Exceptional Children, 26:*, 1960, p. 464.

Carr, J.: The teacher's role in promoting mental health. *Volta Review, 63:*, 1961, p. 65.

Charles, E. N.: Social adjustment of a deaf child. *Volta Review, 36:*, 1937, p. 271.

Costello, M. R.: Changing concepts in audiology. *Volta Review, 60:*, 1958, p. 395.

Costello, P.: Where does Mike belong? *Volta Review, 62:*, 1960, p. 66.

Davis, H. and Silverman, S. R.: *Hearing and Deafness—A Guide for the Layman,* revised ed. New York, Holt, Rinehart and Winston, 1960.

Fant, L. J.: Say it with hands. Washington, D.C., 1964.

Fast, J.: Body language. M. Evans and Company, 1970.

Furth, H.: *Thinking without Language: Psychological Implications of Deafness.* New York, The Free Press, 1966, p. 461.

Furth, H. G.: A comparison of reading test norms of deaf and hearing children. *American Annals of the Deaf, 111:*, 1966.

Garrett, C. W.: *Quo Vadis:* A pilot study of employment opportunities for hearing impaired. *Volta Review, 66:*, 1964, p. 669.

Gessell, A.: The psychological development of normal and deaf children in their pre-school years. *Volta Review, 58:*, 1956, p. 117.

Groht, M.: *Natural language for deaf children.* Washington, D.C., A. G. Bell Association for the Deaf, 1955.

Hart, B. O.: *Teaching reading to deaf children.* Washington, D.C., A. G. Bell Association for the Deaf, 1963.

Heider, G. M. and Heider, F.: The adjustment of the adult deaf: After school problems as the psychologist sees them. *Volta Review, 45:*, 1943, p. 389.

Heider, G. M. and Heider, F.: The adjustment of the adult deaf: Comments from the deaf about after school problems. *Volta Review, 45:*, 1943, p. 325.

Heneger, M. E. and Cornett, R. O.: *Cued speech handbook for parents.* Washington, D.C., 1971.

Hudgins, C. V.: A method of appraising the speech of the deaf. *Volta Review, 51:,* 1949, p. 597.

Knight, M. H.: Emotions of the young deaf child. *Volta Review, 44:,* 1942, p. 69.

Leshin, G. H. and Stahlecker, L. W.: Academic expectancies of slow learning children. *Volta Review, 64:,* 1962, p. 599.

Levine, E. S.: *The Psychology of Deafness: Techniques of Appraisal for Rehabilitation.* New York, Columbia University Press, 1960.

Lowell, E. L. and Stoner, M.: *Play it by Ear.* Los Angeles, John Tracy Clinic, 1960.

Lykos, C.: *Cued Speech Handbook for Teachers.* Washington, D.C., Department of Health, Education, and Welfare, 1971.

Mangan, K.: Rehabilitation of the Deaf. A speech before Vocational Rehabilitation Counselors at Northern Illinois University, 1969.

Mayer, J. H.: My deafness. *Volta Review, 56:,* 1954, p. 440.

Menninger, K. A.: The mental effects of deafness. *Volta Review, 25:,* 1923, p. 439.

Meyerson, L.: A psychology of impaired hearing. In Cruickshank, William H. (Ed.): *Psychology of Exceptional Children.* New York, Prentice-Hall, 1955.

Monaghan, A.: Educational placement for the multiply handicapped hearing impaired child. *Volta Review, 66:,* 1964, p. 383.

Montague, H. A.: Tad Chapman at home. *Volta Review, 54:,* 1952, p. 58.

Mykelbust, H. R.: Diagnosis, learning and guidance. *Volta Review, 64:,* 1962, p. 363.

Nace, J. S.: A superintendent looks at the future of vocational technical education. *Volta Review, 67:,* 1965, p. 688.

Neyhus, A. I.: The personality of socially well adjusted adult deaf as revealed by projective tests. Unpublished doctoral dissertation, Northwestern University, 1962.

Neyhus, A. I.: The social and emotional adjustment of deaf adults. *Volta Review, 66:,* 1964, p. 319.

Nitchie, E. B.: Some assets of deafness. *Volta Review, 15:,* 1913, p. 204.

Pintner, R.: Deductions from tests of mentality in schools for the deaf in comparison with schools for the hearing. *Volta Review, 22:,* 1920a, p. 197.

Pintner, R.: Deductions from tests of mentality in schools for the deaf. *American Annals of the Deaf, 65:*, 1920b, p. 278.

Pintner, R. and Brunschwig, L.: Some personality adjustments of deaf children in relation to two different factors. *Journal of Genetic Psychology, 49:*, 1936, p. 377.

Pintner, R. and Brunschwig, L.: An adjustment inventory for use in schools for the deaf. *American Annals of the Deaf, 82:*, 1937, p. 152.

Pintner, R. and Paterson, D.: The Binet Scale and the deaf child. *American Annals of the Deaf, 60:*, 1915, p. 301.

Pintner, R. and Paterson, D.: Some conclusions from psychological tests of the deaf. *Volta Review, 20:*, 1918, p. 10.

Phillips, R. M.: Experiences in the community. *American Annals of the Deaf, 103:*, 1958, p. 382.

Quick, M.: Role of the administrator in the guidance program. *Volta Review, 62:*, 1960, p. 418.

Quigley, S. P.: *The Influence of Fingerspelling on the Development of Language, Communication and Educational Achievement in Deaf Children.* Department of Health, Education and Welfare, Washington, D.C.

Riekchof, L. L.: *Talk to the Deaf.* Springfield, Missouri, Gospel Publishing House, 1963.

Rosenstein, J.: Social and vocational planning for the adolescent. *Volta Review, 64:*, 1962, p. 433.

Scouten, E. L.: Helping your child to master English through fingerspelling. *American Annals of the Deaf, 105:*, 1960, p. 226.

Shere, M. O.: The cerebral palsied child with a hearing loss. *Volta Review, 62:*, 1960, p. 438.

Shontz, F. C.: Reactions to crisis. *Volta Review, 67:*, 1965, p. 364.

Stewart, P.: I am one of the lucky ones. *Volta Review, 55:*, 1953, p. 41.

Streng, A.: *Children with Impaired Hearing.* Council for Exceptional Children, 1960.

Switzer, M. E. and Williams, B. R.: Life problems of deaf people. *Archives of Environmental Health, 15:*, August, 1967, p. 249.

Thompson, R.: What speech and lipreading mean to me. *Volta Review, 52:*, 1950, p. 115.

Thompson, R.: Counseling and the deaf student. *Volta Review, 66:*, 1964, p. 511.

Watson, T. J.: *The Use of Residual Hearing in the Education of Deaf Children.* Washington, Volta Bureau, 1961 (Pamphlet).

Whitehurst, M. W.: *Auditory Training for Children,* A manual, rev. ed. Armonk, New York, Hearing Rehabilitation, 1966.

Wier, R. C.: Impact of the multiple handicapped deaf on special education. *Volta Review, 65:,* 1963, p. 287.

Wooden, H. Z.: Deaf and hard of hearing children. In Dunn, L. M. (Ed.): *Exceptional Children in the Schools.* New York, Holt, Rinehart and Winston, 1963.

Yale, C.: A plea for the instruction and after-school care of the feeble minded deaf. *Volta Review, 19:,* 1917, p. 578.

Chapter XV

THE PATH OF LIGHT

Alfred A. Nisbet

The human eye is a small but mighty organ. The life of a person may be altered by its failure to function adequately. The globe is a miniature camera about an inch in diameter which nestles in the bony cavity called the orbit. It is cushioned in fat, protected by eyelids, enveloped by a fibrous capsule, moved by externally attached muscles, supplied with nourishment by arteries, relieved of waste products by veins and lymph vessels, and directed by nerves. The optic nerve which connects it to the central nervous system is not really a nerve but a stalk of the brain.

The eye is an end organ for receiving light. This light is converted through electrical impulses which are carried to the visual area of the brain for distribution or interpretation. Thus, a break in the path of light at any point is important. It may be reparable if it is in the anterior part of the eye but usually not if in the posterior portion of the eye, in the optic nerve or in the brain.

Light, upon entering the eye, passes through critically important structures. From the air it strikes the cornea, which is a transparent, avascular, watch-crystal–appearing structure in the front of the white, fibrous globe wall. Next it enters a clear, watery fluid, then passes through the pupil (a round opening in the colored curtain, or iris) entering the crystalline lens as it does so. After the lens, it passes through the jelly-like fluid called vitreous, which fills the posterior two thirds of the eye, to be focused on the interior wall posteriorly. Here it is received by the nervous tissue wall covering called the retina. The retina is the ocular antenna and its nerve fibers are collected to form the optic nerve.

Lesions of the cornea are important because the arrangement of cells allows it to be transparent, but injury results in scar, which is opaque. Any change in curvature causes irregular

329

bending of light rays. Thus, the image on the retina is out of focus.

If corneal scars are superficial, the outer layers may be surgically removed, restoring some visual acuity. Deep scars may be treated by removing a full-thickness window, including the scar, and replacing it with a clear window from a donor eye. Corneal transplant procedures are now quite successful in selected cases.

The lens focuses the incoming rays but must be clear to do this efficiently. When it is unclear for any reason, we name it a *cataract*. If cloudy at birth, it is congenital, and often associated with other defects. If cloudy later from disease, age, or injury, it is classed as acquired. When this is the only defect in the path of light, the possibility for return of good vision is favorable with surgery. This surgery consists of removing the cloudy lens by a procedure having a percentage of success in the nineties. When the cloudy lens has been removed, the eye no longer focuses properly, and in order to see clearly it is necessary for the patient to wear a forward-fitting lens in a spectacle frame. It is also possible to fit this aphakic eye with a contact lens. This is particularly valuable for a person who has had a cataract removed from one eye and has good vision in the other. Ordinarily, the size image difference between a corrected, aphakic eye and one still having its lens is so great that it is not possible to team them. If a contact lens is used and a small size image difference is tolerated by the patient, binocular vision may be restored.

Glaucoma is a term used to describe an ocular condition in which the fluid balance within the eye is altered positively. This may result in increased formation of fluid or the eye may be unable to adequately filter a normal amount of fluid to the exterior. In either situation, the pressure within the eye elevates. If this pressure becomes about three times normal, pain may result and this is known as acute glaucoma. In some ways, this is favorable because the patient is thus aware of pressure. The other kind of glaucoma is the chronic and simple, in which the pressure is only slightly above normal but stays up without making its presence known. After a variable time, the pressure reduces the nourishment to the nerve cells of sight in the retina and the optic nerve, causing permanent loss of vision. This latter glaucoma is known as the "thief in the night," for it is at that time that ocular pressure is usually higher. The glaucoma patient may sleep his sight away without knowing it.

Diagnosis of this blinding disease is important. About 15 percent of the half-million legally blind people in the United States have glaucoma. Whereas once glaucoma was thought to be a disease of the elderly, all patients over the age of forty years are now routinely tested. It is found at a younger age, but here it seems more difficult to differentiate between a mild elevation of ocular tension and glaucoma with its resulting visual loss.

Prevention of visual loss is probably best, because when an increased ocular tension is found, it should be considered glaucoma until proved otherwise.

Usually the acute glaucoma may be controlled by medicine or surgery. When it occurs in one eye, often prophylactic surgery may be performed in the other eye.

Chronic glaucoma may be adequately treated for years after diagnosis has been made. Only a small percentage of patients need to have surgery, but there are procedures available when the ocular tension is no longer controlled medically.

The retina is that important receptor for the incoming beam of light. Any damage to its sensitive cells breaks the necessary connection with the brain. As just mentioned, pressure on its fibers may reduce vision, but inflammation, tumor, loss of attachment to the inner surface of the globe, or decrease in nourishment may also cause danger.

Two types of sensitive nerve cells are present in the retina. The rods are the ones concerned with observing movement and are scattered in large numbers in the retina except at the point of focus, which also happens to be the point of most acute vision. At this tiny point, there is a great concentration of the other kind of cell—the cone. This cell is for color and discriminative vision. Thus any damage to this part of the retina may involve only a relatively small area but can cause a person to be permanently industrially blind because he is unable to read.

External muscles move the eye. They are attached posteriorly to the apex of the orbit and anteriorly to the globe. Movement is partially under voluntary control. Thus you may decide to look right or left but you are unable to direct the coordinated movement of both eyes. If you read at near distance, you must converge the eyes, then move them together while holding them in fixed convergence. Then another muscle must act. It is within the eye and attached to the lens. When it contracts, the lens changes shape, resulting in a change of focus. None of this action is under voluntary control, so any minor break in this complex sequence may prevent functioning of the entire process, and a person requiring binocular vision may be incapacitated.

Color vision is often assumed to be normal, and no tests are performed in childhood. Often boys are thought to be color-ignorant when they are really color-defective. The disease is hereditary and occurs more often in boys. Usually the defect is for red and green but seldom for yellow and blue. The degree of the defect varies, so that the old term "color-blind" is misleading. A person having a color vision defect may be prevented from obtaining or keeping certain occupations. Since there is no treatment for the condition and the person may not be changed, the work requirements must be. Usually placement in some other field is indicated if the defect is so marked that discrimination of bright colors is not possible, for the common red-green defect is also the usual warning-signal combination.

A basically similar heredity-related problem is *constitutional dyslexia*—often called *word blindness*. The affected individual is unable to properly recognize groups of letter symbols as units having a specific meaning. Perhaps this is due to imperfect visual imagery. Although not a true eye defect, it is important because about 10 to 20 percent of the school population is affected and about 4 percent are reading cripples. Recently there has been an interest in recognition of the problem, but little is being done in its management. Since there are varying degrees of severity, a reasonable approach would be to teach reading to the limit of the individual's ability. Then, if he is still deficient, attempts should be made to build up his funds of information through audiovisual means. Further, when he is being tested for what he has learned, it may be necessary to give oral examinations, unless misspelling of words is disregarded.

REHABILITATION BY VISUAL IMPROVEMENT

Return of satisfactory function is first attempted by visual aids. The most common one is obtaining proper spectacles for the correction of refractive errors. Unfortunately, many people have the idea that all ocular problems may be solved with glasses. When told that such is not true, they are unbelieving. Only those optical errors of far-sightedness, near-sightedness, and regular astigmatism may be helped. Often an adult with a high refractive error, when corrected for the first time, will not tolerate glasses, even though they improve his vision. Frequently such cases are not corrected to what is considered normal visual acuity.

A recently popularized visual aid is the contact lens. Contact lenses will correct an irregular astigmatism such as found with corneal scarring. Spectacles will not do this as well. Low-vision aids are numerous but usually depend on magnification. Thus the image, though blurred, is enlarged sufficiently for the patient to recognize the object. In most large cities there are visual aid clinics, but in any city large enough to have an ophthalmologist, a patient may get reliable advice.

Rehabilitation by surgery is often limited. The vision which is restored may not be sufficiently acute or of the quality to allow a person to return to his former occupation if visual demand had been great. Following a severe chemical burn, the cornea may be so scarred that a corneal transplant is indicated, but even when performed successfully, it may be discovered that the vision is not adequate. So we must remember that in any reconstructive procedure, there may be a great difference between a successful surgical result and the hope or expectation of surgeon and patient.

Cataract and glaucoma cause about one third of all the blindness in the United States. Rehabilitation of patients with these conditions may be quite complicated. Both are usually found in the elderly, and limited function may be all that is required. If nothing except cataract is present, a percentage of success in the nineties may be expected. In contrast, a person with an advanced glaucoma can expect little return of function regardless of treatment. Visual-field loss from glaucoma does not return.

Some patients have both cataracts and glaucoma. When the cataract is successfully removed, it is discovered that little vision remains. In contrast, a relatively young person with only cataracts may expect years of useful vision following operation. To be sure, it is a new kind of vision which is clear, with vivid colors. The image size is larger, so objects appear to be closer. If spectacles are used, the area of clear vision is restricted to the central portion of the lens. Looking through the peripheral part of the lens results in distortion of objects. This may not be usual vision but is certainly useful.

Loss of vision due to retinal damage is permanent. Peripheral retinal detachment may cause little noticeable field loss until the macula—or area of most acute vision—is involved. Then, even if the retina is returned to its proper place and remains there, reading vision may never return. People who have had this type of surgery may be reassured that they will not be blind but will be able to get about by themselves as they use their peripheral vision.

Retrolental fibroplasia is a disease of the premature newborn which occurs when excess oxygen was used to save the infant's life. It appears a few weeks after birth. Vessels in the retina enlarge, fibrous tissue forms, the retina is pulled loose by adhesions, and the posterior part of the eye becomes disorganized. The degree of damage varies and no treatment is available after the onset, so prevention is the only hope and this has been successful in recent years.

Deviations of the eyes with onset early in life may be successfully treated, some with spectacles and a few with brief periods of training (orthoptics). Then, finally, surgery may be performed. With it, some patients may get the eyes mechanically aligned and develop binocular vision. More often, a cosmetic result is obtained in which the person may use the eyes alternately but not simultaneously. After visual patterns have been established, trauma that causes weakness of extraocular muscles results in *double vision (diplopia).* Surgery on extraocular muscles is performed with the hope that the double vision will be completely eliminated or at least reduced to such an extent that the residual deviation may be neutralized with prisms in spectacles.

Tumors of the eye that require removal of the globe will permanently handicap those persons whose occupations require binocular vision. This is not as disabling as one would suspect because a person who is trained will be able to compensate sufficiently to continue his occupation.

Chapter XVI

PSYCHOLOGICAL ADJUSTMENT
TO BLINDNESS

John G. Cull

It is true that our clients are much more like us than unlike us, but they differ in one major respect. They have suffered the psychological impact of disability and have adjusted or are in the process of adjusting to this impact. In this chapter, we shall discuss the factors which affect the psychological adjustment to blindness and the mechanism by which an individual adjusts to his blindness.

During the first and second world wars, behavioral scientists noticed increased incidence in conversion reactions. Conversion reactions are (APA, 1965) a type of psychoneurotic disorder in which the impulse causing anxiety is "converted" into functional symptoms in parts of the body rather than the anxiety being experienced consciously. Examples of conversion reactions include such functional disabilities as anesthesias (blindness, deafness), paralyses (aphonia, monoplegia, or hemiplegia), and dyskinesia (tic, tremor, catalepsy).

The study of these conditions along with other studies led to the development of a discipline known as psychosomatic medicine. Psychosomatic medicine is concerned with the study of the effects of the personality and emotional stresses upon the body and its function. This psychological interaction with physiology can be observed in any of the body systems.

After the establishment of psychosomatic medicine, behavioral scientists (psychiatrists, psychologists, social workers, etc.) began observing the converse of this new field. Instead of studying the effects of emotional stress on bodily functioning, they studied the effects of physical stress on emotional functioning. Their concern was directed toward answering the question, what are the emotional and personality changes which result from physical stress or a change in body function or physical configuration?

ROLE OF BODY IMAGE IN ADJUSTMENT
TO BLINDNESS

This new area of study became known as somatopsychology. The basis for this study is the body image concept. The body image is a complex conceptualization which we use to describe ourselves. It is one of the basic parts of the total personality and, as such, determines our reaction to our environment. According to English and English (1966), the body image is the mental representation one has of his own body.

There are two aspects of the body image concept—the ideal body image (the desired body image) and the actual body image. The greater the congruity between these two images, the better the psychological adjustment of the individual; conversely, the greater the discrepancy between these two parts of the self-concept, the poorer an individual's psychological adjustment. This is very understandable. If an individual is quite short and views himself as such but has a strong ideal body image of a tall person, he is less well adjusted than he would be if his desired image were that of a short person. This is a simplistic example, but it portrays the crux of the psychological adjustment to blindness.

In order to adjust to the psychological impact of blindness, the body image has to change from the image of a sighted person to the body image of a blind person. Early in the adjustment process, the actual body image will change from that of a sighted person to the actual body image of a blind person; however, for adequate psychological adjustment to the blindness, the ideal body image must make the corresponding adaptation. Therefore, in essence, psychological adjustment to a disability is the acceptance of an altered body image which is more in harmony with reality.

FACTORS ASSOCIATED WITH ADJUSTMENT

There are three groups of factors which determine the speed or facility with which an individual will adjust to his disability. They help an individual understand the degree of psychological impact a particular disability is having on a client and the significance of his adjustment.

The first of these three groups of factors are those directly associated with the disability. Psychological effects of disabilities may arise from direct insult or damage to the central nervous system. These psychological effects are called brain syndromes and may be either acute or chronic. In this instance, there are a variety of behavioral patterns which may result directly from the disability. In disabilities involving no damage to brain tissue, the physical limitations imposed by the disability may cause excessive frustration and in turn result in behavioral disorders. For example, an active outdoorsman and nature lover may experience a greater psychological impact upon becoming blind than an individual who leads a more restricted and physically limited life, since the restrictions imposed by the disability demand a greater change in the basic life style of the first person. Therefore, factors directly associated with the disability have an important bearing upon an individual's reaction to disability.

The second group consists of those factors arising from the individual's attitude toward his disability. An individual's adjustment to his disability is dependent upon the attitudes he had prior to his disability. If his attitudes toward the blind were quite negative and strong, he will naturally have a greater adjustment problem than an individual with a neutral or positive attitude toward disability and the disabled, or specifically the blind and blindness. A part of this attitude formation prior to blindness is dependent upon the experiences the client had with other blind individuals and the stereotypes he developed.

The amount of fear a client experiences or the emotion he expends during the onset and duration of the illness or accident leading up to the disability will determine the psychological impact of the disability. Generally, the greater the amount of emotion expended during onset, the better the psychological adjustment to the disability. If an individual goes to sleep a sighted person and awakens a blinded person, his psychological reaction to the disability is much greater than if a great deal of emotion is expended during a process of becoming blinded.

The more information an individual has relating to his disability, the less impact the disability will have. If the newly blinded individual is told about his blindness in a simple, straightforward, mechanistic manner, it is much easier to accept and adjust to the disability than if it remains shrouded in a cloak of ignorance and mystery. Any strangeness or unpredictable aspect of our body associated with its function immediately creates anxiety and if not clarified rapidly can result in totally debilitating anxiety. Therefore, it is important for psychological adjustment to a disability that the individual have communicated to him, in terms he can understand, the medical aspects of his disability as soon after onset of disability as possible.

When we are in strange or uncomfortable surroundings, our social perceptiveness becomes keener. Social cues which are below threshold or are not noticed in comfortable surroundings become highly significant to us in new, strange, or uncomfortable surroundings. Upon the onset of blindness, the client will develop a heightened perceptiveness relative to how he is being treated by family, friends, and professionals. If others start treating him in a condescending fashion and relegate him to a position of less importance, his reaction to the psychological impact of the blindness will be poor. Professionals can react to the client from an anatomical orientation (what is missing) or a functional orientation (what is left). The anatomical orientation is efficient for classification purposes but is completely dehumanizing. The functional orientation is completely individualistic and as such enhances a client's adjustment to his disability.

Perhaps a key concept in the adjustment to blindness is the evaluation of the future and the individual's role in the future. In many physical medicine rehabilitation centers, a rehabilitation counselor is one of the first professionals to see the patient after the medical crisis has passed. The purpose of this approach is to facilitate the patient's psychological adjustment. If he feels there is a potential for his regaining his independence and security, the psychological impact of the blindness will be lessened. While the counselor cannot engage in specific vocational counseling with the patient, he can discuss the depth of the vocational rehabilitation program and through these preliminary counseling sessions, the counselor can help the newly blinded person evaluate the roles he might play in the future.

The last factor which determines the adjustment process is based upon the individual's view of the purpose of his body and the relationship this view has with the type and extent of disability. The views individuals have of their body may be characterized as falling somewhere on a continuum. At one end of the continuum is the view that the body is a tool to accomplish work; it is a productive machine. At the other end is the view that the body is an esthetic stimulus to be enjoyed and provide pleasure for others. This latter concept is much the same as we have for sculpture and harks back to the philosophy of the ancient Greeks. Everyone falls somewhere on this continuum. To adequately predict the impact of a disability upon an individual, one has to locate the placement of the individual upon this continuum and then evaluate the disability in light of the individual's view of the function of this body.

As an example of the above principle, consider the case in which a day laborer and film actress sustain the same disabling injury—a deep gash across the face. Obviously, when considering the disability in conjunction with the assumed placements of these two upon the functional continuum, the psychological impact will be greater for the actress; since we have assumed the day laborer views his body almost completely as a tool to accomplish work and the disability has not impaired that function, the psychological impact of the disability upon him will be minimal. However, if the disability were changed (they both sustained severe injury to the abdomen resulting in the destruction of the musculature of the abdominal wall), the psychological impact would be reversed. In this case, the actress would view her disability as minimal, since it did not interfere with the esthetic value of her body, while the day laborer's disability would be overpowering, since it had substantial effects upon the productive capacity of his body.

The most obvious conclusion to be drawn from the above three factors is that the degree of psychological impact is not correlated with the degree of disability. This statement is contrary to popular opinion; however, disability and its psychological impact is a highly personalized event. Many counselors fall into the trap of equating degree of disability with degree of psychological impact. If the psychological impact suffered by a client is much greater than that considered "normal," the counselor will often become impatient with the client. It should be remembered that relatively superficial disabilities may have devastating psychological effects. The psychological impact of total blindness is not necessarily greater than partial blindness or, for that matter, more anatomically superficial physical disabilities.

ROLE OF DEFENSE MECHANISMS IN ADJUSTMENT

While the three groups of factors discussed above determine the length of time required for adjustment to blindness, the path to adjustment is best described by defense mechanisms. Defense mechanisms are psychological devices used by all to distort reality. Often reality is so harsh it is unacceptable to us. Therefore, we distort the situation to make it more acceptable. Defense mechanisms are used to satisfy motives which cannot be met in reality; they reduce tensions in personal interactions; and they are used to resolve conflicts. To be effective, they must be unconscious. They are not acquired consciously or deliberately. If they become conscious, they become ineffective as defenses and others must replace them. For the major part of the remainder of this chapter we will look at the defenses most often employed by the disabled in the general order of their use.

Denial

Denial is an unconscious rejection of an obvious fact which is too disruptive of the personality or too emotionally painful to accept. Therefore, in order to soften reality, the obvious fact is denied. Immediately upon onset of disability, the individual denies it happened. Then, as the fact of the disability becomes so overwhelming its existence can no longer be denied, there is a denial of the permanency of the disability. The newly blinded individual, while utilizing the defense of denial, will adamantly maintain that he shall see again. There will be a miraculous cure or a new surgical technique will be discovered.

While there are few steadfast rules in human behavior, one is that rehabilitation, at best, can be only marginally successful at this point. Rehabilitation cannot proceed adequately until the client accepts the permanency of the disability and is ready to cope with the condition. This is what is meant by many professionals when they say a client must accept his blindness. Most clients will never accept their blindness, but they should and will accept the permanence of blindness. Denial is the front line of psychological defense but it may outlast all other defenses.

Withdrawal

Withdrawal is a mechanism which is used to reduce tension by reducing the requirements for interaction with others within the individual's environment. There are two dynamics which result from withdrawal. In order to keep from being forced to face the acceptance of the newly acquired blindness, the individual withdraws. As a result of the client's changed physical condition—blindness—his social interaction is quite naturally reduced. His circle of interests as determined by friends, business, social responsibilities, church, civic responsibilities, and family is drastically reduced. Thus the client becomes egocentrically oriented until finally his entire world revolves around himself.

Rather than functioning interdependently with his environment to mutually fulfill needs as our culture demands, he is concerned exclusively with his environment fulfilling his needs. As his world becomes more narrowed, his thoughts and preoccupations become more somatic. Physiological processes heretofore unconscious now become conscious. At this point he begins using another defense mechanism—regression.

Regression

Regression is the defense mechanism which reduces stress by avoiding it. The individual psychologically returns to an earlier age that was more satisfying. He adopts the type of behavior that was effective at that age but now has been out-grown and substituted by more mature behavior—behavior which is more effective in coping with stressful situations.

As the newly blinded individual withdraws and becomes egocentric and hypochrondriacal, he will regress to an earlier age which was more satisfactory. This regression may be manifested in two manners. First he may, in his regression, adopt the dress, mannerisms, speech, etc., of contemporaries at the age level to which he is regressing. Secondly, he may adopt the outmoded dress, mannerisms, speech, etc., of the age to which he regressed. This second manifestation of regression is considerably more maladaptive, since it holds the individual out to more ridicule which, at this point in his adjustment to his blindness, quite possibly will result in more emphasis on the defense mechanism of withdrawal.

While utilizing the first three defense mechanisms, if reality is being harshly pushed on him and his defenses are not working, he may, as a last resort, become highly negative of those around him and negative in general. This negativism is demonstrated as an active refusal, stubbornness, contradictory attitudes, and rebellion against external demands. He may become abusive of those around and may become destructive in an effort to act out the thwarting he is experiencing. This negativistic behavior is an indication that the defense mechanisms he is employing are not distorting reality enough to allow him to adjust to his newly acquired disabled status. If, however, he is able to adjust and the defense mechanisms are effective to this point, he will employ the next defense.

Repression

Repression is selective forgetting. It is contrasted with sup-pression, which is a conscious, voluntary forgetting. Repression is unconscious. Events are repressed because they are psychologically traumatic. As mentioned above, the attitudes the client had relative to blindness and the blinded have a major bearing upon his adjustment. If these attitudes are highly negative, the client will have to repress them at this point if his adjustment is to progress. Until he represses them, he will be unable to accept the required new body image.

Reaction Formation

When an individual has an attitude which creates a great deal of guilt, tension, or anxiety and he unconsciously adopts the opposite of this attitude, he has developed a reaction formation. In order to inhibit a tendency to flee in terror, a boy will express his nonchalance by whistling in the dark. Some timid persons, who feel anxious in relating to others, hide behind a facade of gruffness and assume an attitude of hostility to protect themselves from fear. A third and last example is that of a mother who, feeling guilty about her rejection of a newborn child, may adopt an attitude of extreme overprotectiveness to reduce the anxiety produced by this guilt of rejection. This example is seen more often in cases of parents with handicapped children.

In this new, dependent role, the blinded individual will feel a varying degree of hostility and resentment toward those upon whom he is so dependent—wife, relatives, etc. Since these feelings are unacceptable, he will develop a reaction formation. The manifest behavior will be marked by concern, love, affection, closeness—all to an excessive degree.

Fantasy

Fantasy is daydreaming. It is the imaginary representative of satisfactions that are not attained in real experience. This defense mechanism quite often accompanies withdrawal. As the client starts to adjust to a new body image and a new role in life, he will develop a rich, overactive fantasy life. In this dream world he will place himself into many different situations to see how well he fits.

Rationalization

Rationalization is giving socially acceptable reasons for behavior and decisions. There are four generally accepted types of rationalization. The first is called blaming an incidental cause: the child who stumbles blames the stool by kicking it; the poor or sloppy workman blames his tools. Sour grapes rationalization is called into play when an individual is thwarted. A goal to which the individual aspires is blocked to him; therefore he devalues the goal by saying he did not really want it so much. The opposite type of rationalization is called sweet lemons. When something the individual does not want is forced upon him, he will modify his attitude by saying it was really a very desirable goal and he feels quite positive about the new condition. The fourth and last type of rationalization is called the doctrine of balances. In this type of rationalization we balance positive attributes in others with perceived negative qualities. And conversely, we balance negative attributes with positive qualities. For example, beautiful women are assumed to be dumb, bright young boys are assumed to be weak and asthenic, and the poor are happier than the rich.

The blinded individual will have to rationalize his disability in order to assist himself in accepting the permanence of the blindness. One rationalization may be that he had nothing to do with his current condition but that something over which he had no control caused the blindness. Another dynamic which might be observed is the adherence to the belief on the part of the client that as a result of the blindness there will be compensating factors. He will develop in other areas, such as additional senses or aptitudes and talents he previously did not possess, e.g. an aptitude for music.

I once had a client whose rationalization of his disability ran something like this: All of the men in his family had been highly active outdoor types. They all had died prematurely with coronaries. He, the client, was a highly active outdoors type; however, now that he was severely disabled, he would be considerably restricted in his activities. Therefore, he would not die prematurely. This logic resulted in the conclusion that the disability was positive and he was pleased he had become disabled. Granted, rationalization is seldom carried to this extreme in the adjustment to blindness, but this case is illustrative of a type of thinking which must occur for good adjustment.

Projection

A person who perceives traits or qualities in himself which are unacceptable may deny these traits and project them to others. In doing so, he is using the defense mechanism of projection. A person who is quite stingy sees others as being essentially more stingy. A person who is basically dishonest sees others as trying to steal from him. A person who feels inferior rejects this idea and instead projects it to others; i.e. he is capable but others will not give him a chance because they doubt his ability. These are examples of projection. With the blinded person, many of the feelings he has of himself are unacceptable. Therefore, in order to adjust adequately, he projects these feelings to society in general. "They" feel he is inadequate. "They" feel he is not capable. "They" feel he is inferior and is to be devalued. This type of thinking normally leads directly into identification and compensation which are, in reality, the natural exits to this maze in which he has been wandering around.

Identification

The defense mechanism of identification is used to reduce an individual's conflicts through the achievement of another person or a group of people. Identification can be with material possessions as well as people. A person may derive his social adequacy and psychological adequacy through his clothes ("The clothes make the man"), his sports car, his hi-fi stereo paraphernalia, etc. People identify with larger groups in order to take on the power, prestige, and respect attributed to that organization ("Our team won"). This larger group may be a club, lodge, garden club, college, or professional group.

In adjustment to his blindness, the client will identify with a larger group. It may be a group of other blind persons, an occupational group, a men's lodge, or a veterans' group. But at this point in the adjustment process, he will identify with some group in order to offset some of the feelings he has as a result of the projection he is engaging in. If successful, the identification obviates the need to employ the mechanisms of denial, withdrawal, and regression.

Compensation

If an individual's path to a set of goals is blocked and he finds other routes to achieve that set of goals, he is using the defense mechanism of compensation. A teen-ager is seeking recognition and acceptance from his peers. He decides to gain this recognition through sports. However, when he fails to make the team, he decides to become a scholar. This is an example of compensation. Compensation brings success; therefore, it diverts attention from shortcomings and defects, thereby eliminating expressed or implied criticism. This defense mechanism is most often used to reduce self-criticism rather than external criticism. As the individual experiences successes, he will become less preoccupied with anxieties relating to his disability and his lack of productivity.

Identification and compensation usually go together in the adjustment process. When the client starts using these two defenses, he is at a point at which he may adequately adjust to the new body image and his new role in life.

IMPLICATIONS FOR PROFESSIONALS WORKING WITH THE BLIND

Almost everyone in our society views handicapping and disabling conditions from an anatomical point of view rather than functionally. It is imperative that the newly blinded be helped to view their disability functionally rather than anatomically. The client should gain an appreciation of the abilities he has left rather than classifying himself with a group based solely upon an anatomical loss. The worker with the blind should make sure the information which the client has is factual, concise, and clear. He should be sure the client's perception of his disability is correct and the cause is completely understood. This understanding greatly enhances the adjustment of the client to his blindness.

The client should be helped in exploring his feelings regarding the manner in which he is currently being treated by family and friends. Help him to understand the natural emotional reactions he will have resulting from his newly acquired blindness; and help him to understand that the feelings of family and friends are going to be different for a period of time while they adjust to his disability.

Do not fall into the trap of thinking that the degree of blindness is correlated with the degree of psychological impact. Realize that each individual's disability is unique unto that individual and his reaction to his disability will be unique.

Lastly, in summary, the most important role anyone can play in assisting a client in the adjustment to blindness is to be a warm, empathic, accepting individual who is positive in his regard toward the client and who is pragmatic in counseling and planning efforts with the client.

REFERENCES

American Psychiatric Association: *Diagnostic and Statistical Manual of Mental Disorders.* Washington, D.C., American Psychiatric Association, 1965.

English, H. B. and English, A. C.: *A Comprehensive Dictionary of Psychological and Psychoanalytical Terms.* New York, McKay, 1966.

APPROXIMATE NORMAL LABORATORY VALUES OF CLINICAL IMPORTANCE

Readings above these upper limits or below these lower limits may indicate disease.

BLOOD

Chemical Constituents

Albumin, serum	4.0-5.2 gm/100 ml
Bilirubin, total serum	0.1-0.8 mg/100 ml
Direct	0.1-0.2 mg/100 ml
Indirect	0.1-0.6 mg/100 ml
Calcium, serum	9-11 mg/100 ml
	4.5-515 mEq/L
Cholesterol, total serum (Schoenheimer-Sperry method)	160-270 mg/100 ml
Cholesterol as esters, serum	100-180 mg/100 ml
Cholesterol ester fraction of total cholesterol, serum	60-75%
Circulation time	Arm to tongue, 9 to 16 seconds (Decholin®—a derivative of ox bile)
Creatinine, serum	1-1.5 mg/100 ml
Fat, neutral, serum	150-300 mg/100 ml
Fibrinogen, plasma	0.2-0.4 gm/100 ml
Globulins, serum	1.3-2.7 gm/100 ml
Glucose (fasting), blood	70-110 mg/100 ml

(Courtesy of U. S. Department of Health, Education, and Welfare. *Descriptions of Common Impairments.* Washington, D. C., U. S. Govt. Printing Office, 1959.)

Hemoglobin, blood:

    Males ....14-18 gm/100 ml

    Females ....12-16 mg/100 ml

Icterus index, serum ....4-7 units

Nitrogen, nonprotein, serum ....15-35 mg/100 ml

Oxygen capacity, blood ....18-22 vol %

Oxygen content, arterial blood ....17-21 vol %

Oxygen percent saturation,
arterial blood ....94-96 vol %

Oxygen percent saturation, venous
blood, arm ....60-85 vol %

Oxygen tension, serum ....95-100 mm Hg

CO_2 tension ....40 mm Hg

pH, serum 7.37-7.45

Phosphatase, acid, serum:

    (Gutman or King-Armstrong method) . 1-4 units/100 ml

    (Bodansky method) ....8-14 units/100 ml

Phosphatase, alkaline, serum:

    (Bodansky method) ....1-4 units/100 ml

    (King-Armstrong method) ....8-14 units/100 ml

Phospholipids, serum ....230-300 mg/100 ml

Phosphorus, inorganic, serum ....3-4.5 mg/100 ml

Potassium, serum ....4.0-5.0 mEq/L

Protein-bound iodine, serum ....4-8 mg/100 ml

Proteins, total serum ....6.5-8.0 gm/100 ml

Proteins, total plasma,

    electrophoretic fractions: ....

    Albumin ....3.5-5.5 gm%

    Globulins ....1.3-3.2 gm%

    Fibrinogen ....2-.4 gm%

Urea Nitrogen (BUN) ....10-20 mg/100 ml

HEMATOLOGIC LABORATORY TESTS

Cells, differential count:

Erythrocytes, per cu mm .... 4.2-5.5 million

Leukocytes, per cu mm .... 5-10 thousand

Platelets, per cu mm .... 200-500 thousand

Reticulocytes, per cu mm .... 0.5-2.0% red cells

Hematocrit (vol % of red cells) .... 40-54% males

37-47% females

Hemoglobin, adults:

Females .... 12.8-15.2 gm/100 ml

Males .... 14-17 gm/100 ml

Hemoglobin, children:

Varies with age .... 10-18 gm/100 ml

KIDNEY FUNCTION TESTS

1. PSP test (Phenolsulphonphthalein). This test is based on the ability of the kidney to excrete a solution of PSP which has been injected intravenously. Normal excretion is 60-75 percent of the dye in two hours.

2. Dilution-concentration test. Six 2-hour samples (8 A.M. to 8 P.M.) Total volume: ability to dilute to 1001 or 1003, ability to concentrate to 1021 or higher.

3. Urea clearance test. This test measures the kidneys' ability to clear blood of urea. The rate depends on the rate of urine production. The patient should first be adequately hydrated and if 1 cc or less than 2 cc of urine is produced per minute, any clearance in excess of 40 cc represents adequate function. If the kidney produces more than 2 cc per minute, clearance should exceed 75 cc of blood.

Appendix II

ABBREVIATIONS COMMONLY FOUND IN MEDICAL RECORDS

a.c.	before meals (p.c., after meals)
ASHD	arteriosclerotic heart disease
AP	anterior posterior (PA, posterior anterior)
b.i.d.	twice daily; t.i.d., three times daily; q.i.d., four times daily
BUN	blood urea nitrogen
BMR	basal metabolism rate
B.P.	blood pressure
$\bar{c}$	with; $\bar{s}$, without
C	colored
C.C.	chief complaint
CVA	cerebrovascular accident
ECT	electroconvulsive therapy
EKG or ECG	electrocardiogram
EEG	electroencephalogram
E.S.T.	electric shock therapy, occasionally ECT
E.E.N.T.	eye, ear, nose, and throat
E.S.R.	erythrocyte sedimentation rate
GI	gastrointestinal
GU	genitourinary
GYN	gynecology
HCVD	hypertensive cardiovascular disease
h.s.	at bedtime
HMCT	hematocrit
Hb	hemoglobin
IVP	intravenous pyelogram (dye injected intravenously so that urinary tract can be x-rayed)
I.V.	intravenously

I.M.	intramuscularly
K.U.B.	kidney ureter, bladder test (x-ray)
L.M.P.	last menstrual period
OPD	outpatient department
o.s.	left eye
o.d.	right eye
p.r.n.	as needed
PI	present illness
PH	past history
PID	pelvic inflammatory disease
P.T.	physical therapy
qod	every other day
q	every
R	respiration
RUQ'	right upper quadrant
℞	prescription—treatment prescribed
RBC	red blood count
SOB	shortness of breath
S.I.	seriously ill
STS	serologic test for syphilis
T	temperature
Tsp	teaspoon
Tbsp	tablespoon
URI	upper respiratory infection
VDRL	slide test—venereal diagnostic research laboratory slide test (flocculation test for venereal disease)
WBC	white blood count

SUBJECT INDEX

AUTHOR INDEX